THE STREETS OF EUROPE

THE
STREETS
OF
EUROPE

The Sights, Sounds, and Smells
That Shaped Its Great Cities

Brian Ladd

The University of Chicago Press

Chicago and London

The University of Chicago Press, Chicago 60637
The University of Chicago Press, Ltd., London
© 2020 by The University of Chicago
All rights reserved. No part of this book may be used or reproduced
in any manner whatsoever without written permission, except in
the case of brief quotations in critical articles and reviews. For
more information, contact the University of Chicago Press, 1427
E. 60th St., Chicago, IL 60637.
Published 2020
Printed in the United States of America

29 28 27 26 25 24 23 22 21 20   1 2 3 4 5

ISBN-13: 978-0-226-67794-1 (cloth)
ISBN-13: 978-0-226-67813-9 (e-book)
DOI: https://doi.org/10.7208/chicago/9780226678139.001.0001

Library of Congress Cataloging-in-Publication Data

Names: Ladd, Brian, 1957– author.
Title: The streets of Europe: the sights, sounds, and smells
        that shaped its great cities / Brian Ladd.
Description: Chicago: The University of Chicago Press, 2020. |
        Includes bibliographical references and index.
Identifiers: LCCN 2019035376 | ISBN 9780226677941 (cloth) |
        ISBN 9780226678139 (ebook)
Subjects: LCSH: Streets—England—London—History. |
        Streets—France—Paris—History. | Streets—Germany—
        Berlin—History. | Streets—Austria—Vienna—History. |
        Streets—Social aspects—Europe—History. | Sociology,
        Urban—Europe—History.
Classification: LCC HT153 . L265 2020 | DDC 307.76094—dc23
LC record available at https://lccn.loc.gov/2019035376

♾ This paper meets the requirements of ANSI/NISO Z39.48-1992
(Permanence of Paper).

Contents

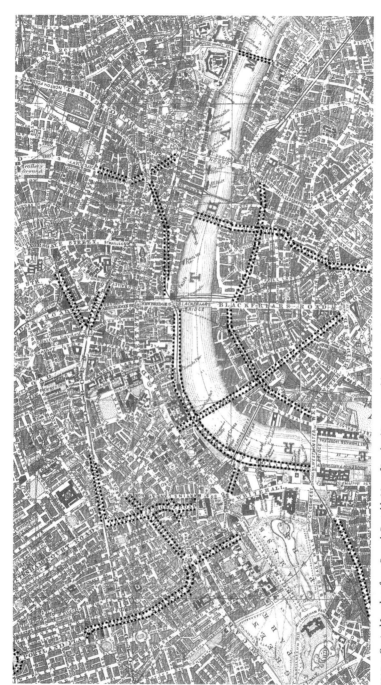

MAP 1. Central London, from *Bacon's Portable Map of London* (George Washington Bacon), c. 1899, with bold dotted lines highlighting new streets built during the nineteenth century.

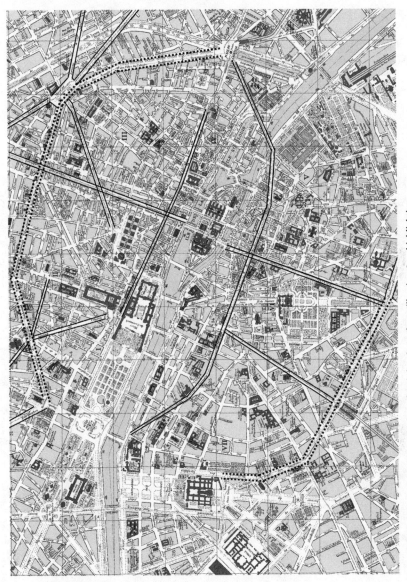

MAP 2. Central Paris, from Hachette map of Paris by Alexandre Vuillemin, 1892, highlighting eighteenth-century circuit of Grands Boulevards (*dotted lines*) and new post-1850 streets (*solid lines*).

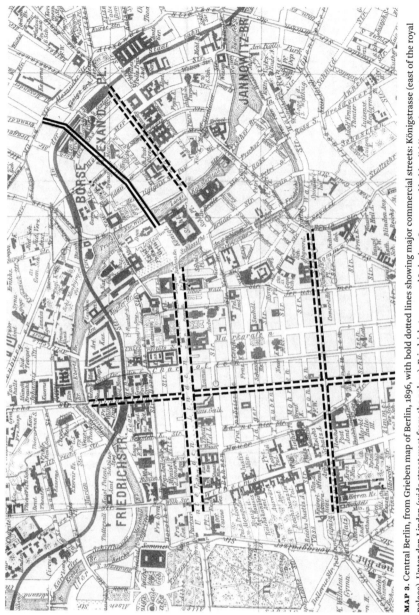

MAP 3. Central Berlin, from Grieben map of Berlin, 1896, with bold dotted lines showing major commercial streets: Königstrasse (east of the royal palace), Unter den Linden (wide street west from the palace), Friedrichstrasse, and Leipziger Strasse; and bold solid lines showing the new Kaiser-Wilhelm-Strasse (1888). The bold curving line on the original map marks the new elevated rail line (1882).

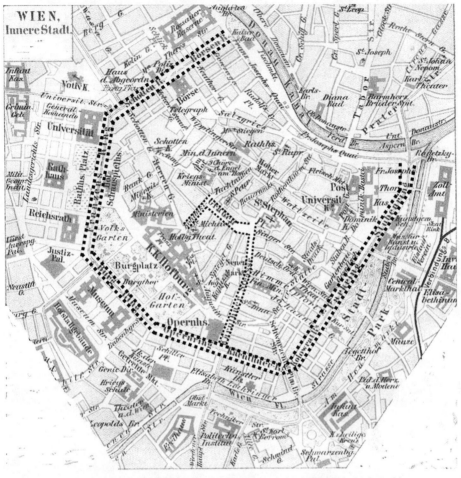

MAP 4. Center-city inset of Vienna map from *Meyer's Konversationslexikon*, 3rd ed., 1878, with bold dotted lines showing circuit of new Ringstrasse and major inner-city shopping streets: Kärtnerstrasse, Graben, and Kohlmarkt.

Introduction

The Form and Use of City Streets

The twenty-first century is the urban century. For the first time in history, a majority of the world's population lives in cities, with all the amenities and all the nuisances they have to offer. Life in close proximity to so many strangers demands compromises but also provides opportunities. Despite worries about their growth and crowding, cities may be more appealing than ever before. For ambitious young people in particular, the economic and cultural attractions of city life seem to outweigh the fears of crime, grime, and slime that repelled many of their elders.

Cities are, or can be, the places where everyone coexists, where old hierarchies crumble, and where barriers of ethnicity, class, and gender break down. One of their attractions is the possibility of human contact—visual, verbal, and tactile, especially the serendipitous encounters that happen only in crowds and public places. Theorists of economic development and of psychological well-being argue that opportunities for face-to-face contact are beneficial, and that they can be further enriched by the ethnic diversity of urban populations.

The quintessential place of crowds and strangers, of stimulation and surprises, is the city street, especially in the enclosed form it developed up to the nineteenth century. There has been a recent revival of interest in this kind of street, as cities across the world have proclaimed or pursued a resurgence of street life. Civic leaders hope to recover something that was lost during the twentieth century when street life was deliberately impoverished or abandoned. For much of that century, disgust with streets, if not fear of them, outweighed any lingering affection. Urban development broke radically with tradition, dispersing buildings away from streets and from each other. Advocates of urban revitalization, aghast at the results, believe that old streets can bring new life to cities, and they have sought to revise the historical picture by recalling both the pleasures and the practical advantages of the public street. They offer a useful corrective to older prejudices. The rosy history they tell can, however, be as one-sided as the bleak image they seek to counter, which portrayed streets as filthy and dangerous. Apart, perhaps, from exceptional and fleeting moments of political or religious alchemy, the street has rarely been a place of harmony. Friction and conflict have been more typical—and in fact are essential to productive urban life. To understand the appeal and the value of streets, we need to acknowledge their inherent tension but also to understand how it contributes to their pleasures and benefits.

An old painting or photo or film of a crowded street can appeal to many of us because it seems to promise a thrilling social experience. But a desire to recover the glories of the past also risks ignoring the deep chasm that separates us from it. The resemblance between urban crowds of different eras may be less than meets the eye. Pictures and descriptions of apparently harmonious street scenes from the nineteenth century can be deceiving because they do not reveal that the visible order depended on participants who observed invisible distinctions of deference and subservience, with nearly everyone conforming to more or less clearly defined class and gender roles that constrained their behavior. Some of those roles live on, but most have changed beyond recognition, replaced by other tacit or even unconscious rules that ensure outward harmony in our own streets today. As a result, many of us can be drawn to a charming street because either physical designs or visible authorities keep the poor, the homeless, or the ethnically other at a safe distance. As in the past, for many women a sense of comfort in the streets still depends on obvious or subtle signals that make them feel safe from harassment and sexual violence. In this we find echoes of the nineteenth century: although profound changes in gender roles and women's expectations entail different signals and customs, bold women are once again rewriting codes of public conduct.

We can learn from the urban past only if we remember that our needs have changed—in dwelling, working, and shopping. Our expectations, too, are different: for privacy or solitude; for sights and smells we welcome and others that we don't. Across the centuries, we can trace gradual changes in the ways people of different classes and genders used their streets and interacted with, or avoided, their neighbors. It is obvious that people in the twenty-first century can satisfy more of their needs without leaving their homes or coming into direct contact with strangers. A torrent of manifestos at the turn of the new century declared our imminent liberation from space and locality and even materiality. Some of them also predicted the imminent death of city life, reviving an old anti-urban tradition that feeds on fears of crowds and strangers. Of that demise there is little sign, but the use of urban space—its role in our lives—continues to change.

Reformers who lament that our streets have degenerated into automotive "traffic sewers" hope that a thoughtful restoration of pre-automotive features can create more humane spaces. It is indeed possible to draw contemporary lessons from historic streets, since some of them still function well. But creating streets that invite people to linger is trickier than building roads to rush them along. Although it sometimes helps to remove the cars, we are still left with the human beings who so eagerly drove them. Architects and retailers study successful streets, past and present, to learn what attracts people and what repels them. They examine the ways these streets connect places where people live and work, and how they balance the needs for enclosure and visibility, for leisure and mobility.[1] Successful streets, by any definition, need appropriate dimensions, architecture, and amenities, but they also have to transmit the cultural signals—visible or not, consciously received or not—that attract the right sort of people, and perhaps repel the wrong sort. Those who look to history for guidance in making better streets, therefore, need to look beyond designs to understand how streets have been perceived and how they have functioned. The invisible differences between the streets of past and present can help explain both the nature and the limits of their contemporary appeal.

This book is inspired by these twenty-first-century efforts, and perhaps also by a naive admiration for European urban traditions born out of the battered cities of the late twentieth-century United States. However, it is organized not around current issues but instead around the experiences that either gratified or horrified the people who used the streets of the nineteenth century and before. I have gathered material that could be used to build a case for either an endorsement or a condemnation of street life, but I do not claim to do either of those things. I offer no definitive answers about the value or the optimal form of streets, and certainly not about their future prospects. My purpose is, instead, to recover their historical richness, by reaching back a century and more in order to convey some sense of how and why streets have mattered. I seek to evoke the social frictions and stinking horrors that repelled contemporaries along with the delight they took in the sights and sounds, and even the smells, of their streets.

European cities are my focus. They were the world's largest and fastest growing in the eighteenth and nineteenth centuries, and they offered models of urban order and design that were imitated or imposed elsewhere. Four major cities furnish most of the evidence. To a remarkable extent, previous histories of urban street life have examined either London or Paris alone. Building on that trove of material, two other imperial capitals, Berlin and Vienna, fill out the picture here, along with relevant examples from elsewhere. In 1900 these were Europe's four most populous cities, matched elsewhere on the globe only by New York and Chicago. Many of the characteristics of modern urban life appeared in them earlier and more dramatically than anywhere else and were therefore more likely to attract comment. Reactions to the crowds, the filth, and the spectacle of the largest cities shaped beliefs and policies across Europe and beyond.

Contemporaries liked to draw distinctions between one city and another, often to praise or criticize their hometowns. Most historians, too, have focused on a single city, and their publications trace some of the developments studied here in greater detail. In ranging widely across centuries and cities, I venture generalizations that can certainly be questioned by specialists. A work of this breadth relies heavily on those scholars who have dug deeply into particular records in one city or another, and whose findings inform my identification of broader trends. Because I do not pretend to exhaust my topic, there would be little value in a bibliography listing every book and article I consulted. Instead, the source notes discharge scholarly debts and identify particular sources of facts, interpretations, and quotations. (Translations are mine except where I cite someone else.)

The year 1900 is my approximate end date, because the twentieth century introduced new thinking, new customs, new designs, and new technology—above all, the automobile—that mark a break in the history of street life. The years around 1900 were also a high point in attention to city streets. With the ranks of big cities rapidly expanding, civic leaders cast their gaze across international borders, as their successors do today. Political and social theorists turned their attention to the urban crowd as a source of vitality or, more often, of worry. The new discipline of sociology, in Germany and elsewhere, grew out of efforts to understand the behavior of people packed into urban tenements, factories, and streets. A broader gauge of interest comes from Google Ngrams, crude tools that nevertheless offer the advantage of synthesizing vast amounts of data. They show a clear trend in the prevalence of the words "street," "rue," and "Strasse" in published books: an increase starting in the mid-1700s that (in French and English) accelerated around 1850 and persisted until just after 1900, followed by a sharp decline. This book follows a similar trajectory, looking primarily at the nineteenth century, with forays into the eighteenth century and earlier in order to trace long-term developments. Along the way it offers some tentative answers to the question of why the interest in streets seems to have peaked and then dwindled.

Part of the explanation is that the early 1900s mark a turning point in the physical form of city streets. Up to then European cities had continued to build streets in their classic and instantly recognizable form: a façade-lined canyon with windows and doors opening directly onto a lively jumble of traffic and commerce. Although the twentieth century embraced other arrangements, this form remains familiar, because many streets have maintained it—some thriving, others lifeless. We also know it from descriptions, prints, photographs, and a few snippets of early film that show us bustling streets just before they were taken over by automobiles. They offer enticing models for recent efforts to promote "mixed use" and "shared streets." It would be a mistake, however, to forget that the streets of 1900 are a particular snapshot in time, products of a long historical development and in some ways as different from those of 1800 as they are from those of today. Although every city and country developed its own street culture, the nineteenth century saw a fundamental revaluation of street space across Europe and beyond.

The book delimits its subject matter just as the building line of a traditional European street visibly separates one set of activities from another. This kind of crisply framed street has served to distinguish public from private spaces, a legal distinction often applied to political ideals of democratic discourse in the town square. But the term "public space" must be approached with caution because scholars have laden it with many meanings.[2] Rather than subsume streets under the amorphous rubric of "public space," this book works the other way around, using the tangible evidence of the street wall to define the spaces that are its subject. I step into the architectural frame and investigate how it connected home, work, commerce, and leisure, and how it shaped collective encounters, private solitude, and public anonymity. Conversely, I also ask how these activities reshaped the architectural setting.

This interaction between form and use has been too little studied. Just as architectural historians do not always put people into their accounts, most social and political historians have paid scant attention to the built environment that framed the activities of their subjects. I bring the insights of architectural historians and urban geographers to bear on the work of social historians who have studied the uses of the street. Unlike most urban histories, this book does not focus primarily on the street crowds' political goals.[3] Its approach is also distinct from that of architectural historians, who typically focus on the buildings themselves and on the kings and architects who imposed a visible form on a street or city.[4] They usually study individual streets and squares, since the systematic reshaping of a major city was all but unknown before the mid-nineteenth century, when the achievements of Emperor Napoleon III and his prefect Georges-Eugène Haussmann drew the world's attention to Paris. Similarly ambitious projects in many cities during the following decades are inseparable from the bundle of initiatives that came together in the new discipline of urban planning, and they culminated in well-known twentieth-century projects that fundamentally reshaped the street. Here we will instead begin not with the king or government or architect but rather with the citizen in the street—shopping, socializing, dodging filth and traffic, and clamoring for, or resisting, official interventions in commerce, sanitation, and transportation.

We can investigate the experience of the street only through the perceptions of it. Physical sensations were the raw material of our historical sources, and they are ours as well. We all have our own acquaintance with streets and crowds, and we cannot help filtering the historical record through our own sense memories as we consider what might have been different or familiar in remote times and places. But our own bodies and senses are inescapably estranged from those old streets. We cannot actually be jostled by the crowds on the eighteenth-century Strand, nor can we imbibe the aroma of revolutionary Paris (not that we would want to). We will always be seeing—or hearing or smelling or feeling—the past through the eyes, ears, noses, and elbows of contemporaries, as transmitted through the words, pictures, and architectural fragments they have left us. Our sources, therefore, are those that describe their perceptions of urban space.[5]

This disembodied source material leaves frustrating gaps, obliging us to cobble together our own vicarious impressions. Even Charles Dickens, justly famed for his vivid descriptions of London streets, typically evoked an atmosphere of decay and poverty more than its material reality. His words leave a great deal to the reader's imagination, and often substitute moral judgment for factual detail. He expected his contemporary readers to be able to call to mind the sights, sounds, and smells of "a black, dilapidated street, avoided by all decent people." We find it more difficult to do so.

Nor does this book profit much from the voluminous attention given to the figure of the "flâneur" who plunged eagerly into the nineteenth-century streets, famously in Paris, in order to heighten his (typically masculine) perceptions of humanity. Certainly the era's fascination with urban crowds is an important clue to the emergence of new forms of public interaction. The street became the place to escape a rigid order of thought or behavior and discover the riches of humanity. However, accounts left us by self-styled urban explorers typically attempt to describe the writer's feelings more than the people and places that stimulated them. The scholarly attention lavished on the figure of the flâneur has sought more to define modern art than to understand the streets. The flâneur is presented as a key to understanding the birth of "modernity" or "the modern world," with modernity typically understood as an unprecedented break with the past and a release from tradition. As such, it has often been identified with the European city, where we find a radical reorganization of communities, of industry and labor, of family life, and of technology. I do not attempt to define the "modern" street as distinguished from its predecessor.[6] A search for "the modern" risks imposing a direction on events that may simplify what was actually going on. Belief in the inevitability of some "modernity" can also lend itself to the conclusion that any longing for premodern street life is sentimental and misguided. This book gathers evidence left us by contemporaries who sought to identify new ways of thinking and living. We would lose the rich variety of their voices if we ranked them on a scale of modernity. Nevertheless, many of the men and women most quoted in these pages might be labeled "flâneurs": inveterate city walkers who were best able to put into words (or pictures) the sights and sounds that enthralled them.

Our witnesses include police and judges; municipal and state officials; social, medical, and moral reformers; journalists and essayists; novelists and poets; painters, cartoonists, and photographers. This book relies heavily on the self-selected minority that recorded its impressions—letter writers, diarists, and memoirists; travel writers; feuilleton journalists; graphic artists—and it is weighted toward outsiders, since fresh impressions were more likely to be recorded than the far more numerous daily routines. The poor workers and destitute vagrants who made up the great majority of people on most streets are badly underrepresented in the historical record. In relying to a great extent on others' observations of them, we need to be vigilant about the reliability of witnesses, who saw things through the veil of their own prejudices and who wrote for purposes other than informing posterity.[7]

Many of our sources are more than mere witnesses. The views of intellectuals and experts mattered because they shaped not only perceptions of street life but interventions in it as well. They recommended new ways to police or design streets and sometimes proposed radical reforms to restrict urban activities or move them off the streets entirely. Social, economic, and technological forces fundamentally changed streets both before and after 1900, but they did not do so by themselves. Political choices were made, swayed by the weight of influential opinion. That is an important part of the story told here.

After a first chapter that identifies some key moments in the history of street form and street life, the book subordinates chronology to a thematic arrangement of chapters, each examining a set of related activities. Chapter 2 looks at the street as a place of labor, especially selling and buying, whether from mobile vendors, temporary stands, or open shopfronts. Chapter 3 focuses more broadly on sociability, moving down the scale from aristocrats to the poor, from formal promenades to everyday encounters and illicit activities. Chapter 4 considers the street's historic and pungent function as a site to dispose of waste, and at the ceaseless if often futile efforts to keep it clean. Chapter 5's topic is transportation. This was always a basic function of streets, but the nineteenth century saw rapid increases in the volume and speed of traffic, along with a fundamental change in attitudes and policies, as authorities increasingly equated streets with mobility to the exclusion of other uses. Chapter 6 looks at the regulation of street life, including policing but also, more broadly, ambitious efforts to design streets that displayed a more visible order.

The long-term trend was to remove many of these activities from the street, especially during the nineteenth and twentieth centuries: production and exchange, formal and informal interaction, and the disposal of bodily, household, and industrial waste all withdrew from the street to a great extent. Accelerated movement, propelled by economics as well as technology, spurred efforts to devote streets more exclusively to wheeled vehicles and to redesign them for that purpose. By 1900 multiple forces were simplifying and impoverishing street life, removing filth and obstructions but also commerce and entertainment and crowds—that is, people. The conclusion considers how a tendency to survey and manage streets from afar reinforced the growing disdain for them—but also spawned a reaction.

The most important technological breakthrough was, ultimately, the automobile. Its arrival accelerated the abandonment of the street, isolating its users while making street space increasingly inhospitable to non-motorists. It is not wrong to say that cars fundamentally transformed city streets.[8] But a deeper understanding of the nineteenth century reveals that a desire to escape from the street predated the automobiles that enabled so many people to do so. In other words, the flourishing street life of the nineteenth century generated conflicts that drove people off the street. And because the transformation of the street was underway before cars arrived, it would be a mistake to exaggerate the benefits of removing them now. Cars only enabled an escape that was already underway.

Through the eyes of contemporaries, we can see the fascination and the horror of the nineteenth-century street. Their words and also their silences reveal a consensus that by 1900 many long-standing problems of the street, notably but not only those of sanitation, were well on the way to being solved. It was, however, a deeply paradoxical solution. Streets had become more pleasant places to work, shop, stroll, and travel, and for a great many people the street was as enthralling as ever. Yet the faster, smoother, cleaner street turned out to be more hostile to social and commercial life. After all, the best way to make streets tidier was to chase people off them. The reformed street became an emptier street, as people took their lives elsewhere or sealed themselves inside their vehicles. Twentieth-century Europe promised at first to be a golden age of street life. Instead it abandoned the street. A century later, new generations, drawn by the allure of the historic street, seek to reclaim it. Perhaps this book can help them better understand the streets they admire.

1

Streets in History

Streets give shape to a city. Buildings strike the eye and have usually been constructed with more care, but they need connective tissue to make them part of something greater. While a building is for somebody, a street is usually for everybody. Streets carry people through their daily lives, bringing them in and out of town and to and from their destinations. On the pavement, people mix, eagerly or reluctantly. They encounter, attract, and enjoy other people and other activities. They stop to embrace and chat, to buy and sell, to assemble and protest. Street space furnishes light, air, and greenery, a stage for monuments and communal ceremonies, and a visible shape for civic identities. Because streets stay in place for decades or centuries, they can serve as repositories of individual and collective memories that endow them with political or religious meaning. Streets are, in short, the quintessential sites of public life.

Most of these activities can take place elsewhere, however, and increasingly over the past two centuries they have done so. For many people today, streets hardly matter. They are lines on an electronic map and open-air tunnels for our cars. They get us to home and to work, despite all the annoying obstacles they put up—stoplights, crashes, pedestrians, demonstrators, hawkers—and at best they offer us some visual diversion along the way. An influential belief during the twentieth century was that streets were obsolete because more efficient modes of transportation could be segregated in exclusive corridors on, below, or above the ground. But dissenters have always argued that we wanted or needed streets, and that we should look to the past and to existing streets to understand how to preserve and create streets worth living in.

What is a street, actually? It might be just leftover land between buildings, or, as is now typical, a sterile transportation corridor. Space and movement are the basic elements of the laconic definition of *rue* in Antoine Furetière's 1690 dictionary: "space between houses that provides passage for the public." We find a richer meaning, though, when we look at the many uses of that space. As an experience, not just a space, a street could be a dismal traffic conduit best avoided, or a tolerably familiar setting for daily routines, or perhaps a place of mystery and excitement, of visceral encounters and prospective adventures, where visible and invisible barriers break down and we literally rub shoulders with people who are very different from us. In other words, a street can be as devoid of meaning as it is of scenery, or it might be richly endowed with both. Where the street offers unpredictable human contact, it unleashes our yearning for connection, or our fear of it, or both. The lonely might venture out in search of human contact, while others with homes and families seek out familiar faces, or try to spice up their comfortable lives with a whiff of danger. The men, women, and children who live on the street, and the larger number who work there, set the scene for the throngs of passersby, making us more comfortable there (sanitation crews, food trucks) or perhaps less so (beggars, the homeless). The sight of a police officer on the beat puts some citizens at ease and sets others on their guard. One street is filled with our kind, another with people unlike us, while others offer a dizzying mixture. Interaction with strangers or with fleeting acquaintances unleashes our capacity for empathy and for sustaining some kind of social order.[1]

People go to the street in search of physical contact—visual, aural, olfactory, and ultimately tactile. The bodies on the street can make us reach out in desire but also draw back in revulsion. The search for connection is recognizably human, a fact of psychology and even biology, but it has a history, too. People's needs and desires are not the same in all times and places, since the roles of families and communities are not, either. Nor do we always have the same opportunities to pursue our desires. The street meant something very different to the urban poor of the eighteenth and nineteenth centuries, who sought employment, solace, and an escape from their miserable homes, than it did to the homebound middle class of 1927 London, where Virginia Woolf wrote her essay "Street Haunting." She favored a late-day walk in order to flee domestic tranquility: "We are no longer quite ourselves. As we step out of the house on a fine evening between four and six, we shed the self our friends know us by and become part of that vast republican army of anonymous trampers, whose society is so agreeable after the solitude of one's own room."[2]

Furetière's combination of space and movement has always ensured an ambiguity about the purpose of streets. They were paths into town and into houses, but they also provided space for outdoor and communal activities. Quarrels over their use were an unavoidable part of daily life. By the twentieth century, the bone of contention was the growing belief that streets were exclusively for traffic, especially automobiles. The acceleration of movement, which predates the automobile, made traffic increasingly incompatible with human contact. Other activities gradually withdrew from the street during the nineteenth and twentieth centuries. Although recent initiatives have sought to reclaim it for other users, the street is not what it used to be, especially in wealthy lands. It might still serve as the setting for rituals that cement communal identities—anniversaries, parades, celebrations—but far less than in centuries past. Many North Americans and Europeans manage to avoid streets almost entirely, except while encased in a car. But others still find the street a compelling place, or would like to. They can look to other parts of the world to find some of the activities that have vanished from prosperous Western cities, whether open sewers and impassable throngs or lively street markets and colorful festivities.

The premodern European street calls up two well-known but contradictory images. One is the kind of evocative village setting that might frame the opening scene of an opera: a colorful but homogeneous community gathered at its market or church. The other is the stinking morass of trash and sewage that city dwellers had to endure before modern bureaucracy and technology fixed problems of waste and drainage (a fix that too many of the world's city dwellers still await). Both images, the good old days and the bad old days, took hold during the late nineteenth and early twentieth centuries, when the world seemed to be emancipating itself from villages and from dung-heaps. Although an amalgam of the two images—villagers merrily prancing in putrid slime—might be the stuff of black comedy, perhaps it begins to approach historical reality. The exchange on a vaguely medieval street in the absurdist comedy film *Monty Python and the Holy Grail* is instructive, if not historically accurate:

> Who's that, then?
> I dunno. Must be a king.
> Why?
> He hasn't got shit all over him.

THE DISCOVERY OF THE STREET

Streets are an invention, if largely an accidental one. Human settlements have always had gaps between houses that functioned as routes in and out of the village. Perhaps the houses were the primary focus, with space left between them; or perhaps they were subordinate to communal sites outside. Either way, the paths took on definite shapes as towns grew, as open land became scarcer, and as more people and activities were funneled into narrower confines. Sometimes, of course, a highway or crossroads came first, and the town developed alongside it. The streets of growing towns became increasingly distinct from rural highways and from mere leftover space. The act of paving them with stone lent them a deliberate and tangible identity. The European street, with its roots in ancient Rome and medieval Italy, became the focal point of public life. In much of the ancient Mediterranean, and in parts of the modern world as well, houses faced inward onto courtyards and left the street as a mere pathway. In some places, though, houses turned outward onto a central street, often because traders prevailed over more parochial interests seeking to preserve walled enclaves. Civic and commercial activity developed along the axes of movement.[3]

For much of the European Middle Ages, streets do not seem to have been a basic source of orientation or identity. Instead, people indicated their location with reference to a block of buildings, or an individual house, or a nearby shrine or market or fountain or crossroads. A gradual change came during the late medieval period as streets acquired a clearer visual and cultural identity, and often a more elongated and linear shape as well.[4] Eventually they became both a common reference point (consider how they begin to appear in early Renaissance paintings) and a site of civic encounters. This is more or less what the influential landscape writer J. B. Jackson meant when he placed "the discovery of the street" in the eleventh century, based primarily on evidence from German archaeological excavations. He believed that the demarcation of marketplaces in the commercial towns of northern Europe amounted to a "discovery" of the street because it revealed the emergence of a new sense of communal identity, one that became visible in the public space of the street.[5]

Jackson is one of the more insightful of many writers who have used the built form of cities—either as it is still visible, or as it was recorded—to draw conclusions about the ways residents negotiated their collective lives. This is the approach typically, and often fruitfully, taken by architectural historians. Even more than architecture, though, medieval historians have recourse to laws as evidence of a discovery of the street. Town governments and ruling princes asserted their authority in order to control various activities, whether paving, or refuse removal, or trade, or acts deemed immoral—and, conversely, they acknowledged the limit of that authority at the thresholds of houses. These governments—German free cities, English town corporations, Italian city-states, and monarchies— adjudicated conflicts among users and neighbors, codified local customs, and built up a body of municipal law. Ordinances increasingly demarcated the open space of the street and regulated the activities there. Along the way, streets acquired an identity rooted not only in daily use but in acknowledged customs and written laws.[6] And their basic shape endured. In European towns dating to the Middle Ages, the most durable feature has been the street plan. Traces of Roman street grids even remain in some of them.

Broadly similar arrangements of walls, gates, streets, and façades developed across much of Europe, as ancient Roman rules on street alignments were revived by the thriving towns of medieval Italy while German settlers built new towns in familiar patterns as far away as Estonia and Transylvania. The street became the most valuable land in a European town, even in a village. Clear evidence of this fact is found in the typical property lines in much of Europe. Because street frontage was scarce and valuable, houses and lots were narrow, with deep plots extending back from the street. Where courtyards and backyards were built up as well, the most desirable rooms and apartments were usually those facing the street—until the automotive age.

The concentration of people, buildings, and activities gradually gave shape to streets during the Middle Ages. In successful towns— those that grew from mere settlements into something more— a loose collection of religious foundations, a castle, and a market typically coalesced around a core or spine. As these towns grew, buildings were aligned to form clearly defined street walls, especially on the main streets, so that a continuous line of façades marked the street's edge. This edge could be ragged, however, and often shifted over time, as property owners encroached on the roadway, while town governments pushed back to assert collective rights of access. Centuries of ordinances sought to limit encroachments onto the street, whether in the form of ground-floor building extensions, projecting upper stories, cellar stairs, water spouts, or shop counters.

The clearly delineated street served both practical and decorative purposes. Where towns had walls, as was typical in medieval Europe, their gates usually opened into well-defined streets lined with houses, greeting new arrivals with a stately vista. The buildings defined the open space of the street, and vice versa: the form of the street often dictated the size and shape of the houses that faced it. In a self-governing commercial town, rows of ornate façades lent a distinctive visual identity to the organized bodies of merchants and artisans who governed the town and who cherished it as their collective patrimony, worthy of comparison to any lord's castle. Only a few prominent buildings such as churches and town halls were permitted to step forward from the street line. By the fourteenth century, Italian town governments had enacted architectural rules to ensure that street walls were continuous, harmonious, and dignified.[7] Many other jurisdictions eventually followed, notably in a 1607 French royal decree that confirmed the king's power to enforce the alignment of façades. The word "façade" also spread to several European languages after the Italian *facciata* came into use during the fifteenth century to describe the architectural "face" that a building presented to the street.[8] The renowned architectural innovations of fifteenth-century Florence were more than a mere matter of style: powerful families expressed confidence in their town's security when they hired architects such as Alberti and Michelozzo to replace towers and fortified compounds with outward-facing palaces along major streets. These imposing stone façades spoke a language of strength that was more symbolic than functional.

Architectural styles varied from town to town, and even from street to street, depending on local construction skills and materials but also on the residential character of streets. A city's characteristic appearance can be traced partly to these organic traditions, but civic leaders often codified them as enforceable rules. In 1297, for example, Siena's government mandated that the façades of all buildings on the main piazza had to follow the model of the grand new town hall.[9] Self-governing merchant towns like Nuremberg and Amsterdam crafted ordinances that prescribed the dimensions, materials, and adornment of street façades, ensuring that their city maintained a distinctive appearance, sometimes over several centuries — even up to the present in cities that have embraced their ver-

FIG. 1. Giovanni Stradano, *Jousting Tournament in Via Larga, Florence*, 1561–62, with Medici palace on right. Photo credit: Alinari/Art Resource, NY.

nacular traditions. More predictably, princes enforced similar rules in their capitals. The customs and codes in many northern European towns preserved an informal harmony among the vertical lines of their gabled houses, while princely rulers more typically followed French classical models of horizontal order, and British elite taste eventually abandoned the gabled style in favor of the more formal rhythms of Georgian houses. What the various local styles had in common was a shared belief that the buildings lining major streets could lend a city dignity and a visual identity.[10]

Rulers also displayed their sovereignty over a town by lengthening or widening its streets, and especially by creating entirely new streets for ceremonial purposes.[11] In the Renaissance and after, as kings and other rulers increasingly settled in capital cities, their urban interventions became more extensive and more enduring. They laid out new, wide streets and erected buildings that gave their processional routes a more splendid backdrop. Late medieval Siena and Florence were pioneers, wealthy city-states that issued regulations to ensure that reconstructed streets were straight, well paved, and lined with

FIG. 2. Versailles: royal palace, Place d'Armes, and three radiating avenues. © ToucanWings/ Wikimedia Commons, CC-BY SA 3.0: https://creativecommons.org/licenses/by-sa/3.0/legalcode.

buildings that displayed harmony and grandeur. Similar sentiments became common among civic leaders across Europe, even if the will to enforce them was often lacking. An ambitious early example is Genoa's sixteenth-century Strada Nuova, where the duke supervised the design of the palaces his rich merchants built. In the seventeenth century, the city-state of Dubrovnik, rebuilding after a fire, enforced a uniform style on its main street, the Stradun. During the early eighteenth century, King Friedrich Wilhelm I compelled his subjects to build houses in identical forms along many new streets in Berlin and Potsdam. Dresden offers a similar if grander example from the same period.

By the seventeenth and eighteenth centuries, princes embracing the style we call Baroque built grand avenues and squares that framed a path to a palace or other monument. Some of the most striking examples take the form of three straight avenues converging on a single point. Rome's Piazza del Popolo is an early example from the sixteenth century. Perhaps more influential was the framing of the palace façade by three radiating avenues in Louis XIV's newly created town of Versailles. Eighteenth-century princes in Germany, Spain, and Italy imitated his model as they built their own palaces. We find it as well, on a distinctly more modest scale, in the expanded Friedrichstadt of Friedrich Wilhelm I's Berlin in the 1730s, and also at the same time in Russia's new capital, St. Petersburg. These mostly wide streets might have served practical purposes of commerce and traffic, but their design was clearly intended to lend the city an unprecedented visual unity, often by making a palace the visually dominant structure.[12]

This was a different kind of street, intended more for show than for use, and best viewed from above or afar. The fact that form trumped function was especially apparent where, as in Genoa, the ruler mandated uniform façades along the length of a ceremonial avenue or square. These façades were not intended to display the tastes of the nobles or merchants who lived in the houses behind them, nor to provide practical connections between street and house. Instead they served to frame the urban space as a dramatic backdrop for official ceremonies. They became some of the most magnificent and least typical streets in Europe. Seventeenth-century Turin offers particularly successful examples of a ruler's imposition of uniform alignments, heights, and façades along entire streets, in an effort to extend the style of the ducal palace through his city.[13] French kings enforced this kind of uniformity most visibly on squares, notably Henry IV's Place Royale (now Place des Vosges), but also built streets of identical façades such as the rue Royale. In geometry and scale, these streets and squares offered a striking contrast to the winding lanes of most towns. The grandest of them dwarfed all but the largest crowds.

These designs have often been compared to the theaters that kings were sponsoring at the same time. A city street designed like a theater might be lively but would display a clear order, unlike the unplanned street of serendipitous encounters. The Baroque street or square was designed as a whole, able to be taken in at a single glance. Any crowd in it was supposed to be orderly if not ornamental, with everyone knowing his or her place. The will to enforce its visible order was at once aesthetic and political, with visual unity not only reinforcing an aura of authority but also enabling access and surveillance, and often extending central authority into quarters once controlled by clans or guilds. After the French Revolution, this approach to urban design increasingly appealed to rulers who feared unruly crowds.

Before the late nineteenth century, this kind of street was a rare exception—a wider, straighter, more uniform version of the typical main street that had developed over centuries in response to the desires of merchants, mayors, and princes. However, even more modest efforts to create beautiful streets were accompanied by attempts to regulate the activities there, by favoring, for example, aristocratic processions over petty commerce, or carriage traffic over pedestrians, or at least cleanliness over casual waste disposal. Governments and rulers gradually asserted their authority over the townscape, as they came to recognize that these façade-lined spaces shaped both the practical functions and the visual identity of the European city.

In defining a street as "a space between houses," Furetière's 1690 dictionary distinguished it from a rural road by alluding to its role in the alignment of buildings. A few years earlier, the definition in Pierre Richelet's rival dictionary had assigned a more decisive role to the buildings: a "road [*chemin*] in towns and villages that is lined on both sides by houses."[14] A similar definition, in the same French tradition, came much later from the European street's most vehement foe, the Swiss architect who called himself Le Corbusier. He declared that it was imperative to "kill" the "corridor street," by which he meant "streets in narrow trenches walled in by seven-storied buildings set perpendicular on the pavement and enclosing unhealthy courtyards, airless and sunless wells."[15] This was the judgment of the early twentieth century: a declaration of war on centuries of European urban history, because the street was a monstrous historical mistake that could be fixed by rational planning. To a considerable extent, that war was won.

But that is the story of the twentieth century. For centuries before that, these streets shaped daily sights, journeys, and encounters. Street walls enclosed most exterior urban space and framed nearly every view. In much of Europe, especially where half-timbered construction prevailed, upper stories were cantilevered over the narrow streets, sometimes nearly blocking out the sky. Even the rivers that traversed most towns opened up fewer vistas than we might expect. Quays were crowded with buildings, and bridges were lined with overhanging houses that blocked the view of nearly everything except their façades. That was true of all of Paris's Seine bridges, Berlin's Mühlendamm bridge, and London Bridge, that city's only Thames crossing before 1750. From the inside, these bridges were virtually indistinguishable from streets, which for most purposes they were. The Pont Neuf in Paris, opened in 1604, was notably "new" in not having houses on it, and also in having raised footways on each side. It became a kind of public square and marketplace as well as the best spot to enjoy a view of the river.

The multistory, window-lined street wall became the visual emblem of the European city, at a time when Europe meant power and progress. Tsar Peter the Great, the ruthless Westernizer, thought so: he ordered his nobles to erect their St. Petersburg mansions "like the buildings of other European states . . . on the line . . . and not in the middle of the courts."[16] During the eighteenth and nineteenth centuries, change was incremental and piecemeal. Influenced by showcase projects, one building or a few might be rebuilt with taller or more fashionable façades. The distinction between street and building, between public and private space, only became clearer as courts, closes, and alleys were sealed off and street walls became crisper, straighter, and more boldly defined, and as greater streams of traffic flowed alongside them. The enduring result was the European street as we know it.

The finest of the new streets drew attention and comment from visitors. Contemporaries heaped particular praise or opprobrium on one city or another, with the major capitals attracting the most attention, sometimes for their architecture but more often for the activity it framed. Three thumbnail sketches can reveal some of the phenomena that most struck them.

LONDON IN THE 1700S

Visitors to London had never seen anything like it. The houses and streets sprawled on and on, yet they teemed with people from dawn

FIG. 3. Gerrit Adriaenszoon Berckheyde, *The Jansstraat in Haarlem with the St.-Bavo Church in the Background*, c. 1680.

until dark and even later. Eighteenth-century London was on its way to becoming the most populous city in Europe since imperial Rome, and soon the largest the world had ever known. Most people were unfamiliar with the statistics, but they knew they were seeing something new and extraordinary. A few minutes on the Strand exposed many of them to more strangers than they had seen in their entire lives. They saw more opulence and, in its midst, more misery than they had ever imagined.

Everyone had seen crowds before, but the presence of a throng had always signaled a special occasion: a procession, a fair, or perhaps a major market day. London's crowds were different. Visitors were so routinely dumbfounded by the deluge of humanity that their typical reaction became a cliché. Tobias Smollett, in 1771, put it into the letter of a fictional character who reeled at the "crowds of people that swarm in the streets. I at first imagined, that some great assembly was just dismissed, and wanted to stand aside till the multitudes should pass; but this human tide continues to flow, without interruption or abatement, from morn till night. Then there is such an infinity of gay equipages, coaches, chariots, chaises, and other carriages, continually rolling and shifting before your eyes, that one's head grows giddy looking at them; and the imagination is quite confounded with splendour and variety."[17] As Smollett knew, many real-life visitors carried home this explanation of what William Wordsworth called the "moving pageant": like the greatest crowd you had ever seen at a fair or a royal procession, except that it never ended.

Late in the century, the young Wordsworth's formative experience of "the great tide of human life" surging across this "monstrous ant-hill on the plain" informed a key section of his autobiographical poem *The Prelude*. He was fascinated and frightened by "that huge fermenting mass of human-kind" and by his own anonymity in a sea of strangers:

How oft, amid those overflowing streets,
Have I gone forward with the crowd, and said
Unto myself, "The face of every one
That passes by me is a mystery!"

Wordsworth ultimately spurned the crowd in favor of the pastoral life, but his friend Charles Lamb affirmed a passion for "streets, streets, streets." In a letter to Wordsworth, he explained:

Separate from the pleasure of your company, I don't much care if I never see a mountain in my life. I have passed all my days in London, until I have formed as many and intense local attachments, as any of you mountaineers can have done with dead nature. The Lighted shops of the Strand and Fleet Street, the innumerable trades, tradesmen and

customers, coaches, waggons, playhouses, all the bustle and wicked-
ness round about Covent Garden, the very women of the Town, the
Watchmen, drunken scenes, rattles,—life awake, if you awake, at all
hours of the night, the impossibility of being dull in Fleet Street, the
crowds, the very dirt & mud, the Sun shining upon houses and pavements, the print shops, the old book stalls, parsons cheap'ning books,
coffee houses, steams of soups from kitchens, the pantomimes, London itself a pantomime and a masquerade,—all these things work
themselves into my mind and feed me, without a power of satiating
me. The wonder of these sights impells me into night-walks about her
crowded streets, and I often shed tears in the motley Strand from fulness of joy at so much Life.[18]

Its sheer size and unpredictability ensured that the London crowd
loomed as a menace to the powerful and comfortable. The mob
could be provoked—by a bread shortage, perhaps, or by a rumor that
a criminal was escaping justice. This horde was not really the head-
less beast that it seemed to be: many kinds of invisible order functioned in the streets. Rarely did the wealthy and powerful fear the
mob's wrath as a grave threat to their position. More typically, in fact,
they could turn it to their own purposes. But the daily spectacle of the
street reminded kings, lord mayors, and constables that the London
crowd was far beyond anyone's ultimate control.

Walking the streets was guaranteed to be an adventure, of sorts.
The Reverend John Trusler offered his *London Adviser and Guide*
(1786) as practical advice for visitors, but the brief chapter "On
Walking London Streets" reads more like a recommendation to stay
away entirely. The standard advice to "keep the wall" seems helpful
enough: stay close to the buildings to avoid unpleasant encounters
with traffic of all kinds. But he immediately warns that the wall may
not always be your friend: "Don't dispute the wall with a cart or carriage, lest you should be crushed." In fact, the proximity of houses
offered anything but shelter: "If you wish to walk safe, never pass
under any goods &c. that are drawing up to the top of a house by a
crane, nor pass a house where the bricklayers are at work, lest any

The Art of Walking the Streets of London Plate 2ᵈ

FIG. 4. George Cruikshank, *The Art of Walking the Streets of London*, 1818. Captions: How to stop up the Passage; How to make the most of the Mud; How to carry a Stick; How to get into the Watch House. Digital Commonwealth.

thing should fall on your head." And he alludes delicately to another notorious danger: "Do not walk under a pent-house, lest persons watering flower-pots, or other slops, should drop upon your head." His readers knew that those "other slops" came from chamber pots, not flower pots. At any distance from the wall, other dangers loomed: "Be careful, if you meet a porter carrying a load upon his head, that you do not get a blow that may be fatal." Whereas "in frosty weather it is adviseable to walk in the coach-ways, which are not so slippery as the foot-paths; and to bind a piece of cloth-list round one of your shoes, it will save you many a fall," Trusler also warned, "Don't hastily cross a street when a coach is coming up, lest your foot should slip and you be run over." And it was foolish to forget the perils of even the cleanest thoroughfare: "Never stop in a crowd, or to look at the windows of a print-shop or shew-glass, if you would not have your pocket picked."[19]

FIG. 5. *Pickpocket and Fashionable Gent.* Print by Joseph Lisle, *The Spectator*, 1828. © The Trustees of the British Museum/Art Resource, NY.

A later chapter at least assured his readers that when calamity struck, the law might be on their side. Indictable "nuisances" included "pigs, foul drains, privies, overflowing cisterns, rotten water-pipes, decayed vegetables thrown out in foot-ways, obstructions in foot-ways, flower-pots dropping on people's heads, &c. &c," as well as "coaches or carts obstructing a footway" and "persons placing obstructions or filth in the streets."[20] In all, scarcely reassuring news. And this was at a time when London streets had been much improved and were widely admired by visitors, their paving and clean-liness ranking with Vienna's, and far above that of Paris or Berlin or squalid provincial backwaters.

Yet the London streets could also be alluring, just as Lamb at-tested. A new literature of urban adventure around 1700 was pro-duced by men (only men) who found these streets both pleasant enough to enjoy and exciting enough to be worth writing about. Ned Ward's sensational tales of "the London Spy," Joseph Addison and Richard Steele's articles in *The Spectator*, and John Gay's long poem *Trivia: or, The Art of Walking the Streets of London* all led readers through the streets and recounted the pleasures as well as the perils to be encountered by day and by night. They were the pioneers of a literature of urban exploration that flourished throughout the cen-tury and into the next one.

PARIS IN THE 1800S

Paris could claim to be even more crowded than London, and noisier too. In 1700, each city had about half a million residents, with Paris's squeezed into a much smaller area. In the narrow lanes of Paris, the congestion was greater and the going was slower, but for sheer lack of space the crowds were not as overwhelming. Rich and poor lived in closer proximity. The unchallenged capital of fashion and ele-gance remained the city where inequality was most blatant. Whether the poor of Paris really lived their lives on the street more than those of London, as was often claimed, is difficult to know, but their pres-ence on the streets was more visible to outsiders.

By the late eighteenth century, the upper classes in both cities had begun to fear the unruly masses as never before. The Wilkite demon-strations in the 1760s and the Gordon Riots of 1780 showed London-ers that the people might, by acting en masse, intervene in national politics. Much more frightening were the developments in Paris be-ginning in 1789, when the poor rapidly created their own means of political expression and enforced their views through sheer numbers assembled in the streets. There, in the streets of Paris, the era of rule by the masses—as a hope or a threat, if seldom a reality—had begun. Throughout the next century, the Paris crowd repeatedly seized the reins of power, if only for brief moments. The crowd gave city life a new, historically portentous import.

Apart from the brief revolutionary outbreaks, however, overt political tensions remained mostly invisible—always in the background, never entirely forgotten, but submerged in the daily struggles of the crowd. Paris, more than London, became the city where rich and poor learned to share the street. The deference of the poor (usually) and the consideration shown by the rich (sometimes) lubricated their daily interaction. Disputes, verbal and physical, might be settled by the intervention of strangers, the assertion of customary neighborhood authority, or the arrival of official force in the person of the constable or soldier.

A growing number of nineteenth-century intellectuals plunged eagerly into the crowd to observe the public faces of rich and poor alike. Around 1840 Parisian intellectuals began to write a great deal about the "flâneur," a loner said to wander the streets anonymously to observe the urban crowd. The early twentieth-century Berlin critic Walter Benjamin identified the flâneur as the characteristic figure of Paris, the "capital of the nineteenth century." His quintessential flâneur was the poet Charles Baudelaire, whose prose poem "Crowds" exalts the man who "melts into the crowd" to "take a bath of multitude" with its "feverish ecstasies." Many scholars have followed Benjamin's lead and heralded the flâneur as the harbinger of a new artistic consciousness. Whether they are correct, particularly in seeing nineteenth-century Paris as fundamentally more modern than eighteenth-century London, is impossible to say. Clearly, though, the anonymous urban crowd had become an enthralling spectacle as well as a sobering reminder of human vanity in England too. Already in 1749, Henry Fielding put the essence of flânerie into the mouth of a character in his novel *Tom Jones*: "I hastened therefore back to London, the best retirement of either grief or shame, unless for persons of a very public character; for here you have the advantage of solitude without its disadvantage, since you may be alone and in company at the same time; and while you walk or sit unobserved, noise, hurry, and a constant succession of objects, entertain the mind."[21]

If eighteenth-century English writers took note of the urban crowd, nineteenth-century Parisian art and literature plunged into it. Both the visual and the verbal arts portrayed characters bombarded, if not overwhelmed, by the torrent of people and sensations on the street. Writers—Balzac, Hugo, Flaubert, Zola—placed their characters on the streets they knew. Their novels evoked the crowd and the street more than those of eighteenth-century London. Parisian newspapers invented the laconic report of local sensations, the *faits divers*, and also created the feuilleton, a newspaper supplement that invited urban commentary—and subsequently spread across the Continent. Prints and paintings increasingly showed bustling streets rather than placid urban landscapes. Artists such as Louis-Léopold Boilly brought their viewers directly into intimate and even claustrophobic street scenes, painting, for example, a bourgeois family crossing a gutter on a narrow plank put down by a petty entrepreneur who holds out his hand for payment.[22] Strolling in the streets was not an entirely new custom for the upper crust, but the fashionable promenade seems to have given artists license to take stock of the diverse crowd rather than look only at the select few. A remarkable aspect of this fascination with the crowd was a thirst to plumb the depths of the dark lanes and the "dangerous classes," those exotic, larcenous, and violent denizens of the shadows, an indulgence documented in sober statistical treatises on disease and prostitution but perhaps most evident in the extraordinary popularity (and widespread imitation) of Eugène Sue's cliché-ridden but gripping novel *Les Mystères de Paris*, serialized in 1842–43.

A greater emphasis on public display—of manners, clothes, and façades—ensured that Paris, more than London, sparkled in the eyes of visitors. At least that is what they told us. The awestruck young Italian writer Edmondo De Amicis, riding past the shops and throngs of the boulevards upon his arrival in 1878, decided that "those who have not seen it will never be able to envisage the spectacle of that living stream which flows without rest between those two endless

FIG. 6. Louis-Léopold Boilly, *The Downpour*, c. 1804.

walls of glass, amid that verdure and that gold, beside that noisy tumult of horses and wheels, in that wide street whose end one cannot see." The visible crowd also turned his mind to the memories of eminent personages who had once walked the same streets: "One experiences a kind of pleasure in being there on that pavement scattered with crushed ambitions and dead glories."[23]

Nineteenth-century Paris also led the way in reshaping streets to suit the new age. The prefect Georges-Eugène Haussmann, acting on the authority of Emperor Napoleon III, set the international standard for radical urban renewal in the 1850s and 1860s by piercing the inner city with broad new boulevards lined with stately buildings. The self-styled "baron" was able to create what other civic leaders had long dreamed of, and now sought to emulate: streets where middle-class commerce and leisure flourished, air and traffic (and soldiers) flowed freely, clean water gushed in and wastewater poured out.[24] The many pre-1850 descriptions of Parisian strolls attest to the fact that Haussmann did not invent the fashion for wandering amid the crowds. His reforms did, however, magnify its appeal. Without destroying all the charms of old Paris, the inventive and ruthless

Haussmann made it easier for fastidious people to enjoy them, and thus he ensured Paris's stature as the paramount city of stimulation and delight, and as the headquarters of twentieth-century theorists of flânerie.

BERLIN IN 1900

Berlin was a latecomer to the ranks of great metropolises. In 1800 its population of 150,000 ranked behind such capitals as St. Petersburg, Naples, Amsterdam, and Lisbon, and far below London and Paris. Even within the German lands, it was no match for the imperial grandeur and lively crowds of Vienna. A century later, Berlin rivaled Paris as Europe's second-largest city (they were third and fourth in the world after London and New York). Its rapidly expanding belt of gargantuan factories and teeming tenements marked it as the most modern of cities, a "German Chicago" as dynamic and unsettling as its North American counterpart. German intellectuals began to ruminate about the world-historical significance of city life. Much of what they saw would not have surprised an eighteenth-century Londoner, though: crowds of strangers thronging the streets, hawkers clamoring for their attention while obstructing their path, the rich brushing elbows with the poor.

Two things were fundamentally different, however: the looming threats of urbanization and democracy. Whereas eighteenth-century London was an urban behemoth in a rural world, the industrial revolution had meanwhile transformed far more than just a few big cities. By 1850 England became the first country with a majority of its population living in towns. Germany caught up rapidly, crossing the same threshold around 1900. When German theorists tried to characterize metropolitan personalities, they knew they were describing the twentieth-century world, not just a peculiar corner of it. Wordsworth's consternation at the anonymous London crowd was soothed by the assurance that he could retreat to a place where he belonged. His great city was a freak show, a frightening aberration, or an astonishing spectacle. Hardly anyone thought it was the future. By 1900 it was common to look at Berlin that way.

The nineteenth century was engulfed by the urban crowd. In 1800, when London's population reached one million, its only rivals in size were faraway Edo (Tokyo) and Beijing. By the 1840s, Paris passed the million mark while London was piling more millions on the first. Late in the century, the imperial capitals of Berlin, Vienna, and St. Petersburg also joined the million club, along with New York, Chicago, and Philadelphia, with other second cities (Manchester, Hamburg, Budapest, Moscow) not far behind. More visitors to more places, and of course far more city dwellers themselves, knew how it felt to be overwhelmed by a crowd. The experience of being part of the throng, once exceptional, became commonplace.

The visible challenges of the city spawned a generation of urban reformers, many of them employed by German municipal governments and determined to root out the filth and poverty they saw. Their remedies included bold plans to rebuild cities along more decentralized lines. Not the least of their targets were the crowded and disorderly streets. New schemes for housing, industry, sanitation, and transportation foresaw replacing the chaos of the street with something tidier—something that was perhaps not a street at all. Inspired by Haussmann's Paris, planners hoped not merely to emulate his boulevards but to guide their cities' rapid growth along more rational lines.

The statistical facts of urban growth were better known to scholars and policymakers than to ordinary people negotiating the streets. What might have mattered more to most Germans was the changing relationship between social classes. The poor far outnumbered the wealthy, just as they always had. The chasm between rich and poor remained immense, in wealth and in social standing. Yet something was different. Perhaps social distinctions were more fluid, although the baker's son or daughter had occasionally risen to wealth and social position before. The difference was rather the baker's— and, more important, the factory worker's—sense that his status as a citizen gave him a kind of equal rank, a belief increasingly ratified by law, as civil equality and hesitant steps toward democracy began to fulfill the promise of the French Revolution.

The change in attitude began in the street, or at least was most visible there. Conservatives were horrified by the lack of deference working-class urbanites showed to their betters. Others hoped to see more such behavior: they urged the newly urbanized Germans to conduct themselves as a metropolitan people, not a subject people. Unlike Londoners and Parisians, Germans were not used to finding crowds when they stepped out their doors. By the 1840s Adolf Glassbrenner could express delight at the spirited crowds on Königstrasse, the main thoroughfare of Berlin's old center (now Rathausstrasse, and unrecognizable), which he called "Berlin's stomach" because its countless shops and restaurants attracted a perpetual throng of excited consumers.[25] As late as 1879, though, the Londoner Henry Vizetelly reported that it was still the only street in town "where one gets jostled by a crowd."[26] Nevertheless, Karl Gutzkow opened his 1877 Berlin novel *Die neuen Serapionsbrüder* with his characters discussing "a new nervous ailment" called "sidewalk disease," induced by the involuntary intimacy of the narrow pavement.[27] Soon the animated crowds of Friedrichstrasse and Potsdamer Platz became an indispensable ingredient in every description of Berlin, and the experience of the street sparked anguished debates about the psychic burden it imposed. At the end of the century, the Western world, but especially Germany, saw widespread unease and occasional panic about an epidemic of neurasthenia caused by the stress of urban life.[28]

The crowds multiplied during these decades of astonishing growth, as hundreds of thousands of migrants arrived from the provinces. Visitors from London and Paris grumbled that Berliners behaved like hayseeds, obstructing the walkways with their sluggish movement and clumsy comportment. The die-hard Berliner Arthur Eloesser saw a deeper problem: his fellow Germans in 1909 were only beginning to cast off their "atavistic tendency to draw distinctions and presume too much." He believed that a metropolitan crowd expressed its modernity by refusing to acknowledge class and caste. In insisting on social distinctions amid the crowds, Germans "come across as provincials" even as they unforgivably "obstruct the tempo" of the street.[29]

Berlin
Friedrichstrasse,
Ecke Leipzigerstrasse

FIG. 7. Berlin, Friedrichstrasse. 1914 postcard.

In its darker corners, though, the Berlin of 1900 became notorious as the most daringly modern of cities, where provincial diffidence changed overnight into metropolitan brashness. Visitors sought out notorious nightspots on back streets, where they could check their bourgeois proprieties at the door along with their hats. Berlin became famous as the place for experiments with alternative sexualities, whether in Magnus Hirschfeld's pioneering laboratory of "sexual science" or in racy nightclubs sought out by tourists hoping to be shocked, titillated, or liberated.

German writers and artists grasped for ways to explain what was new about an urban world. Young Friedrich Engels had been a pioneer with his excruciating descriptions of Manchester and London slums in the 1840s. He and Karl Marx thought English factory workers and Parisian street crowds would upend the social order that produced such misery. More fearful theorists turned their attention to the frightening manifestations of crowd psychology, while others tried to make sense of new identities. The pioneering sociologist Ferdinand Tönnies drew an influential distinction between the social bonds of the traditional organic "community" and the artificial urban "society."[30] The first years of the twentieth century saw painters such as Ernst Ludwig Kirchner and Ludwig Meidner produce the garish portraits of Berlin street crowds that became the defining images of German expressionism, if not of the modern city in general. Writers proposed to let the physical artifacts of the city wash over them to create a new poetry, as Alfred Döblin declared in his 1913 "Berlin Program" for authors: "I am not me, but rather the street, the lamp, this and that event, nothing more." The poems and paintings have often been seen as expressing terror, but in them we can also recognize what the architect August Endell invoked in 1908 as "the beauty of the metropolis" in all its unsentimental grandeur.[31] Meanwhile, visionaries sketched architectural forms that might shape or at least suit new ways of living.

During the 1920s and 1930s, the Berliner Walter Benjamin tried to assemble a monumental account of how the modern social order became visible in the nineteenth-century Parisian shopping arcade. His friend Siegfried Kracauer offered the hotel lobby, prominent in film and detective fiction, as the exemplary site of modern encounters and the hollow substitute for a church in a godless world. Both of them drew on the work of the older sociologist Georg Simmel, who argued that the street's sensory overload produced a cool defensive response that he characterized as the "blasé attitude" (and who also applied his knowledge of Kant and Plato to a brief treatise on "flirtation").[32] These Germans, together with their English and French forebears, launched the study of mass society that has continued ever since.

DECLINE AND FALL

Nineteenth-century Paris and turn-of-the-century Berlin have frequently been heralded as the birthplaces of modernity or "the modern," which in turn have often been situated in the city street. But modernity is also blamed for the demise of the street. According to the avowedly modernist view that prevailed in the twentieth century, the decline of the street was a story of progress, spread out over a cen-

FIG. 8. Ernst Ludwig Kirchner, *Women on Potsdamer Platz*. Woodcut, 1914.

tury or two. Technological breakthroughs, greater wealth, respect for privacy, better sanitation, and perhaps moral progress all combined to draw one activity after another off the street and into its own designated space. Streets, in other words, ceased to host a jumble of varied pursuits that had no other home, and thereby lost their traditional purpose. Whether the result—our contemporary streets—really represents progress eventually became a matter of dispute.

The chapters that follow examine these activities in their heyday and in decline, tracing the simplification of the street and the disentangling of its traditional functions. The street hawkers, markets, and open-fronted shops described in chapter 2 yielded to enclosed shops

that sometimes ceased even to face the street. The formal promenades, informal socializing, and street entertainment examined in
chapter 3 mostly withdrew to more private spaces. A more universally applauded development is the topic of chapter 4: the eventual
end to the street as a waste disposal site. Meanwhile, transportation,
the subject of chapter 5, gradually became the dominant function
of streets, as movement accelerated and claimed more and more
space. The efforts of rulers, police, and planners to maintain public
order, described in chapter 6, tended to restrict non-transportation
activities on the street, culminating in designs for streamlined transportation corridors. In all, it is a story of social and sensory impover-
ishment (except perhaps for noise) but also of efficiency and cleanliness, of control and segregation as well as democracy and order and
comfort.

Most activities retreated from the street gradually and unevenly.
After rulers moved many of their ceremonies indoors, mass politics
sometimes claimed the street, but even that mostly dispersed, as
institutions arose to organize popular participation and give it enclosed facilities. Religious processions do continue to pass through
many streets, but in Europe they have seldom maintained their central role in communal life. Although clusters of street vendors and
outdoor markets are still to be found, most commerce has long since
become an indoor activity, as has the production of nearly all goods.
People still socialize on the street, but far less so than they once did.
Likewise, street entertainment has become the exception, not the
norm, and the kind of social display once associated with public
promenades has largely removed itself to more exclusive environments if not to virtual sites.

If the only legitimate function of the street remaining was motor-
ized transportation, it made sense to imagine that the street could be
dispensed with entirely and replaced by more specialized facilities
such as elevated railways, underground trains, and limited-access
highways. The twentieth century saw no shortage of visionary designs to sweep away the accumulated detritus of centuries. But there
was a lot of history to overcome.

2

Wheeling and Dealing

The Street Economy

The street economy could be very lively. J. W. von Goethe's walks
through Naples in 1787 persuaded him to reject the standard complaint that the city's streets teemed with idlers. He observed the
notorious Neapolitan crowd busily engaged in all kinds of useful
tasks: chopping and carving wood, preparing food, carrying goods
to and from markets, and selling them in the streets. Perhaps, he
thought, the more relaxed pace of life in the Mediterranean climate
fueled northerners' prejudices, as did the people's visible pleasure
in their work: "It appears that they all want to enjoy and contribute
to the great festival of delight that is celebrated daily in Naples."[1]
Similar if fewer complaints dogged the hordes swarming Victorian London's chillier streets, where Nathaniel Hawthorne, too, saw
enterprise, not indolence: "It is strange to see how many people are
aiming at the small change in your pocket; in every square, a beggar-
woman meets you, and turns back to follow your steps with her miserable murmur; at the street-crossings, there are old men or little
girls with their brooms; urchins propose to brush your boots; if you
get into a cab, a man runs to open the door for you, and touches his
hat for a fee, as he closes it again."[2]

For centuries, a great many people claimed the street as their
workplace. Changes in production, exchange, and street design during the past two centuries have not only removed a great deal of toil

from the streets, they have also more firmly separated indoor and outdoor employment, isolating the remaining street workers from the rest of the labor force. Before this gradual but momentous transformation, labor and trade were essential components of street life, and the street was a vital place of commerce for vocations high and low.

We seldom think of banking and finance as outdoor occupations, and indeed it has been centuries since eminent merchants and brokers huddled in the streets of Venice and Antwerp and London to make their deals, but Paris's Pont au Change was once called Pont des Changeurs because the city's money-changers were obliged to ply their trade in the open air of the bridge. Other kinds of labor remained on the street much longer. Artisans' work spilled out the front doors of their workshops to take advantage of sunlight, space, and sociability. Hawkers accosted their customers or exhorted them to approach booths or barrows. Waiters patrolled the outdoor terraces of cafés, or delivered breakfasts through the neighborhood. Where commerce flourished and crowds gathered, street entertainers were sure to follow, offering music and magic and puppets—and more: itinerant commedia dell'arte troupes in eighteenth-century Paris maintained a side business in tooth pulling, which itself could be a rather theatrical enterprise.[3] Street preachers sometimes drew crowds as well, where religious toleration permitted them to proselytize. Muscular laundresses lined the banks of some inner-city streams and canals, such as the Seine and the Canal Saint-Martin in Paris, whose murky waters lent feeble assistance to their Sisyphean struggle against the encrusted street dirt on everyone's clothes. At designated times and places, job seekers swarmed the street, either at a customary site for hiring servants or day laborers such as the Place de Grève in Paris, or, by the late nineteenth century, outside newspaper offices to get a look at the job advertisements as soon as they came off the press.

Communications and transportation supplied a growing number of outdoor jobs as the eighteenth century turned into the more mobile nineteenth. Teamsters and conductors offered to carry your

goods in a wagon or yourself in a taxi or bus. Messengers and porters, whether freelance or in someone's employ, stood ready to take
your burden and your coin. Nineteenth-century Berlin boasted a
famously visible caste of porter-messengers, who displayed their official licenses on armbands (similar to their counterparts elsewhere)
as they waited at their posts outside major buildings. Because they
were stationed at conspicuous sites, they were universally known
as "Eckensteher"—corner-standers—and they became notorious
for their indolence, insolence, and copious consumption of cheap
spirits. They were credited with nurturing the famously sharp-
tongued Berlin humor, even as they became the favorite target of
the city's most popular humorist, Adolf Glassbrenner. Their refusal
to debase themselves before potential clients lent them a subversive air of dignity. "They have a deal of sly cunning and drollery; a
dry manner; will have the last word; and are sure to turn the laugh
against their antagonists, be they high or low, educated or uneducated. . . . They are always ragged, fond of drink, and ready with their
repartee," explained William Howitt in 1842, as he drew on familiar
ethnic stereotypes to describe them to his fellow Englishmen: "They
are a most un-German sort of fellows—the Irish of Berlin."[4]

The men, women, and children at the very bottom—the dregs of
society—were particularly visible, since they devoted their lives and
exertions most exclusively to the streets. Beggars, prostitutes, and
criminals were fluid categories with a great deal of overlap, as desperate people risked their dignity, health, and freedom in order to
survive. Prostitutes often went unmentioned but were seldom invisible, whether or not they were legally permitted to solicit on the
street. Some managed to project an air of elegance, but more typically they were desperately poor women (or men) with nothing left
to sell but their ravaged bodies. In the eighteenth century, they may
have been as much pitied as reviled; the nineteenth century was
more moralistic but also tried to help more. In 1751 Samuel Johnson published a story that powerfully evoked the miseries of a girl
dragged into prostitution. Although James Boswell often paid for the
services of street prostitutes, he and Johnson "talked of the unhappy

situation of these wretches" after being solicited on the Strand in 1763.[5] Among those peopling a 1792 description of Berlin's elegant promenade Unter den Linden are the prostitutes who crowded its benches at night, driven by hunger to solicit passersby "without any feelings of shame or honor."[6]

Perhaps the true street people were the beggars, especially those to whom all doors were closed. Many became familiar faces in their neighborhoods. They were variously treated with compassion, contempt, or revulsion, reactions that often concealed fear. A mid-nineteenth-century tendency toward sympathy is apparent in (and was encouraged by) Dickens as well as Victor Hugo's creation of the noble urchin Gavroche. But comfortable citizens assuaged the pangs they felt by telling each other that many beggars were feigning their disabilities and perhaps were not even poor, as in Conan Doyle's Sherlock Holmes story "The Man with the Twisted Lip." In *The Hunchback of Notre Dame*, Hugo revived the hoary tale of the colorful beggars' hideout at the Cour des Miracles. There was in fact such a gathering place until the seventeenth century, although most of the lore associated with it was fictional. The "miracles" were the blind and lame street beggars who limped home every evening and then emerged at night in blooming health. Everywhere, the number and visibility of beggars varied according to the intensity of police repression and the state of the economy: while war might cause inflation and shortages, peacetime was often a disaster, bringing a lull in industrial production and a returning surplus of soldiers and sailors. The respectable public dreaded the daily reminders of the precariousness of urban life, occasionally panicking in fear that the hordes might get out of control. When officials cracked down, beggars might be arrested, expelled beyond the city gates, or transported to the workhouse or the fleet. But they kept coming back. Mendicancy was a visible problem that was never solved.

When starvation loomed, the step from beggar to thief was often a short one, although not every street criminal was desperately poor. Pickpockets and robbers were invisible to all but the most practiced eye, their inevitable (if often exaggerated) presence revealed only when it was too late. Crime rates certainly varied over time and between cities, but reliable statistics are scarce, and the perception of rising crime was probably more common than the reality of it. The presence of thieves, beggars, prostitutes, and other reprobates ensured that constables and watchmen remained among the most visible street workers. Also contributing to official efforts to manage the streets was a growing force of street cleaners and other maintenance workers, tending to the slowly expanding systems of public works.

ITINERANT STREET VENDORS

Street hawkers remain a familiar sight in cities around the globe, but their role in the developed world's economy has become marginal. When shops were fewer and less accessible, and most people had neither the money nor the time to shop for more than their immediate needs, mobile sellers supplied an astounding variety of goods and services: mending shoes and pots and chairs, and selling food and drink for immediate or later consumption, potable water, pots and pans, trinkets and statues, newspapers and prints, shoeshines and rat traps, in addition to offering the trifling pleasures provided by wandering musicians, magicians, and jugglers in exchange for a few coins.

Today's hawkers thrive on car traffic in some cities, but only where traffic jams prevail. In the pre-auto age, the occasional customer came by carriage but most were pedestrians. Many vendors followed established family trades and might even have managed to live in a modicum of comfort. Others appeared to be among the lowest of the low, "a covert mendicancy" (according to Dickens), condemned to a miserable existence in the open air because they could not find more secure employment.[7] Hawkers flourished in the biggest cities, since only immense crowds made it possible to eke out a living in the implausibly specialized niches that many of them sought to exploit, as we know from the reports of astonished visitors from the provinces: selling chestnuts or scraps of iron, rosemary or radishes, tinder boxes or smelts, cat's meat or canaries.

Innumerable descriptions, pictures, complaints, and police regulations give us a sense of the ubiquitous presence of street vendors, even if we have few reliable statistics. One study found over twenty thousand in Berlin at the end of the nineteenth century.[8] Visitors to crowded Paris reported feeling overwhelmed by the swarms of hawkers, but their numbers probably peaked in the teeming streets of Victorian London, where the indefatigable journalist Henry Mayhew's encyclopedic survey of street trades at midcentury counted fifty thousand street sellers, most of them "costermongers," a word that originally meant "apple sellers" but had become the name for hawkers of vegetables, fruits, and fish. Mayhew classified the trades exhaustively: the sellers of fish, poultry, meat, and cheese; vegetables and fruit; "eatables and drinkables"; "stationery, literature, and the fine arts"; manufactured articles; secondhand articles; live animals; and "mineral productions and curiosities." He also surveyed the several categories of street performers (showmen, artists, dancers, musicians, singers, purveyors of games); the street artisans who fabricated things as you watched (metal pins, knit caps and doll dresses, wooden spoons, glass bowls, and much else), or mended goods, or made them at home and sold them in the streets; the street laborers who cleaned, lighted, and watered, or who offered or crafted advertisements; and street servants including horse-holders, porters, and shoeblacks.[9] Most of these street trades, and a few others, could be found in any major city. Some had been around for centuries, while others sprang up with the availability of new products or technologies in the industrial and colonial age — cheap printing, for example. Mayhew's rare achievement in the 1840s and 1850s was to engage sellers in conversation and record their occupational and life stories. There is good reason to doubt the absolute veracity of his verbatim transcriptions of hundreds of interviews, too many of them reinforcing middle-class prejudices, but his sympathy with his subjects was often in evidence and their value as a general picture is unparalleled.

Memoirs recall pleasant encounters with hawkers. Maximilian Rapsilber, describing his youth in nineteenth-century Berlin, remembered feeling a kind of comfort even in the presence of the crippled veterans of Prussian wars settled on their benches in the

FIG. 9. Oyster stall, London, mid-nineteenth century. Print by W. G. Mason adapted from a daguerreotype, in Mayhew, *London Labour and the London Poor*.

shade of Unter den Linden. Another pleasantly piquant memory was that of "the much-loved pickle sellers. With a fork the men pulled out the pickled cucumbers, and regular customers or other good friends were also permitted to take a swallow of the juice." The sandman was a familiar presence, with his pair of brutalized young assistants and his skeletal horse pulling a rickety wagon. He carried his product through doorways by the apronload for women to scour their floors. The "turf women" who sold their cheap fuel from large baskets were infamously filthy, while the dainty milkmaids from still-rural Schöneberg maintained a more wholesome image, despite their notoriously adulterated product, with gleaming metal cans and diminutive carts drawn by wretched dogs.[10] We have many other testimonies across the centuries from satisfied customers who could brighten their day with a fresh bun, or a shoe-shine, or a bunch of flowers. In 1884 Charles Hindley observed agreeably that hot green peas were still being sold in the streets of London by the halfpennyworth or pennyworth, as they had been for centuries, served with a ladle "and eaten by the customers out of basins provided with spoons by the vendor," who would add salt, pepper, or butter on request.[11]

Inevitably, however, the historical record is also filled with complaints about the hawkers obstructing traffic, or molesting pedestrians, or stealing or cheating or obstreperously begging, or simply begriming the streets with their unwelcome presence. Showmen who drew crowds with their adroit displays of exotic goods or mechanical skill were the most likely to raise hackles as well.[12]

In his sketch of Vienna in 1787, Johann Pezzl let public opinion judge the butchers' booths outside St. Stephen's cathedral: "you see how all passersby hold their noses and avert their faces."[13] He also decried the obstruction of traffic by "a breed of insolent, shameless, pushy, deceitful, depraved women, who have occupied every street and lane, every square, every corner and every entrance to churches and houses, year in and year out." He described them as living dictionaries of Austrian provincial insults and complained that they cruelly harassed country dwellers who came into town to sell their goods, not relenting until these poor men surrendered their goods to the city women for resale.[14] Female vendors in Bologna had faced similar complaints two centuries earlier. They stood accused of tainting the good character of the honest market-gardeners (also women) who came from the countryside to sell their produce. Bologna, in fact, banned the urban vendors from the market square during the hours the peasants were selling.[15] This hostility reflected long-standing prejudices against both city dwellers and women. The enduring figure of the stolid peasant, unspoiled by city ways, is ancient and perhaps uneradicable, although the same can be said of its mirror image, the foolish country bumpkin. Obviously the misogyny also has a long history. Respectable women in the city streets—and men, too—had to be protected from immoral influences: fallen women could so easily infect the innocent. The usually unspoken fear was that these public women were prostitutes, eager to ruin men and country women alike.

Shocking improprieties could also serve as entertainment, however. The German clergyman Friedrich Wendeborn showed himself to be somewhat less censorious than many of his English colleagues when he visited London's notorious Billingsgate fish market in 1779: "Whoever wants to witness natural powers of speech, figures of oratory, well chosen epithets, strong expressions, delivered with an audible voice, in the vulgar English tongue, let him offend one of these fish-women."[16] By 1700 the word "billingsgate" had come to mean scurrilous or abusive language, and in 1852 the market was still called "the lowest point to which the English language can descend."[17] But the greatest variety of verbal talents may have been found among news criers, whose business was, after all, fundamentally verbal. Those in London led the way, since its eighteenth-century press was freer and more diverse than that of continental cities.

Hawkers announced their presence boldly, and not everyone was pleased to hear them. Giovanni Paolo Marana, an Italian visitor to Paris in 1692, thought the deaf should be grateful to be spared "such a diabolical uproar."[18] His satirical tone was taken up by many pens. Joseph Addison printed a letter from a (presumably fictional) gentleman who offered to better orchestrate the chorus of London cries, lamenting that they were "so full of Incongruities and Barbarisms, that we appear a distracted City, to Foreigners. . . . The Chimney Sweeper is confined to no certain pitch; he sometimes utters himself in the deepest Base, and sometimes in the sharpest Treble. . . . The same Observation might be made on the Retailers of Small-cole, not to mention broken Glasses or Brick-dust. In these, therefore, and the like Cases, it should be my Care to sweeten and mellow the Voices of these itinerant Tradesmen."[19]

Jonathan Swift claimed he wouldn't have minded the cries of Dublin if they had been intelligible:

> Perhaps there was never known a wiser institution than that of allowing certain persons of both sexes, in large and populous cities, to cry through the streets many necessaries of life; it would be endless to recount the conveniences which our city enjoys by this useful invention, and particularly strangers, forced hither by business, who reside here but a short time; for, these having usually but little money, and being wholly ignorant of the town, might at an easy price purchase a tolerable dinner, if the several criers would pronounce the names of the goods they have to sell, in any tolerable language. And therefore till our law-makers shall think it proper to interpose so far as to make these traders pronounce their words in such terms, that a plain Christian hearer may comprehend what is cried, I would advise all new comers to look out at their garret windows, and there see whether the thing that is cried be tripes or flummery, butter-milk or cow-heels.[20]

Swift, like Addison, was not being entirely serious. He was merely using the familiar sounds as comic grist while he warmed up to a satirical attack on political polemics, pretending to argue that the Dublin dustmen who called for "dirt to carry out" had to be Tory hirelings making malicious reference to Whigs, and that the fishwives who cried "buy my fresh plaices" were in fact advertising the corrupt sale of government offices.

London's intolerable street noise was a recurring theme in English art and literature. The plot of Ben Jonson's 1609 play *Epicœne* turns on the central character's desperate efforts to shroud himself in silence. One of William Hogarth's best-known etchings is "The Enraged Musician" (1741) in which a bewigged violinist despairs at the hubbub of wandering singers, performers, and traders swarming beneath his window. Hogarth may not have been taking sides: among the grotesque figures on the street, a quietly elegant milkmaid exudes more virtue than the fuming violinist. Nor is there an obvious message in Paul Sandby's painting, a few years later, of women apparently delighted at the raucous scene outside their window. Their ear trumpets, and the picture's title, "The Asylum for the Deaf," suggest that they may have been among the few who could abide the street noise.[21] In the next century, Thomas Carlyle grappled with his own ambivalent feelings. Visiting London in 1824, the young Scot wrote to his brother of the "coaches and wains and sheep and oxen and wild people rushing on with bellowings and shrieks and thundering din, as if the earth in general were gone distracted. . . . There is an excitement in all this, which is pleasant as a transitory feeling, but much against my taste as a permanent one. I had much rather visit London from time to time, than live in it."[22] However, this famously dyspeptic Victorian did settle in the midst of London's excitement for the last half-century of his long life. Eventually he had a special soundproof study built into his house to protect him from a "vile yellow Italian" organ-grinder among other street noises.[23] Things were little different in other cities. Carl Herloss thought visitors to Vienna must find "the ceaseless jangling and tootling" of street music intolerable, although the Viennese themselves seemed resigned to its inescapable din.[24]

Victor Hugo and Charles Dickens, on the other hand, claimed to need a backdrop of street noise to sustain their pens.[25] The sights and sounds of the Paris and London streets populated their rich tapestries of urban life. One of Dickens's youthful "Sketches by Boz," a street scene of two housemaids flirting with a baker's boy, could have been the opening scene of a novel. Even as he and other citizens welcomed familiar sounds, some visitors were enthralled by the vendors' oral talents. In 1789 Friedrich Schulz catalogued the ways Paris hawkers drew attention to themselves: clowns, street stages, drums, fiddles, voices of pamphlet sellers loudly reading out juicy excerpts. He marveled that the "sellers and buyers of old clothes buzz parrot-like through their teeth; the rabbit-fur merchants meow almost like cats; the water carriers manage to sound almost like toads."[26] Other visitors described the cacophony of Parisian street vendors as an in-

FIG. 10. William Hogarth, *The Enraged Musician*. Engraving, 1741. Library of Congress, Music Division.

FIG. 11. Paul Sandby, *Asylum for the Deaf*, watercolor, late eighteenth century. © Victoria and Albert Museum, London.

decipherable hubbub, but Louis-Sébastian Mercier, the great chroni-
cler of pre-revolutionary Paris, claimed that servants five floors up
could immediately pick out the distinctive call of a trade whose services they required.[27]

Street entertainment took many forms, including juggling, acro-
batics, dancing, acting, and instrumental music. The mobile Punch-
and-Judy stages with their violent puppets were major attractions.
But singers were probably the most numerous performers. Pathetic
beggars sometimes tried to attract attention with vocal efforts that
were unlikely to awaken sympathy. The tireless classifier Mayhew
introduced street musicians this way: "As a general rule, they may
almost be divided into the tolerable and the intolerable," the latter
"only making a *noise*" in the hope that they might be given money
"merely as an inducement for them to depart."[28] On the professional side, itinerant street singers (*Bänkelsänger*) were a fixture
of the German lands for centuries. The biggest cities had resident
troupes, while others wandered from town to town, seeking out a
central square to intone their ballads of crime and calamity and intrigue, more or less based on recent or historical events. At times
they functioned as singing newspapers. Their origins seem to have
coincided with that of the printing press, and they often made their
paltry living chiefly by selling printed sheet music.[29] The eminent
magistrate John Fielding attested to vocalists' visibility in the London of 1770 when he complained to Parliament "that Ballad-singers
are a greater nuisance than Beggars, because they give Opportunity
to Pickpockets, by collecting People together." He may have divulged
the true source of his animus when he added that "the songs they
sing are generally immoral and obscene."[30] By the nineteenth century, authoritarian leaders like Metternich and Napoleon III sent
police censors into the streets because they feared the subversive
potential of songs and prints.

Hawkers were the "familiar strangers" of premodern urban life
(to borrow a term from twentieth-century social psychology), visible
or audible outside the window and an unavoidable presence in
the streets. The comforting familiarity of their cries marked daily

rhythms and neighborhood identities. An anonymous poem from the early 1700s, "On the Death of Old Bennet the News-Cryer," detects "a sudden silence" in the London air, because "Bennet, the Prince of Hawkers, is no more":

> He, when the list'ning Town he would amuse,
> Made Echo tremble with his bloody News,
> No more shall Echo now his voice return,
> Echo forever must in silence mourn.

Even a familiar figure like Bennet probably remained a stranger to his customers. A social chasm separated hawkers from their more comfortably situated customers; and even among their fellow poor, they often set themselves apart in occupational, family, or ethnic networks that dominated a city's trade in a particular product or service. Where neighborhoods were knit together by networks of kin and labor, the mobile hawkers, however familiar, remained outsiders, perhaps trusted, perhaps not. Although some street traders sold goods produced by local artisans, most lacked any ties to the guilds that dominated commerce in pre-nineteenth-century towns. Often they had scant urban roots at all. Some goods or skills came to the cities via well-established migration routes. Messengers, bootblacks, and other street trades in eighteenth-century Paris became associated with migrants from Savoy, especially children, and "Savoyard" came to mean a street trader there as well as in London, even when the hawkers came from somewhere else. Many trades were in fact dominated by a particular ethnic group. Mercier surveyed them in Paris: "The Savoyards are bootscrapers, clothes-brushers, and sawyers; nearly all the Auvergnats are water carriers; the Limousins, masons; the Lyonnnais are usually porters and chair-men; the Normans, stonecutters, pavers, and peddlers, crockery menders and sellers of rabbit skins; the Gascons, wig-makers or surgeons; those from Lorraine, itinerant cobblers."[31] Vienna drew its hawkers from all corners of the Habsburg realm: linen dealers from Silesia; Croatian onion sellers; Greeks who sold pipes; orange vendors from Car-

niola. Victorian London was known for its Irish apple sellers, Neapolitan and Calabrian ice-cream vendors, German brass bands, and
Italian organ grinders. Among the well-known Italian figures in Berlin and Vienna were those festooned with salami and the statuary
vendors balancing long boards on their heads. Eighteenth-century
Madrid's knife-grinders were usually French, while its water carriers came from Galicia or Asturias.[32] It is proverbial, but nonetheless true, that Jewish old-clothes dealers and Roma fortune-tellers
dominated their disreputable trades in many cities and were usually
viewed with suspicion. Some hawker clans staked out their own residential corners of the city, using tranquil courts as their marshalling
yards every morning.

These exotic figures made the street the most cosmopolitan part
of a city, where strangers and languages mingled in a display of imperial diversity. Visitors to Vienna, capital of a thoroughly multinational European empire, often commented with delight on the astonishing variety of costumes and characters thronging its streets.
Into the nineteenth century, distinctive clothing made it easy to pick
out Greeks, Turks, Armenians, Roma, and Polish Jews as well as the
more familiar Hungarians, Italians, and Slovaks. Meanwhile, London's streets could boast an intercontinental cast drawn from its
far-flung empire. Mayhew was surprised to learn that most sellers
of Christian tracts were "foreigners, such as Malays, Hindoos, and
Negroes," including some who could speak no English and even
some who were Muslims. He also interviewed Indian "tom-tom"
players as well as "Ethiopian serenaders" and ballad-singers. His
interviewees described small and close-knit non-European communities, visible to all Londoners but acquainted with few of them.[33]

Many of the rural-to-urban networks had a seasonal rhythm, dictated by harvests or holiday products. A passage in John Gay's 1716
poem *Trivia* celebrates the seasons through their products:

Successive cries the season's change declare,
And mark the monthly progress of the year.
Hark, how the streets with treble voices ring,

To sell the bounteous product of the spring!
Sweet-smelling flowers, and elder's early bud,
With nettle's tender shoots, to cleanse the blood:
And when June's thunder cools the sultry skies,
Even Sundays are prophan'd by mackerel cries.
Wallnuts the fruit'rer's hand, in autumn, stain,
Blue plumbs and juicy pears augment his gain;
Next oranges the longing boys entice,
To trust their copper fortunes to the dice.
When rosemary, and bays the Poet's crown,
Are bawl'd, in frequent cries, through all the town,
Then judge the festival of Christmas near . . .[34]

A century and a half later, the most fortunate of London's Italian ice-cream vendors spent their winters in rural Calabria, living there (or so fantasized the journalist Adolphe Smith) almost like English country gentlemen.[35]

A standard literary device of urban chroniclers was the essay tracing the course of a day in the city, a modern urban adaptation of an ancient artistic and poetic convention. Already in the early eighteenth century, William Hogarth satirized this pastoral tradition with his series of four paintings and prints of dawn, noon, evening, and night, scenes crowded with the squalid affairs of the London street instead of the gods and shepherds of his classical models.[36] His older contemporary Jonathan Swift was another artist who embraced the sordid realities of human nature. His 1709 poem "A Description of the Morning" was defiantly anti-pastoral, setting the scene with the day's first hackney coaches and

Now Betty from her master's bed had flown,
And softly stole to discompose her own.

before proceeding to the sights and sounds of the street:

The small-coal man was heard with cadence deep;
Till drown'd in shriller notes of "chimney-sweep."

FIG. 12. John Thomson, *Halfpenny Ices*, London, 1870s. Los Angeles County Museum of Art, www.lacma.org.

Many writers employed the genre as a way of bringing order to the cacophony of the streets. Along the way they catalogued as many sights, sounds, and smells as possible, typically emphasizing their pleasant variety. From the diligent predawn market workers to the night watchmen, criminals, prostitutes, and revelers, each hour offered its familiar and often comforting sights, such as the muscular milkmaids so extravagantly admired by the peculiar Victorian poet Arthur Munby and by the Parisian writer Jules Janin, who, writing in the fictional guise of a visiting American, recalls the daily arrival of his delivery: "This was my amusement every morning. How often have I placed myself at the window just to see this youthful and solemn peasant, distributing here and there, right and left, with a parsimonious hand, her pure milk mixed with fresh water!"[37] John Sanderson, an actual American in Paris, chose to entertain his readers by painting the street cries as an unfolding plague:

> First the *prima donna* of the fish-market opens the morning: *Carpes toutes fraiches; voilà des carpes!* And then stand out of the way for the glazier: *Au vitrière!* quavering down the chromatic to the lowest flat on the scale. Next the iron-monger with his rasps, and files and augers, which no human ears could withstand, but that his notes are happily mellowed by the seller of old clothes: *Marchand de drap!* in a monotone so low and spondaic, and so loud as to make Lablache die of envy. About nine is full chorus, headed by the old women and their proclamations,

announcing the news of the day, all "tuned to different keys. All things of this earth seek, at one time or another, repose—all but the noise of Paris. The waves of the sea are sometimes still, but the chaos of these streets is perpetual from generation to generation; it is the noise that never dies."[38]

Much of the daily rhythm was dictated by markets and suppliers. Vendors of fresh flowers, fish, or fruit bought their supplies in a central market at dawn, and then scattered across the city, seeking to empty their baskets before their goods spoiled or their customers vanished. Their predawn pursuits, along with those of late revelers, were in turn sustained by the proprietors of coffee carts—although in the seventeenth century, before coffee became an affordable fixture of European life, Paris's preferred wake-up drink was brandy. The daily rhythm might vary on the weekend, as dictated by custom or by law. John Trusler's 1786 London guide informed the unwary that "milk and mackrell are allowed to be cried about the streets on Sundays, before nine in the morning and after four in the afternoon, but at no other time of the day," and nothing else might be hawked on the Sabbath.[39]

Some jobs were mostly in the hands of children. Many were reliably gender-specific, with the divisions often but not always falling where we might expect. Shoeblacks were usually boys, while girls sold flowers and took charge of child-minding. Milk, in demand every morning, especially after coffee reached a mass market, remained a female product, even though many milkmaids had to balance heavy pails on their shoulder harnesses.

The sentimental Victorians could recoil in disgust from street people, but they might also cherish them as mirrors of a common humanity, as Richard Rowe did in an 1881 description of his neighborhood watercress seller: "If people far more worthy of notice, according to their own conventional notions, than my poor old watercress-woman, only knew how little they are noticed by their neighbours in this everybody-for-himself London—unless some accident makes their existence interestingly recognizable—perchance there would be a little less self-conceit in the world."[40] A similar realization dawns on the narrator of Franz Grillparzer's 1847 novella *Der arme Spielmann*, who comes to admire the simple nobility of a poor Viennese street musician.

Whereas many trades required apprenticeships and shops, and were organized in guilds, others were ceded to the streets. A continuum rather than a clear line separated ambulatory from sedentary vendors. While the most picturesque hawkers carried their tools and goods through the streets in baskets or harnesses, others set up tables or sold from carts or barrows and might do all their daily business at one spot, which was acknowledged to be theirs by right of possession, or agreement with other vendors, or perhaps either the licensing or the connivance of the police. Still more sedentary were those whose temporary stalls became more or less permanent kiosks wherever the police authorized or tolerated them. It was these booths that most often attracted the ire of nearby shop proprietors, who cried unfair competition, and also of upstanding citizens who complained to the authorities or to the press about the ugly encumbrances that blocked traffic or simply blighted the streets.

Street vendors have always been regulated, more or less, and have always faced criticism if not revulsion for their actual or alleged noise, filth, obstruction, harassment, and thievery, all of which could be very real and yet also proxies for visible poverty. Hawkers typically worked in a murky quasi-legality. Sometimes their very presence was plainly forbidden, but more often they maneuvered among unevenly enforced municipal regulations. Accusations of unfair competition might lead to crackdowns, as could the growing attention to street sanitation. At times there were attempts to regulate noise. More broadly, anti-hawking sentiment reflected changing beliefs about the purpose of streets. Complaints about hawkers blocking traffic multiplied as streets became congested. Regulations, and complaints about them—as either too lax or too strict—document the ceaseless tension between a desire to crack down on visible disorder and the welcome presence of vendors. The hawkers' sworn enemies, like Henri Gisquet, Paris's prefect of police during the 1830s, insisted that they shunned regular work, cluttered the streets, evaded taxes, and competed unfairly with shops. Although other officials proved more sympathetic, street vendors could not count on official acknowledgment that they provided useful services to, and employment for, the urban poor.[41]

In many places, street selling thrived through the nineteenth century and beyond. Already in the eighteenth century, though, demands to remove market stalls and other street traders were frequent, if seldom heeded.[42] The spread of permanent shops, for more goods and in more streets, buttressed the argument that hawkers were not needed. Most British towns banned street selling in the nineteenth century, during the same decades that they were building new market halls to replace the stalls that spilled across market squares and into surrounding streets.[43] Berlin placed strict limits on ambulatory vendors as it built its network of municipal market halls in the 1880s and 1890s.[44] However, market halls in the largest European cities often fared poorly in competition with street vendors. Even at Les Halles in Paris, most retail trade was carried on outdoors.[45] Nor did London follow the rest of Britain in banning street vendors: no one there could imagine streets free of them. When the Metropolitan Streets Act of 1867, a milestone in the nineteenth century's fixation on traffic flow, banned the placement of goods any-where on London's streets except for loading and unloading, it effec-tively outlawed street commerce. Although the absurdity of the new law went unnoticed in Parliament, it quickly became notorious on the street, as is apparent from a derisive broadsheet (one of many in its satirical genre) sold in the streets by an enterprising London printer. Among its clauses parodying the new law:

> That no persons shall under any pretence leave any goods in the streets for more than sixteen seconds and a half; and any baker rest-ing his basket for a longer space of time, shall for the first offence, for-feit his basket, and for the second, be compelled to stand three hours in a flour sack.

And another:

> No shoeblack will be allowed to polish up your understandings, nor use the words, "shine your boots, sir," without being duly licensed ac-cording to Act of Parliament . . . and any donkey braying without an order from the Commissioners shall be taken into custody, and fed upon cabbage stumps for one month.[46]

In the face of protests, the Home Secretary hastily amended the bill to relegalize hawking, and street commerce continued to thrive in London. Most continental cities also opted for mild regulation, in practice if not in law. Police regulations, in fact, offer copious evi-dence of recurring and mostly ineffective crackdowns on hawkers. For example, Paris forbade street selling at the edges of public mar-kets and in front of shops offering similar goods.[47] Paris was also typical in its strict requirements for the licensing of hawkers. These rules usually met with limited success, since hawkers were mobile by definition and wary by nature.

STREET CRIES

One remarkable trove of evidence attests to the inescapable and welcome presence of hawkers in European urban life. For centuries, commercial prints of local street traders were produced and sold in many lands, typically as broadsheets arrayed with individual portraits. Eventually there were many variations, some printed singly and others collected in books, or even as playing cards or commercial packaging. For all its variations, though, the genre was immediately recognizable across borders and centuries. Why their production persisted for so long is something of a mystery, beyond the apparent fact that they continued to sell. Many were marketed to tourists as souvenirs, others presumably to local residents. Some were tacked up on the walls of shops, offices, and homes.[48] For residents and visitors alike, they sustained memories of familiar sights, sounds, and smells. Buyers of the prints would not have been the traders themselves but rather the upper-class visitors to the streets—who may indeed have seen themselves as visitors, intruding on the territory of the street folk. For these outsiders, constrained by their class's prevailing codes of behavior, the street sellers were both an everyday sight and an exotic race that performed a colorful show on the most public of stages.

Illustrations and poetic renderings of street cries have survived from the Middle Ages, before artists and printers quickly exploited the new printing presses to launch the tradition of printed sheets. Among early examples from Renaissance Italy, one of the best known and most imitated sets of prints was engraved from drawings made by the Bolognese artist Annibale Carracci in the 1590s. Many of the earliest prints appeared in France. In seventeenth-century Paris, and then in London, they proliferated, with later engravings from the work of such major artists as François Boucher and Edmé Bouchardon. Fewer but still numerous examples can be found by the late eighteenth century in all neighboring lands.[49] We can even follow the prints' return to the street: Mayhew's nineteenth-century survey of London street trades includes a section on ambulatory sellers of prints, which raises the question of whether sellers might sometimes have patterned their postures and cries on prints rather than vice versa.[50] The genre seems to have thrived up to the middle of the nineteenth century. Its decline thereafter paralleled that of street trading to some extent, but the more immediate cause may have been the growth and speed of urban traffic that made hawkers less visible and less audible. The more interesting question, albeit one that eludes any definitive answer, is why they maintained their popularity for so long. Why was it not merely acceptable but actually fashionable, for centuries, to gaze upon images of the urban poor? For some reason, hawkers remained not merely a familiar but also a welcome sight.

The typical broadsheet—perhaps just a few images but often twenty or thirty or even far more—depicted a representative of each street trade, often alone, and arranged the portraits in rows and columns. In this form they simplified, categorized, and froze the tumult of the street. The representatives of most trades remained either reliably male or female across the centuries, probably reflecting reality in most cases, with women or girls selling fruits, vegetables, and flowers while men or boys shined or repaired shoes, played barrel-organs, and hawked pots and pans. Each figure wears the characteristic apparel of the trade and is encumbered with its goods, whether a basket of buns or pails of water or milk secured by a sturdy harness. By the eighteenth century, many prints had become scenes of urban life, with the trader appearing against a background of street scenery or, less frequently, interacting with customers. By the nineteenth, some were evolving into a new tradition of genre scenes. At mid-century they also faced competition from horizontal strip prints of actual storefronts, a new product that reflected the changing shape of retailing.[51]

Each figure was identified by his or her characteristic tools and poses. The theme of some series was the distinctive clothing worn by practitioners of each trade. The rat catcher's ruff and jerkin were conspicuously old-fashioned by the eighteenth century, for example, making him identifiable across Europe even without the box of poi-

LES CRIS DE PARIS.

PORTEUR D'EAU. A l'eau!
à l'eau!

M^d DE POIRES D'ANGLETERRE.
A deux liards tous les Anglas.

M^d D'HABITS. M^d d'habits,
vieux galons!

M^de DE MARÉE. Ah! qu'il est beau
le Maquereau!

M^ar D'OEUFS. A trois desix blancs,
les rouges et les blancs!

M^ds D'HUITRES. A la barque!
à la barque!

M^d DE SALADE. En voulez-vous
de la salade!

M^de DE POIS. Pois ramés,
pois écossés!

M^de DE CERNEAUX.
Mes gros cerneaux!

M^d DE PARAPLUIES. Parapluies!
Parasols!.

M^de DE CHIFFONS. Vieux bas,
vieux souliers, vieux chiffons!

M^d DE TISANNE. A la fraîche,
coco, qui veut boire!

M^d DE CERISES. A la douce cerise,
à la douce!

M^d DE PEAUX DE LAPINS.
Lapins! lapins! lapins!

M^de DE BOUQUETS. Mesdames de
belles roses, achetez donc des roses.

LE COMMISSAIRE.
La paix! la paix!

FIG. 13. *The Cries of Paris.* Printed by Lacour in Nancy, 1831.

son around his neck or the dead rats hanging from his belt.[52] More broadly, the prints reveal just how widely known these types were, and the desire to acquire them also suggests that the traders' familiar presence might somehow have been comforting.

This familiarity was not only visual. In fact, this genre of prints was known as "street cries" or the "cries of Paris" or London or Hamburg. In a world where sound recording was inconceivable, the pictures evoked the customary cry of each trade, with its recognizable phrase, meter, and even melody. Typically the prints show the trader in the act of uttering his or her tune or phrase, and often the words are printed below the portrait. To take a few London examples that require no translation: "Buy a steele or a Tinder Box" (1650); "Ripe yeoung beanes" (1655); "Ha y'any knives to grinde" (1655); "Rats or mice to kill" (1655); "Buy my dish of great eels" (1711 and 1821); "Sweet China oranges, sweet China" (1794); "Old cloaths, any old cloaths" (1799); "Come buy my fine singing birds" (1804); "The King's speech, the king's speech to both houses of Parliament" (1812); "In the Gazette Great News to-day" (1820); "Old chairs to mend" (1839); and of course the legendary if numerically puzzling "one a penny, two a penny, hot cross buns."[53] Some prints also featured quatrains or longer verses. These were typically literary embellishments of actual cries in a tradition reaching back into the Middle Ages — a well-known example being Autolycus's song in Shakespeare's *The Winter's Tale* — and which lives on in nursery rhymes about Simple Simon and the Muffin Man. By the eighteenth century, collections of cries were being published as children's books.[54]

Some prints even included musical scores to notate the tunes sung by sellers of a product. When we think of street music, we think of fiddlers and organ-grinders, but, even more than the performances of street musicians, sellers' cries were the music of the streets. And they also became the music of salons and concert halls. The German bibliophile Zacharias Conrad von Uffenbach, browsing in a London bookshop in 1710, explained the advantage of buying a set of "Cries" that included musical notation: "The extraordinary sounds that they call out or sing can be remarkably well imitated

FIG. 14. Marcellus Laroon, "Buy my fat Chickens," c. 1700. Yale Center for British Art, Paul Mellon Collection.

with the violin."[55] The melodious music caught the ears of prominent Renaissance composers in England and France, including Clément Janequin, Jean Servin, Richard Dering, Orlando Gibbons, and Thomas Weelkes, who incorporated these cries into their own compositions, as did the eighteenth-century French comic opera composers Charles Favart and Charles-François Panard. The tradition lasted into the nineteenth century and beyond, for example in Offenbach's *Mesdames de la Halle*, Puccini's *La Bohème*, Gershwin's *Porgy and Bess*, and the 1960 musical adaptation of Dickens's

Oliver Twist—and even into the YouTube era with Muhammad Sha-hid Nazir, London's "One Pound Fish" man. The growth of popular theater in the nineteenth century may have reversed the direction of influence, with street criers imitating the authoritative models they saw on stage.[56]

Of course we cannot rely on these prints as a documentary record of premodern street life. The artists and printers applied their own styles of portraiture and posture, and they pursued various aims: documenting street life, perhaps, but more likely seeking pictur-esque beauty there, or displaying their facility at portraying bodies and drapery, or giving shape to a moral ideal of working-class life, or enabling their upper-class patrons to feel at ease in the streets of their own city. The figures in the prints were stylized: again and again we see a trade assigned the same gender, the same clothing, the same pose, and the same phrases. To some extent this reflects reality: traders followed established traditions, and they counted on being identifiable to customers by their characteristic dress, ges-tures, phrases, and tunes. Over the centuries, though, the portraits were clearly based more on earlier prints than on live observation. Nevertheless, they offered a kind of map of urban life. Just as illus-trated maps and *vedute* were sold as fashionable mementos of a city, and just as a guidebook could define a city through its acknowledged monuments, so, too, could a matrix of hawkers' portraits serve as an illustrated guide to its visual and aural identity.[57]

It is paradoxical, though, that these images were typically con-joined to the identity of each individual city. Across the centuries, the printed "cries of London" were remarkably similar to the "cries of Paris" and of other cities, as the occasional traveler noted. Images marketed as the local color of London or Paris or Vienna were in fact more like universal urban icons, the sights and sounds that dis-tinguished the city from the country. They were souvenirs of a pan-European urban identity. And within each city, the street traders came to signify the vast urban working class, of which they were the most visible members. Mayhew offered his *London Labour and the London Poor* as an encyclopedic survey of all trades, yet "the London

Street-Folk," a small minority of the London working poor, take up three of his four volumes (with the fourth devoted to "prostitutes, thieves, swindlers and beggars"). The composer Georges Kastner accompanied his symphonic adaptation of cries with an essay describing them as "the voices of Paris."[58] The contrary view was that of their contemporary Karl Marx, for whom these street people were the essence of the "Lumpenproletariat," the ragged fringe of the true working class.

After the mid-eighteenth century, ambitious artists varied the genre even as banal imitations of the old broadsheets persisted. The late eighteenth-century humorists James Gillray and Thomas Rowlandson subjected hawkers to their own styles of grotesque caricature. A few other artists employed the familiar figures for social commentary, evoking either sentimental harmony or painful chasms between rich and poor. An encounter at a doorway or window, for example, might suggest a lighthearted exchange or, less often, a frisson of social tension. Paul Sandby's set of London etchings from 1760 broke with tradition in its portrayal of dirty and dubious hawkers.[59] To a remarkable extent, however, the street criers were not depicted as the "other"; the prints neither aroused pity at their lot nor caricatured them as morally degenerate flotsam. Usually they appeared in dignified poses, neither comical nor misshapen nor even visibly bent under their burdens. For all the care lavished on some of the figures, most represented types rather than known individuals. Into the nineteenth century, with occasional exceptions, their bodies conformed more to classical ideals of the human form and of graceful posture than to the realities of poverty and toil. To some extent the prints were, deliberately or unconsciously, made more appealing to buyers by ennobling the vendors' poverty.[60] Perhaps they expressed hopes of civilizing the poor or simply acknowledged their humanity. The production of these images first flourished at the same time as the aristocracy practiced the ideal postures of classical dance in Louis XIV's France. The movement and interactions invoked by the prints were certainly not the same thing as the "sidewalk ballet" described by Jane Jacobs centuries later, yet in both cases the daily

FIG. 15. Paul Sandby, "Any Kitchen Stuff," from his *London Cries*, 1759. Yale Center for British Art.

interactions in the street reveal human contact and coexistence, if perhaps not harmony, amid a world seething with discord. The floating population of the street offered a source of artistic inspiration, and later of popular memory and identity. It was an odd and limited way of expressing solidarity or sympathy with the visible poor.

Along with the work of the subjects themselves, the portrait tradition was in decline by the late nineteenth century, a time when hawkers probably became less numerous and certainly became less visible, displaced by long-term changes in the retail economy but also by competition for street space as well as aural space, with the clatter of horseshoes, street railways, and iron wheels on stone pavement threatening to drown them out. By then, middle-class buyers of prints were also less likely to do business with them. Even so, hawkers remained a familiar presence in the big cities, and photography gave the genre a new lease, whether in the traditional portraiture of Vienna's Otto Schmidt or London's John Thomson (see figs. 12, p. 57, and 16, p. 72) or the more circumspect approach of the street photographers Eugène Atget (see fig. 38, p. 165) and Louis Vert in Paris, Emil Mayer in Vienna, and Heinrich Zille in Berlin. A more visible revival came with the new picture postcards of the late nineteenth century, which also celebrated lively street scenes that featured hawkers as a typical motif.

FROM ECONOMICS TO FOLKLORE

For centuries these printed images depicted contemporary urban life. After 1800, though, a new hint of nostalgia crept in. The nineteenth-century middle classes could experience hawkers as part of their daily lives and yet also as vestiges of a misty past. After the French Revolution, an educated public more attuned to historical change could be persuaded that hawkers were colorful relics of a bygone era in which the poor had been picturesque and unthreatening. This historicization or folklorization of street vendors is apparent in some nineteenth-century prints and descriptions.[61] A decline in street vending, real or imagined, became an opportunity to reflect on what was being lost.

Well into the nineteenth century, hawkers' vital role in the urban economy was seldom questioned. During that century, though, some trades were vanishing, either supplanted by shops or displaced by changing fashions or newer technologies—sedan-chair carriers, for example, a trade that died out soon after 1800. By 1841, Charles Knight observed that thanks to modern piped water, "it is impossible London can ever again see a man bent beneath the weight of a yoke and two enormous pails, vociferating 'Any fresh and fair Spring Water here?'" While he was certain that vendors would never again sell spring water in the streets, he was also convinced that some things could never change: since "there can be no reservoirs of milk, no pipes through which it flows into the houses" surely "the cry of 'Milk,' or the rattle of the milk-pail, will never cease to be heard in our streets."[62]

Victor Fournel's 1887 book on cries was an elegy for the "unending symphony" that once filled the air of old Paris.[63] But some traditional cries may have persisted even when they served little practical purpose, as sales moved indoors and sounds were supplanted by signs. Charles Booth, observing London's Brick Lane Market in the 1880s, saw "absolute indifference on the part of the buyer to these cries. They seem to be accepted on both sides as necessary, though entirely useless."[64]

Already in 1845, Honoré de Balzac lamented that street life had been impoverished during his lifetime by the disappearance of entire trades, such as the families that had subsisted on the business of lighting and maintaining the city's oil lamps until they were displaced by the introduction of gas lanterns. Balzac also cherished fond memories of the familiar red umbrellas of greengrocers' carts, a trade supplanted by the growth of shops. And the purveyors of folk remedies, "those heroes of the public square, now carry out their business on page four of the newspaper. . . . Those charlatans who braved laughter in their faces, out in public, did not lack courage, whereas the charlatan lurking in a mezzanine is more disgraceful than his drug."[65] A few years earlier, Eduard Kolloff may have sensed the winds of change when he urged his readers to hurry to Paris to hear the sounds of the street. Imagine a world in which all these cries have been silenced, he wrote. "How could our descendants have any understanding of them?" But surely, he thought, "the Parisians will never let this custom die out" since "on the day the cries in its streets are silenced, Paris will be slumbering in its grave."[66]

A decline in the number of itinerant street sellers probably con-

FIG. 16. John Thomson, street doctor, London, 1870s. From J. Thomson and Adolphe Smith, *Street Life in London* (London: S. Low, 1877).

tributed to a decreased awareness of them, but it is difficult to know with any certainty. The same might be said of the lowly beggars. The nineteenth century saw growing public and official attention to beggars, much of it sympathetic, along with a new determination to stamp out begging. Shifts in opinion and policy were particularly abrupt in London, where the establishment of the Metropolitan Police in 1829 was followed by the Poor Law of 1834, which prescribed confinement to the workhouse as the cure for poverty. Those laws accelerated a process that had already begun in England and elsewhere. During the eighteenth century, beggars may have been taken for granted or regarded as local color, whereas later they were more likely to be objects of pity but also, often, of contempt. Poems and essays that acknowledged a shared humanity spurred unprecedented efforts to help them, but this very recognition also may have made their proximity distressing.[67]

Writers and artists of the Romantic generation sometimes resolved their feelings of fellowship by, indeed, romanticizing the beggar as well as the hawker. In 1822 Charles Lamb, for example, lamented the "decay of beggars in the metropolis" while recalling the unimpaired good spirits of

> a well-known figure, or part of the figure, of a man, who used to glide his comely upper half over the pavements of London, wheeling along with most ingenious celerity upon a machine of wood; a spectacle to natives, to foreigners, and to children. He was of a robust make, with a florid sailor-like complexion, and his head was bare to the storm and sunshine. He was a natural curiosity, a speculation to the scientific, a prodigy to the simple. The infant would stare at the mighty man brought down to his own level. The common cripple would despise his own pusillanimity, viewing the hale stoutness, and hearty heart, of this half-limbed giant. Few but must have noticed him; for the accident, which brought him low, took place during the riots of 1780, and he has been a groundling so long. He seemed earth-born, an Anteus, and to suck in fresh vigour from the soil which he neighboured. He was a grand fragment; as good as an Elgin marble. The nature, which should have recruited his reft legs and thighs, was not lost, but only retired into his upper parts, and he was half a Hercules.[68]

Thirty years later Dickens declared that Lamb's "decay has now approached dissolution," as was apparent in streets that "are now purged and live cleanly." Dickens was as capable as any Victorian of genuine sympathy for the downtrodden, in, for example, a tender description of a ragged woman trying to sing for a few coins while passersby jeered at her. Yet he, too, offered a wildly unreal portrait of a vanished street person: "The spirit of street mendicity and mendacity is broken; the genius of beggars' invention has shrunk into the envelope of ill-worded begging letters. Where is there now a man like 'the Scotchman,' who wore four waistcoats and three coats, but was shoeless and hoseless, and had a loose robe, disposed like a lady's shawl about him, and so artistically, that he looked 'a deplorable object?' And did he not gain his thirty, or forty, or fifty shillings a-day by pure begging?"[69] Wordsworth, in *The Prelude*, had been more honest when he recalled having been "smitten / Abruptly, with the view (a sight not rare) / Of a blind Beggar":

> And, on the shape of that unmoving man,
> His steadfast face and sightless eyes, I gazed,
> As if admonished from another world.

Reading this last line, we might accuse Wordsworth of reducing the beggar to, literally, an alien creature; but the poet at least acknowledges that the beggar's "sightless eyes" make his very humanity an unsettling presence.

In 1822 Lamb could not imagine that street cries would fade away, and for him the vanishing beggars were a part of the same vital tapestry: "The Mendicants of this great city were so many of her sights, her lions. I can no more spare them, than I could the Cries of London. No corner of a street is complete without them. They are as indispensable as the Ballad Singer; and in their picturesque attire as ornamental as the Signs of old London. They were the standing morals, emblems, mementos, dial-mottos, the spital sermons, the books for children, the salutary checks and pauses to the high and rushing tide of greasy citizenry."[70] In fact, it was the beggars who endured, and the hawkers who faded away. After centuries of the city's sonic landscape defined by a cacophony of musical cries from human voices, the industrial era drowned them out with its mechanical clatter and roar.

THE (WRITTEN) WORD ON THE STREET

The public display of written words has a long history, as a tool to uphold public order, oppose that order, disseminate news, regulate traffic, and—perhaps most of all—to sell. Newspapers began to supplant criers of news in the seventeenth century, but at first only for a small and literate public. The nineteenth century saw a more profound if gradual shift from oral to written communication, from cries to signs, from the spoken and sung word to the silent scream. The spread of schooling and literacy contributed to the change, as did the enclosure of shops. Goods could be seen through windows, but not touched or smelled from the street. Sellers could no longer hail passersby, unless they stood in their doorways, a tactic that came to be associated with disreputable establishments. Other means of communication had to replace face-to-face contact and speech—or to serve as a prelude to it, by luring customers into shops. Shop signs, though not new, became more numerous and more verbose. They proliferated before the era of rapid transportation and then grew to previously unimaginable size during the automotive age, culminating in billboard landscapes and entire buildings designed as eye-catching commercial logos.

In times of political ferment, the city street has often been the battleground between authority and rebellion. (This, in fact, is where the topic of "streets" is most likely to attract the attention of historians.) Since 1789 the most famous political streets have been those of Paris, although every capital has had its revolutionary moments. Subversive manifestos appeared on walls, as scribbled words or printed posters; they were removed or replaced by official proclamations, which in turn were defaced or ripped down. People gathered to read and share the news, and sometimes they became revolutionary crowds. Twenty-first-century electronic devices heralded as the new tools of liberation are merely the successors to the handbill, the poster, and the shout, capable of rapidly spreading pictures and slogans.

Posted rules have also targeted more mundane threats to public order: stay to the right, keep off the grass, no smoking or spitting or littering, post no bills. Then there are the basic labels of place. Street names are very old, but signs with those names are relatively new, standardized in many cities during the nineteenth century, along with the new practice of numbering houses. The older custom of naming houses, and adorning them with corresponding pictorial signs, lingered only as a quaint survival, now best known on English pubs. Posted instructions for traffic control first appeared in crowded late nineteenth-century streets, directed at pedestrians or vehicles or both. "Walk on the left!" commanded signs in turn-of-the-century Vienna, in a tentative effort to manage the relentless streams of pedestrian traffic.

When we think of words on the street, however, we mostly think of commercial appeals. Shop signs in the Middle Ages, and long after, were pictorial symbols associated with a trade, often in the form of massive boards or sculptures suspended over the street: a shoe or a key, shears or a pretzel, the apothecary's mortar and pestle, St. Lawrence's grill (for vendors of roasted meat), or the spiral stripes of the barber's pole. As they accumulated in busy shopping streets, the visual cacophony could be either stimulating or overwhelming. Or dangerous: low signs knocked heads, and heavy ones sometimes came crashing down. In response, Paris restricted the size and height of signs during the late seventeenth century. In the 1760s both Paris and London banned hanging signs entirely, requiring them to be mounted flat against walls. Thereafter they oozed across every available surface. With the spread of literacy and of cheap printing, words often replaced symbols, and the written texts of advertisements and posters supplanted the oral communication of hawkers and stall keepers. London led the way, thanks to its high level of literacy and its booming commercial sector. Already in 1782 Carl Philipp Moritz was amazed by the sight of houses covered "from top to bottom with large letters painted on signs."[71] Pictures still competed with words in the Paris of 1822, according to the Frankfurt journalist Ludwig Börne:

The name of the shopkeeper and his product appears ten times on the doors and over the windows. The façade looks like a schoolboy's exercise book, repeating a few words over and over. The goods are hung in front of doors and windows, not just samples but entire arrays, sometimes festooned all the way from the third story down to the pavement. The shoemaker has painted the exterior of his entire house with shoes of all colors, arrayed in battalions. The locksmith's symbol is a six-foot-high golden key that would be big enough for the gates of heaven. Painted on the sock seller's shop are four-yard-high white stockings. In the darkness they give you a fright, since you think white ghosts are floating by. Each shopkeeper has baited a large hook for the smallest fish he wants to catch.[72]

The Austrian writer Adalbert Stifter described Vienna in 1844 as a city awash in vibrant language: in addition to the newspapers for sale, "on the street corners hang gigantic letters of all colors, but especially red ones." In some places "large stretches of wall are entirely covered from top to bottom, such that several hours would be required to read these things thoroughly. Here you see a giant, there a dwarf; dances, balls, diversions, entertainments, menageries, railway journeys, charabancs, music, and more."[73] On the boulevards of Paris in 1878, Edmondo De Amicis presumably exaggerated his despair at the suffocating spectacle: "You raise your eyes upward, but alas, there is no freedom even in heaven. Above the highest roof of the quarter, traced in delicate iron characters against the blue of the sky, is the name of a cloudland artist who wishes to take your photograph." Casting your eyes down at your café table brings no relief, since it, too, is covered with advertisements, as are the back of your chair and the floor and pavement below. The city "is a kaleidoscopic, inexhaustible, enormous graphic decoration, aided by grotesque images of devils and puppets, high as houses, which besiege you, oppress you, and make you curse the alphabet."[74]

Municipal and state authorities struggled to channel the flood of words. At midcentury, their desire to regulate commercial speech and urban aesthetics was overtaken by the fear of revolution, and

FIG. 17. John Orlando Parry, *A London Street Scene*, 1835.

they took aim at the political posters they had seen during the 1848 uprisings. A solution emerged in 1854 when the Berlin police granted the printer Ernst Litfass an exclusive concession to erect stout round advertising pillars on streets and squares. These ubiquitous Litfass columns, as they are still known in many cities, attracted the idle, the curious, and the information-hungry with their announcements of court news, music and theater, and much else, all subject to official approval.[75] In 1868 the printer Gabriel Morris obtained a similar franchise in Paris for his "Morris columns" (eventually acquired and exported by the multinational ad firm JCDecaux). Kiosks erected for the sale of newspapers or refreshments also served as billboards. Booksellers' shop windows often drew crowds, particularly to the racy or pornographic works for which London's Holywell Street became notorious.

Mobile advertising was another nineteenth-century innovation.

FIG. 18. Berlin, Litfass column. Drawing by Friedrich Stahl, 1888. *Die Gartenlaube* (1888): 667.

Sandwich men (and later women too), those peripatetic human texts, proliferated by the 1830s.[76] Around the same time, advertising vans made themselves unwelcome hindrances to traffic wherever they were permitted. A letter to *The Times* in 1846 bemoaned the "accursed vehicles" devoted to such debased purposes as "the promulgation of the merits of Holloway's ointment in curing diseased legs."[77] A few years later, Max Schlesinger (Germans seem to have been especially struck by the verbal landscape) declared that "their numbers are incalculable. . . . The Advertisement is omnipresent."[78] It spread still further when buses and trams became mobile billboards. Late in the century, electric lighting gave the written word a striking new prominence, especially at night. So did the simultaneous explosion of mass-market newspapers, most of which were hawked on the street.[79]

SHOPS AND STREETS

Written words and symbols came to the fore when masonry, glass, distance, or decibel levels defeated the human voice. The crucial change was the removal of commerce from the street. Shopping moved off the street slowly, unevenly, and never completely. Part of the story is the enclosure of shops, an important long-term development. The shopper's attention gradually shifted from the hanging sign (and hanging goods) to the display window. At that point, however, commerce returned to the street as window-shopping, which became a growing attraction of the afternoon or evening promenade.

Where shops supplanted ambulatory vendors, it became plausible to forbid the hawkers' presence, as happened in some places during the nineteenth century. The same fate befell many fixed street stands, such as the familiar "tobacco booths" of Vienna. An assemblage of stalls, tents, and mobile vendors made the Pont Neuf one of Paris's liveliest marketplaces until an official crackdown banned all structures in 1756, then reauthorized a limited few, before ultimately removing them amid the nineteenth-century promotion of mobility. Elsewhere in Paris, shallow wooden booths, just a meter wide, were built against walls, typically at street corners. In the mid-nineteenth-century era of Haussmann, they vanished rapidly, deemed incompatible with new standards of hygiene, the aesthetics of the wide street, and the new emphasis on traffic flow. An 1867 eulogy mourned the loss of these stalls from "the public street to which they brought life and gaiety."[80]

Clusters of temporary stands could usually lay claim to official

FIG. 19. Jean Henri Marlet, *Les charbonniers*, c. 1820. In front of a street-corner booth, next to men carrying bags of coal, a woman tries to stop a fight. Library of Congress, LC-DIG-pga-11630.

permission or at least long-term custom. These street markets have a long and varied history. Urban planners predicted and plotted their demise throughout the twentieth century, but they have never disappeared entirely. In many places they have thrived without interruption; in others they have been revived as a more indigenous and personalized alternative to chain stores and malls, buttressed by venerable traditions. In the European Middle Ages, most shopping took place in streets and squares, in daily, weekly, or seasonal cycles. The "market" became the name and recognized identity of at least one open space in every town, perhaps with a market cross or tower or fountain marking it as a place of peace and justice. The name "Les Halles" became attached to an entire neighborhood of central Paris, a bustling market district until its activities were moved to a suburb in 1971 and limited to wholesale business. Other large cities dispersed trade among several specialized markets. London's Covent Garden was the place to buy fresh produce and flowers from the seventeenth century to 1974, for example, while the central meat market was at Smithfield and fish sales remained by the docks at Billingsgate. At markets, people bought mostly food, with nearly all of it—fruits and vegetables, meat, eggs, dairy products—coming from the surrounding countryside, traditionally but not always sold directly from the hands of its producers. Farmers hauled their produce into town on carts, in baskets, or on their backs, and offered it at stands arrayed in a market square or along major streets—typically once or twice a week, although larger towns had daily markets. Many of the purchasers were hawkers who then resold the merchandise on the streets. The sale of other goods such as textiles traditionally took place at seasonal fairs that doubled as teeming entertainment venues, for example Bartholomew and Southwark Fairs on the edge of London and those of St. Germain and St. Laurent in Paris. The sites of fairs sometimes evolved into more permanent markets.

A long but uneven trend of moving shopping off the street (or square) was driven partly by official regulation and partly by entrepreneurial initiative. Town governments typically led the way in building market halls. Roofed or partially enclosed markets were erected in many cities across Europe from the late Middle Ages onward, but their heyday was the nineteenth century, the most striking examples being the twelve iron and glass pavilions Victor Baltard designed to house Les Halles in the 1850s. Market halls offered shelter to merchants, goods, and customers; they made sanitary improvements possible; and they cleared the streets for wheeled traffic. They might serve either wholesale or retail trade, like the outdoor markets they replaced. By the nineteenth century, market stalls increasingly had to compete with fully enclosed and autonomous street shops, and their proprietors often adapted accordingly, enclosing individual stalls more completely, separating messy trades (notably butchers) from others, and even building storefronts into the street façades of market buildings.

This is one of the origins of the shop as we know it: the market stall or street stand made permanent. Another line of descent comes from artisans' workshops, opening onto the street and doubling as sales rooms for the goods produced there by tailors, shoemakers, and carpenters, as well as butchers and bakers. Often there was a gradual transformation from the producer-retailer to the shopkeeper who sold goods that had been manufactured elsewhere. Artisanal work frequently spilled out onto the streets, as Goethe saw in the Verona of 1786: "There is not so much as a door in the shops or workrooms. The entire width of the house is open and you can see everything that goes on within. The tailors sew and the shoemakers work, all of them half on the street. The shops take up part of the street. In the evening, when the lights are on, things are very lively."[81]

The result might be noisy or smelly, but in quiet lanes of small towns or close-knit neighborhoods, passersby expected to see familiar faces doing familiar jobs. Bigger cities were more vulnerable to unhappy encounters between strangers. Already in the thirteenth century, the booming towns of Tuscany banned spindles and work benches from their streets.[82] Centuries later in the crowded lanes of Paris, middle-class residents and visitors grumbled about workers who seemed to think they owned the street. In 1835 the English writer Frances Trollope fumed at the presumption of Parisian street laborers: even on the fashionable boulevard des Italiens it was impossible to avoid "being frequently obliged to turn aside, that you may not run against two or more women covered with dust, and probably with vermin, who are busily employed in pulling their flock mattresses to pieces in the street. There they stand or sit, caring for nobody, but combing, turning, and shaking the wool upon all comers and goers; and, finally, occupying the space round which many thousand passengers are obliged to make what is always an inconvenient, and sometimes a very dirty *detour*." She was even more outraged by the fact that no one objected to the very idea of workers occupying the street. When she observed "a well-dressed gentleman receive a severe contusion on the head, and the most overwhelming destruction to the neatness of his attire, in consequence of a fall occasioned by his foot getting entangled in the apparatus of a street-working tinker, who had his charcoal fire, bellows, melting-pot, and all other things necessary for carrying on the tinning trade in a small way, spread forth on the pavement of the Rue de Provence," she was astonished to see that, despite solicitude for the gentleman's misfortune, "not a syllable either of remonstrance or remark was uttered concerning the invasion of the highway by the tinker; nor did that wandering individual himself appear to think any apology called for, or any change in the arrangement of his various chattels necessary."[83] Little did she know that it was only a few years since medical students had been ordered to cease dissecting cadavers in the lanes of the Latin Quarter.[84] This was precisely the era in which traffic flow was beginning to take priority over other uses of the street. The Englishwoman clearly thought the French were behind the times.

In large cities, shops clustered on major streets and gradually took over their entire frontage. London's Cheapside, to take an early example, was a solid double row of shops by the late Middle Ages. Shops in this era were permanent but not entirely enclosed. Typically their unglazed windows were closed at night with two horizontally hinged shutters. During the day the top board was raised to serve as an awning, while the other folded down to become a sales counter, displaying merchandise while separating the shopkeeper from the customer in the street. (The German word for the shutters, "Laden," also became the word for a shop. Similarly, the Spanish "tienda," meaning both shop and tent, recalls shop awnings.) Goods on interior shelves were visible but typically not accessible to customers. In other words, shopping streets had permeable street walls. They functioned much like open-air markets, which the earliest shops often faced. Shopkeepers greeted (or accosted) customers across the counter or in the doorway. In some times and places, though, it was customary to hang all kinds of goods around and outside shop windows and doors, where they could be readily seen, smelled, or placed in customers' hands. Cheapside shopkeepers' wives were said to sit in front of their shops to lure customers, although we should read that lore with caution, since it may merely reveal incomprehension of the fact that many Cheapside shops were owned by women.[85] Sometimes the connections between shopping and sex became more explicit. Censorious observers condemned the seductive smells and tastes on display in shopping streets and suggested that nearby brothels partook of the same methods.[86] Covent Garden in London was just one example of a busy market adjoining a brothel district. Its particular distinction was its flower market: young flower

FIG. 20. Jan and Caspar Luiken, *The Brushmaker*, 1694. From the New York Public Library Digital Collections, The Miriam and Ira D. Wallach Division of Art, Prints and Photographs: Print Collection.

girls, a favorite subject of sentimental art, were tacitly understood to be teetering on the brink between innocence and prostitution (as the fiercely unsentimental George Bernard Shaw knew his audience for *Pygmalion* would at first see the self-proclaimed "good girl" Eliza Doolittle).

In shops as well as in outdoor markets, all business was transacted in the open air of the street, a custom sometimes enforced by municipal or guild statutes. An honest bargain was expected to be made in public view. With food sales, there was the additional concern that it was too easy to pawn off spoiled or adulterated goods in the dim light of a shop.[87] Obvious hazards of the open air included wind and rain as well as dexterous thieves. It was the luxury shops, offering gold, jewelry, silk, and spices, that initiated a long and grad-ual revolution in shop design. The desire to protect merchandise was one motive. Another was the wish to shield wealthy customers from the indignities of the street—visual or olfactory or tactile—and offer them an enclosed and even lavish setting for the leisurely perusal of goods as well as an uninterrupted sales pitch. Some luxury shops specialized in perfume, a product suited to enclosed spaces. Tradi-tional department stores still place their perfume counters just in-side the street entrance as if to shield the rest of the store from the foul street air.

Luxury shops emerged in close association with the exchanges where the city's leading merchants, those engaged in long-distance trade, gathered their intelligence and made their deals. These were the centers of new mobile wealth in the mercantile cities of early modern Europe. At first the merchants gathered in the street itself—in London's Lombard Street, for example, named after the Italian goldsmiths who made it a thriving commercial hub. After 1691 they could meet in Lloyd's coffeehouse. Long before that, however, in 1571, Thomas Gresham's nearby Royal Exchange offered its arcaded courtyard for merchants to assemble and negotiate. As John Stow observed a few years later, it was built so that they could avoid the unpleasantness of "walking and talking in an open narrow street" where they would have to "endure all extremities of weather."[88] The arcade also housed a row of luxury shops that could claim an aura of exclusivity by their separation from the street. Gresham borrowed the idea of combining a mercantile exchange with a shopping arcade from the Nieuwe Beurs of Antwerp, which dated to 1531. Similar estab-lishments could be found in the other major commercial cities of the era, including the exchanges in Bruges and Amsterdam, the Rialto Market in Venice, and the Casa Lonja in Seville, all of which housed the cities' luxury shops. In seventeenth-century Paris, the same niche was filled by stalls lining the gallery of the Palais de la Cité, with the financiers operating out of the adjoining Place Dauphine. The with-drawal from the street could be a mixed blessing: within a few years, Gresham's building acquired a dubious reputation on Sundays, holi-days, and at night as a gathering place of "rogues" and "whores."[89]

During the seventeenth century, London's finest shops abandoned it for the more respectable New Exchange opened in 1609 on the Strand, with its broad arcaded façade designed by Inigo Jones for the Earl of Salisbury. Its shops included haberdashers, stocking-sellers, linen-drapers, tailors, goldsmiths, jewelers, milliners, perfumers, silk mercers, hood-makers, stationers, confectioners, girdlers, and dealers in china, pictures, books, maps, and prints. Here the wealthy could shop for imported luxuries while strolling and mingling with their own kind.[90] As a further precaution against the uncouth ways of the street, the New Exchange's rules forbade its shopkeepers to "pull or hale any man as he cometh by."[91]

More generally, cities saw a gradual enclosure of shops, mainly from the mid-1700s to the mid-1800s, although some exclusive London shops, including at the New Exchange, glazed their windows before 1700. In 1782 Jacques-Hippolyte Ronesse blamed glazing for the fact that the streets of Paris were filthier than they had been twenty years before, when most shops still had open fronts and shopkeepers had scrubbed the pavement diligently to reduce splattering on their goods.[92] Shops on Vienna's premier shopping street, the Graben, mostly ceased to display merchandise in the open air during the last two decades of the eighteenth century, instead enclosing it in glass cases set before the shop doors. Soon after 1800, the display cases migrated inside the shop door.[93] Technological improvements made plate glass available in larger panes, encouraging the use of window displays, first in exclusive shops and then more generally. Large and inexpensive sheets of plate glass became widely available by the mid-1800s. There was no sudden breakthrough, however. Even the small panes used in the eighteenth century could be carefully mounted to dazzling effect in the new bow windows. The German scientist Georg Christoph Lichtenberg marveled that the small-paned shop fronts on Cheapside in the 1770s "seem to be made entirely of glass."[94]

After 1800 established city shops were usually closed off from the street. The purchase of goods became an indoor activity, not for all shoppers or all items, but for many. The lure of the shop was reduced to the visual, and shop owners recognized the vital importance of catching the passerby's glance. The entire shop façade might be re-

FIG. 21. George Scharf, *The Strand from the Corner of Villiers Street, London*, 1824. © The Trustees of the British Museum/Art Resource, NY.

designed to suit the goods for sale. Luxury shops competed to amass classical design elements—pilasters, friezes, pediments—that proclaimed elegance and exclusivity. Balzac declared that they had "become commercial poems,"[95] but Dickens saw an "epidemic" of madness: "The primary symptoms were an inordinate love of plate-glass, and a passion for gas-lights and gilding. The disease gradually progressed, and at last attained a fearful height. Quiet, dusty old shops in different parts of town, were pulled down; spacious premises with stuccoed fronts and gold letters, were erected instead; floors were covered with Turkey carpets; roofs supported by massive pillars; doors knocked into windows; a dozen squares of glass into one; one shopman into a dozen."[96] Increasingly the façade gave pride of place to the display window. Larger windows, plus improved lighting, invited the new practice of window-shopping: looking without touching or smelling, and usually without any interaction with the shopkeeper. Mere piles of goods were replaced by elaborate window displays. After 1850 the big new department stores borrowed the practice from their smaller predecessors while raising the art to new heights, hiring artists who specialized in window displays.

Window-shopping changed the dynamic of the nineteenth-

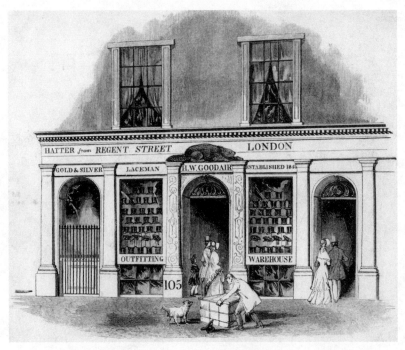

FIG. 22. Regent Street shop, c. 1850. Print by William Dickes. © The Trustees of the British Museum/Art Resource, NY.

century street. It did not entail the interaction of seller and buyer, whether the goods for sale were oranges or rubies; nor did it fit the rules of the formal promenade, where the people, not the goods, were on display. The purely visual focus of attention was the window display, and the crowds were invited to stroll and stop, to gather in front of the windows, and of course to step through the door and make a purchase.

Sellers of printed pictures were among the most successful pioneers in window displays. Prints and descriptions of street scenes, especially in London, show clumps of people gathered in front of print shops, gawking and perhaps exchanging opinions about the pictures on view. By 1782 Carl Philipp Moritz proclaimed the Strand to be London's greatest showcase of both entertainment and education:

It seems to me that here in London there is no need for textbooks or prints to instruct children. You merely have to lead them into the

FIG. 23. Piercy Roberts, *Caricature Shop of Piercy Roberts, 28 Middle Row, Holborn*, 1801. Metropolitan Museum of Art, The Elisha Whittelsey Collection, The Elisha Whittelsey Fund, 1953.

streets of the city and show them the things themselves as they really are. Here every product of art and industry is put on public display. Paintings, mechanical devices, and precious objects: all are available for convenient viewing behind the large panes of glass and the bright shop windows. Spectators are never lacking: here and there they stand still in the middle of the street and gaze at some mechanism or other. Such a street often resembles a carefully curated cabinet of curiosities.[97]

A few years later, another German visitor to a Strand print shop, Sophie von La Roche, possibly influenced by Moritz, also credited the English with promoting enlightenment via shop windows:

Here again I was thrilled to see the admirable arrangement and order produced by the combination of the search for profit and the national taste: everything is so prettily displayed in the large shop windows that it not only decorates the street and lures purchasers, but also publicizes a thousand inventions and ideas, and disseminates good taste, as the excellent pavements permit hundreds of people to stop and inspect the new exhibits. Here and there a genius is surely awakened this way; much labor is improved by competition; and many people have the pleasure of seeing something new.[98]

But the competing window displays also became a matter of commercial survival, as her countryman Ludwig Börne recognized in 1822 in Paris: the shopkeeper needed to catch a potential customer's fancy instantly, before another of the city's innumerable attractions diverted his or her attention. "It is a matter of a minute, of a step, for the power of attraction to work. A minute later or a step farther and the passerby is standing in front of another shop where he can find the wares he seeks. The eyes have to be compelled as if by force: one *must* stop and look."[99]

A faster pace of life affected even shops that resisted the move toward enclosure, as is apparent in Robert Southey's fictionalized description of London in 1808: "I happened to go into a pastrycook's shop one morning, and enquired of the mistress why she kept her window open during this severe weather which I observed most of the trade did. She told me, that were she to close it, her receipts would be lessened forty or fifty shillings a-day; so many were the persons who took up buns or biscuits as they passed by and threw their pence in, not allowing themselves time to enter."[100] Here too, the traffic patterns of the street were governed by the window displays. But also vice versa: as traffic speeded up, first with pedestrians in a hurry, then with fast carriages and automobiles, window displays were designed to be taken in at a glance.

MOVING SHOPPING OFF THE STREETS

The withdrawal of shopping from the street went hand in hand with a growing commitment to mobility, as the nineteenth century saw mounting friction between slow-moving shoppers and faster traffic. Street sellers were targeted as obstructions to traffic, as was merchandise stacked in front of shop doors. In 1815 Dr. Nikolaus Theodor Mühlibach demanded that the display of wares in Vienna's narrow streets be forbidden as a health hazard.[101] In 1842 Brussels banned both shopkeepers and street vendors from displaying their wares on the street, probably in order to improve the flow of traffic.[102] By then the Paris police had issued a string of similar ordinances, apparently with limited success.[103]

Conversely, traffic could annoy or even endanger shoppers. Luxury shops were well suited to the traditional promenades that were a city's widest streets, such as Vienna's Graben and Unter den Linden in Berlin. Problems arose where the shopping streets were also crowded traffic arteries, and window-shoppers had to dodge lumbering wagons, speeding carriages, and hordes of rushing pedestrians. Carl Herloss's 1827 guidebook lamented that the passing crowds made it impossible to appreciate Vienna's magnificent shops, even on the Graben.[104] Johanna Schopenhauer faced the same problem in Cologne's "dark, narrow" streets in 1828: "All around, and in tempting diversity, works of art and all imaginable luxury articles are displayed in large shops behind bright glass windows, but you don't dare linger in front of them to look, as you would in London or Paris, since here there are no sidewalks for pedestrians."[105] London and Paris had by then made conditions much better for shoppers and other pedestrians, not only by installing raised sidewalks, as she noted, but also by opening wide new streets like Regent Street and the rue de Rivoli, which often attracted the finest shops. The shoppers of Vienna and Cologne had to wait for decades before their cities demolished old fortifications to make room for spacious boulevards.

A more radical solution was to move shopping off the street entirely. A unique precursor to this development can be found at the old Rows of Chester, raised above the high street, modernized with plate-glass storefronts in the nineteenth century, and, as an 1856 guidebook explained, offering a great convenience "for old ladies of weak minds who quail at meeting cattle."[106] It is scarcely surprising that younger and sturdier shoppers were just as averse to meeting cattle. The early nineteenth century in London, and to a lesser extent in Manchester and Paris, saw a brief flourishing of so-called bazaars, developed at private initiative. These large roofed structures were divided into dozens of counters for independent vendors. In London the sellers were women, which made the premises morally dubious in the eyes of many respectable citizens, although the usual suspicion that shopping was a cover for prostitution seems to have been unfounded.[107] The bazaars followed the model of the Royal Exchange and Palais de la Cité, with rows of stalls sheltered from the street. More substantial shops first moved off the street in large numbers in Paris, a city renowned for both luxury goods and congested streets. The model for the new arrangement was the Palais-Royal, a spacious palace in the city center with an enclosed garden that had become a fashionable place to stroll. In the 1780s its owner, the Duke of Chartres (later Orléans), built a large commercial arcade in the garden. When the city's most fashionable shops and cafés moved in, it became the beau monde's place to gather, day and night, to browse for luxury goods, linger in garden cafés, dine in splendor, and attend the theaters.[108] Patrons avoided the street's filth, traffic, and rabble, except for the prostitutes who dominated the scene in the evening. As the duke's private property, it was off-limits to the king's police, which helped make the Palais's cafés the breeding grounds of the 1789 Revolution.

The retail aspect of the Palais-Royal soon attracted imitators. Within a few years after the Revolution, Parisian entrepreneurs assembled parcels of property extending through blocks and built enclosed arcades opening onto streets at each end. The arcades were open to pedestrians, but not to horses or vehicles. Their street frontages and exterior façades were narrow and modest. Light came through glass roofs instead of front windows, and their attractions were all but hidden from the street. The early twentieth-century German critic Walter Benjamin famously identified the Paris arcades as the paramount sites of urban modernity, where the wondrous display and sale of goods became the central spectacle of the capitalist city. He also recognized that their attraction began with the separa-

FIG. 24. Paris, Galerie Vivienne, 1820s.

tion of traffic and shopping.[109] The arcades offered a distilled and purified version of the street. They were lined with small shops selling mostly luxury goods. Like the shopfronts of the previous century, they were open to the street, except that it was a "street" without rain or dung. Although they had a few aristocratic predecessors like the Royal Exchange, the Palais de la Cité, and the Palais-Royal, the arcades first made an undiluted shopping experience widely available.

This Parisian model spread to many cities during the nineteenth century, eventually attaining unprecedented heights of scale and ostentation in, for example, Milan's Galleria Vittorio Emanuele.[110] In Paris and most other cities, however, the arcades went into decline later in the century, partly because of the rise of the department store, which effectively consolidated the attractions of the older shops into a single enterprise, substituting internal courts and aisles for an arcade or street. Benjamin, though, thought the cause of their decline lay in a new attractiveness of the street: "widened side-walks, electric light, a ban on prostitutes, a culture of fresh air."[111] Certainly the new boulevards torn through central Paris beginning in the 1850s—another widely imitated Parisian development—drew strollers and shoppers outside and revitalized street-side window-shopping, particularly in the department stores' window displays, which were dazzling at night, especially when electric lighting was installed after 1880. A later and firmer rejection of the street would eventually lead to an enormously successful revival of the Parisian arcade in the form of the enclosed shopping malls that were invented in the United States in the 1950s and subsequently exported around the world. The mall went a step beyond the earlier separation of shop from street. Now the street façade was dispensed with altogether. Shoppers were funneled into the mall, as with the Parisian arcades, and saw it from the inside. Since shop windows no longer faced out-ward, the street, or more likely the parking lot, could be lined with blank walls. Devoid of windows or other architectural foci, and of hawkers and shoppers, the street ceased to hold any interest, except as a conduit for traffic.

Most European shops did not vanish into malls, although some once-grand streets suffered sharp declines in status and allure. Nor did street commerce die out. Only draconian enforcement kept hawkers from returning. Where streets still had enough pedestrians, they attracted hawkers and carts and eventually food trucks. Where cars ruled, traffic jams, those embarrassing failures of the automo-tive city, created opportunities for hawkers to circulate amid the stalled vehicles. Some street commerce evolved new forms, such as the milk wagons that gradually replaced the girls with pails and har-nesses at the end of the nineteenth century and increasingly deliv-ered their products into houses rather than sold them on the street. London saw an early twentieth-century revival of street markets, as ambulatory vendors clustered together rather than leave the streets entirely.[112] After midcentury, some open-air markets made the tran-sition to a more upscale niche. Vienna's Naschmarkt and Munich's Viktualienmarkt, for example, continued to thrive on food sales, and by the twenty-first century every prosperous city boasted similar market revivals.

But the broader twentieth-century trend was away from the street. This was a long-term development that began before malls and automobiles. Gradually and fitfully, familiar presences vanished. After shopkeepers enclosed their sales counters and ceased to linger in their doorways, fewer potential customers loitered in the street, and fewer hawkers as well. The transition was never complete: shops flourished on some twentieth-century streets, sometimes aided in Europe by official restrictions on suburban mall construction. Nor was there a single cause. The growth of traffic played a role, as did the desire for sanitation. Noise was an issue, and street crime, too, in some places. Technology mattered in the form of plate glass and lighting, but the impetus came from elsewhere. Immense economic forces were at work: the hawker on the street was no match for department stores and retail chains, especially where fewer people still lived hand-to-mouth.

Conventional wisdom deemed street vendors to be relics of the past. In an 1891 petition directed against their mobile competitors, Hamburg greengrocers tried to ennoble their various grievances by placing themselves on the right side of history: "Street selling is unworthy of a major city. The sellers' shrieking disturbs instruction in schools; sick people in their houses are bothered; and so forth."[113] Berlin property owners complained that "the morals and manners of our streets" and especially of children suffered from the sight of these "uneducated and poor" people.[114] Street stands belonged in market halls, and even market stands were obsolete, best replaced by enclosed shops. With varying effectiveness, hawkers were banished from city streets. In Europe and America, and in much of the rest of the world, they were not merely obstructions to traffic in the automotive age. Medical authorities could point to measurable problems with the hygiene of their goods, but more important was a vaguer sense that they were incompatible with a clean, modern street. They were an embarrassment: a reminder of primitive times, or perhaps simply of poor people. The twentieth century seemed determined to conceal one of the defining characteristics of the European city. Cities were places where strangers met, and, as Georg Simmel observed in his classic excursus "The Stranger," the archetypal stranger ("who comes today and stays tomorrow") was a trader, arriving to engage in commerce.[115] Whatever the fate of those strangers, they no longer had any place on the street.

The desire to remove customers, goods, and shopkeepers from the street also revealed unspoken beliefs about social prestige. Shopping for anything but the barest necessities has always been a means of establishing status and distinction. Already in the eighteenth century, the most exclusive shops catered to what became known as the carriage trade, customers who arrived by carriage and were escorted directly inside. As these shoppers became more numerous, shops increasingly boasted of their exclusivity and comfort. The sights, sounds, and smells of the street might stimulate shoppers' appetites, but they could also become too democratic, or perhaps too human.

3

Strolling, Mingling, and Lingering

Social Life on the Street

European streets have long been theaters of public life, with an ever-changing cast of performers and spectators. In the Middle Ages, they hosted resplendent entertainments such as jousting tournaments (see fig. 1, p. 20).[1] Of more lasting importance were the identities they acquired from organized parades and processions that marked out a course through town. Some of these were staged by the mayor and municipal government, either to welcome a noble ruler or to stamp streets and landmarks with their own authority. More frequent were religious processions in honor of saints, sponsored by local guilds, tracing a traditional route to a church and lending the streets a Christian identity, one that might be reinforced throughout the year by crosses or shrines. Many of these processions have continued, year after year, even up to the present, sometimes enriched (or contaminated) by more secular entertainments.

After the Renaissance, however, fewer of these events called for citizens' participation, and many noble ceremonies moved indoors.[2] Streets became defined by the informal interaction that had always taken place. Especially in the larger and more diverse cities, old hierarchies were less visible, encounters between strangers were more typical, and street life was lively, varied, and unpredictable. As accepted forms of deference fell into decline, wealthier townspeople increasingly chose to limit their exposure to street crowds. But these changes were gradual, uneven, and never complete.

THE PROMENADE

During the seventeenth and eighteenth centuries, urban display took a new form. As the proliferation of carriages made walking optional for the wealthy—a luxury, not a necessity—strolling became a fashionable pursuit on aristocratic promenades across Europe. The promenade lacked the formal arrangement of a procession, yet participants were expected to observe strict rules of dress and comportment that drew on court etiquette. They engaged in more or less ritualized slow walking (or leisurely carriage rides) while interacting with others of acceptably high social rank. Bows and curtseys, doffing of hats and brief exchanges of verbal formulas—ostentatious displays of modesty, so to speak—displayed a regimen of bodily discipline. The promenade served many purposes: announcing one's presence in town; exchanging news; affirming communal ties and social position; flaunting fine clothes as well as eligible daughters; and of course seeking fresh air and exercise, as increasingly recommended by eighteenth-century physicians. The vogue had local roots in many places, but the main influence was Parisian, as was the case with much aristocratic fashion.

At first, this activity was often confined to royal gardens and very exclusive company, even to closed parks such as the Cours-la-Reine, a gated garden open only to the carriages of the titled few. For a time this formal garden's tree-lined walkways and carriage drives were the favorite rendezvous of the Parisian elite, although it shared the honors with the nearby Tuileries garden and, later, the extension of that garden's axis through the adjoining Champs-Elysées. Many other cities imitated the fashion. In London the closest equivalent was the Mall in St. James Park, created by order of the francophile King Charles II in the 1660s. Later the fashionable world moved on to Rotten Row (possibly a corruption of *route du roi*) in Hyde Park or to commercial pleasure gardens such as Vauxhall. In eighteenth-century Vienna, Emperor Joseph II opened the royal parks of the Prater and Augarten to the public. He also had a tree-lined walkway

FIG. 25. Vienna, Prater garden, 1794.

laid out amid the fortifications that ringed the city, as several other cities had done long before. Others followed Amsterdam's example of canal-side or quayside walkways.[3]

These early promenades, set in formal gardens rather than public streets, had their origins in the Italian Renaissance and were introduced to France by Queen Marie de' Medici, who brought the ritual of coach rides from her native Florence. The Cours-la-Reine was created in 1616 at her behest. Increasingly, however, promenades moved onto public streets, or became public streets. Even parks took on a more urban character, with strollers behaving as if they were funneled into a narrow lane. By 1848 the Polish poet Karol Forster claimed that the Tuileries garden was usually empty, except for two central allées where people crowded together to the point of rubbing elbows, because they came for the social contact, not the trees.[4] A pseudonymous account from 1823 made the same point about the aristocrats who gathered in Hyde Park between five and seven o'clock, shunning its broad lawns in favor of "the limited and ill-chosen space between Piccadilly and Cumberland gates."[5] In late eighteenth-century Vienna, too, the throng packed the central allée of the Prater, and in Berlin, the crowds in the Tiergarten squeezed themselves into a path lined with restaurants and ballrooms, called "In den Zelten" ("in the tents") after the temporary shelters erected there in the eighteenth century, soon to be replaced by permanent buildings. In 1805 a Parisian wit captured the paradox of fashion: for a promenade "to be frequented, it is necessary that it be fashionable; so however crowded, lacking in air, and inconvenient a place may be, everyone wants to go there. . . . In a word, in Paris we only like to take air in places where we suffocate."[6]

The urban promenade became a bourgeois and even a working-class pastime as well. The first promenades were intentionally and visibly separated from places of labor and commerce and quotidian bustle. But overlaps developed, as cities became larger and more crowded, and as the design and uses of urban buildings changed. The most important example is Paris's Grands Boulevards, which were created after 1670, when King Louis XIV decreed the removal of the city's fortification walls and their transformation into a promenade. (This is where the word "boulevard," which shares a root with the English "bulwark," acquired its modern meaning.) Over the following decades, the circuit around the city was landscaped with a wide central roadway flanked by walkways, each framed by a double row of trees.

From the beginning, the boulevards were open to all, unlike the Tuileries and other royal gardens. In the course of the eighteenth century, they became the city's most popular place to stroll, first for the upper classes, then for a wider public. Their trees, a rarity on European city streets, and their great breadth, far exceeding that of Paris's old streets, gave the boulevards a bucolic setting. At first they were very much on the urban fringe, even well beyond the built-up city in the west, and the construction of buildings along them was prohibited. As the city grew outward, however, property owners and entrepreneurs pushed back against the ban and gradually acquired the right to open adjacent terraces and to fence off their properties, arguing that they could best safeguard the propriety and cleanliness

La Promenade des Remparts de Paris.

FIG. 26. Promenade on Grands Boulevards, Paris, eighteenth century. Engraving from a work by Augustin de Saint-Aubin. Metropolitan Museum of Art, The Elisha Whittelsey Collection, The Elisha Whittelsey Fund, 1951.

of the boulevard's periphery. Step by step, the building restrictions were circumvented or repealed. The earliest structures were raised terraces overlooking the boulevards, followed by enclosed garden cafés, and eventually the boulevards became lined with mansions and multistory urban buildings that housed shops and places of public entertainment. Many of the trees were sacrificed in favor of pavement or buildings. As Anaïs Bazin recalled in 1833, "First the gardens disappeared; then the inevitable five-story buildings with their flattened façades and narrow windows, their meager balconies and shops, covered the places where we once gazed at shrubs and flowers."[7] One part or another of the boulevards always drew crowds (remaining the plural "boulevards" because the name changed at every bend). Their status as a place apart from the narrow lanes of inner Paris was marked by the shoe cleaners who stationed themselves at the intersections where city streets emptied onto the boulevards, offering to relieve strollers of Parisian street mud before they displayed themselves on the promenade.[8]

FIG. 27. Café and garden Turc, Paris, boulevard du Temple, c. 1810. Engraving by Jean-Pierre-Marie Jazet. Courtesy National Gallery of Art, Washington.

During the late eighteenth century, the liveliest scenes took place on the boulevard du Temple, where strolling aristocrats set the fashion, attracting diverse crowds to garden cafés such as the famous Café Turc. Benches and rental chairs also provided places to rest and watch people go by. By 1800 new upper-class residential districts had grown out to the more remote western promenade, and fashionable strolling drifted westward to the boulevard des Italiens, home to new theaters and splendid street cafés like Tortoni and the Café de Paris, which by the mid-nineteenth century were serving customers at outdoor tables with an unobstructed view of the passing throng. (The more salubrious streets of Vienna, particularly the Graben, were decades ahead of Paris in this development.) Although everyone could come to watch the crowd — or sell to it or steal from it — its reputation for exclusivity was ensured by the presence of the die-hard royalists who had returned from exile after the fall of Napoleon.

The largest crowds of ordinary Parisians still flocked to the popular theaters of the boulevard du Temple. It became known as the "boulevard du Crime" not because of its numerous pickpockets but rather because of the sensational melodramas that constituted the

FIG. 28. Boulevard des Italiens, Café Tortoni, 1877. Engraving by A.-P. Martial. Bibliothèque nationale de France.

typical theater fare. The theaters, circuses, and garden concerts competed with strolling musicians, jugglers, and other entertainers who drew crowds amid the spacious sidewalks and central promenade. This is the era evoked a century later in Marcel Carné's 1945 film *Les Enfants du Paradis*. A contemporary description gives us a flavor of the scene, if perhaps with some exaggeration:

> Here, crying, lying, dancing, and stealing, are mountebanks, clowns, jugglers, and freaks. Ointments, pastilles, metal files, sabers that extract teeth in a flash, women who have breasts on their knees, hens with human faces sculpted on them, mechanical giants five or twelve

feet tall, two-headed children, sea monsters from the canal de l'Ourcq, savages from the rue de Bondy, albinos from the square, dogs that play the trumpet, rabbits that belong to the Academy, carp that leap like sheep, storytellers, games that the house always wins, marionettes, aerial spectacles, great wax men, painted scoundrels, gravel eaters, file swallowers, incombustible or invisible men, tightrope walkers, physicians, astrologers, astronomers, astrophages—all of them conspire against the purse and the curiosity of the passerby.[9]

That was only the entertainment. Also accosting the crowds were vendors of eggs, fruit, oysters, handkerchiefs, underwear, herbal teas, matches, rags, roasted chestnuts, sausages, fried potatoes, apples, fowl (living and cooked), and coconut water, among much else.[10]

The spectacle came to an abrupt end in the 1860s when the prefect Georges-Eugène Haussmann dispersed the unloved crowds by demolishing most of the theater district to create the square now known as Place de la République. The rest of the old boulevards were integrated into the network of new "boulevards" Haussmann tore through the city center. In bringing the boulevard model into the inner city, Haussmann issued systematic specifications for trees, sidewalks, and carriageways; for lampposts, benches, and kiosks; for uniform rows of balconied apartment buildings; for shopfronts and café terraces; and he imposed the same standards on the old boulevards as well, creating the grand urban avenues best known through the paintings of Monet, Pissarro, and Renoir.[11]

Aristocrats could have fled to the more exclusive confines of the Tuileries or the Bois de Boulogne, yet they still came to "see and be seen" (an established phrase in multiple languages by the eighteenth century) and were followed by a disconcerting assortment of stolid bourgeois and faux aristocrats who carefully copied the prevailing codes of dress and behavior. The same complex social interactions took place in far-flung capitals—on the paseos of Madrid, Dresden's Hauptstrasse, and Nevsky Prospekt in St. Petersburg—as well as in lesser towns, notably the fashionable spas where the rich and titled gathered. Even in democratic New York, the nineteenth-century upper crust took to Broadway for carefully choreographed promenades.[12] In each city, certain hours of the afternoon or evening were known to be the only acceptable times for the beau monde to put itself on display. In Europe no less than in America, however, the fashionable elite shared the street with shoppers, peddlers, entertainers, and crowds of poor folk who came to enjoy the scene, although working-class promenades like the "monkey parades" of English youth often claimed their own times, places, and agendas.[13] Women who put themselves on display usually took great care to adhere to accepted rules in both their appearance and their coterie, for fear of being seen as prostitutes, while male peacocks had more leeway to stand out from the crowd even while conforming to the ephemeral fashions of the dandy, swell, or *Gigerl*.

Distinctions between participant and observer, between stage and spectator, broke down by the eighteenth and especially the nineteenth century, as everyone was in motion and the classes mingled to some extent. Social distinctions might be most visible in the means of conveyance in places where aristocrats and perhaps the higher bourgeoisie did not proceed on foot. Some kings and queens took daily rides alongside their nobles and lesser citizens. In the early nineteenth century, for example, King Victor Emmanuel I of Sardinia (on horseback) and Queen Maria Teresa (in a coach) mingled regularly with the evening strollers on Turin's Corso, taking the air and displaying themselves to their subjects.[14] By the end of the century, the crowds that lined Unter den Linden as Emperor Wilhelm II took his daily ride to the Tiergarten were dominated by people who just happened to be passing. Long before that, the crowd pressed old customs into collision with new worlds, as Samuel Pepys observed in the London streets in 1660, on his way "to Westminster, overtaking Captain Okeshott in his silk cloak, whose sword got hold of many people in walking."[15] It took more than a century for the sword to be supplanted by the less lethal and distinctly more bourgeois umbrella.

The social composition of the promenade has probably always

been in flux, and, consequently, so has its meaning in any community. It has a longer history in southern Europe. In 1581 Michel de Montaigne marveled that "the most ordinary exercise of the Romans is to promenade in the streets; and usually the effort of leaving the house is made solely to go from street to street without a purpose or a destination; and there are streets especially intended for that purpose."[16] The name of Rome's Via del Corso became synonymous with the promenade, which thrived through the twentieth century as the paseo or passeggiata of smaller Mediterranean towns, where it continued to serve as a showcase of fashion, a marriage market, and a place where social status was displayed and negotiated. By general if tacit agreement, certain streets maintained their identity as sites where bodily comportment and precisely calibrated rituals either fulfilled or challenged conventional expectations, while men and women of subtly different social strata sorted themselves into their own routes.[17]

Unter den Linden, which became Berlin's main promenade, is another instructive example. It connected the city center and royal palace to the Tiergarten, the royal game park that became the city's other fashionable place to stroll and ride. Unter den Linden was laid out at the city's edge in the mid-seventeenth century, and it gradually changed its character as Berlin grew around it. In its early years, any comparison to Paris was laughable: a 1690 decree from the prince-elector asked residents to keep their pigs away from his trees.[18] Still, from the beginning it stood out as Berlin's grandest street, its great width divided into a central pedestrian promenade, a bridle path, vehicle roadways, and sidewalks by the six (later four) rows of the linden (lime) trees after which it was named. Over the decades, royalty was a regular sight, often on horseback, accompanied or saluted by soldiers. (In May and June 1878, two different assassins attacked the elderly emperor Wilhelm I on his daily ride down Unter den Linden in the royal carriage. He survived both attempts on his life; the political rights of socialists did not.) Army officers and other aristocrats set the tone, but nearly anyone could join the procession. E. T. A. Hoffmann's 1809 story "Ritter Gluck" observes the "colorful stream of people walking through the linden trees toward the Tier-garten: dandies, solid citizens in their Sunday best parading with wives and children, clergy, Jewish girls, law clerks, prostitutes, pro-fessors, cleaning women, dancers, army officers—on and on."[19]

In the late eighteenth century, at the behest of King Frederick the Great, the street was lined with three- and four-story palaces and mansions in an unbroken row reaching to the Brandenburg Gate, which opened into the Tiergarten. By the early nineteenth century, elegant shops took over the ground floors of these buildings. In keeping with the street's residential character, the shopfronts were anything but ostentatious, lacking display windows and typically marked only by the proprietor's name on a discreet sign mounted above the ground-floor windows.[20] After midcentury, though, the street's appearance as well as its function began to change, as it became a busier and more commercial thoroughfare, and many old palaces were replaced by massive new commercial buildings. Hotels, shops, and cafés proliferated, and Berlin belatedly joined the revolution in storefront design. The crowds became larger and more diverse, including middle-class shoppers as well as swarms of working-class families on their Sunday strolls. Although the Kranz-ler coffeehouse pioneered an outdoor seating terrace in the 1840s, that Parisian fashion did not otherwise catch on in Berlin for another half-century, ensuring that the street as a whole remained a tame af-fair in comparison with the Parisian boulevards, as a scornful visitor from eastern Prussia reported in 1849: the lively scene of strollers and shoppers and riders lacked the spark of Paris or even Vienna, because the only café terrace was the wretched Kranzler, where "per-haps two or three guard lieutenants and a few junior barristers satis-fied their ice-cream cravings."[21]

The diverse crowds, buildings, and activities made Unter den Linden and other promenade routes into true city streets, enclosed by street walls and characterized by a complexity of design, sight lines, and functions. Along with all the social and architectural variety we associate with city streets, the melding of the formal stroll and the city crowd presented myriad opportunities for social friction,

FIG. 29. Berlin, Unter den Linden at Friedrichstrasse, 1907. Photograph by Max Missmann.

upper-class unease, and misunderstandings. A daring radical wrote in 1747 that "a cobbler won't give way to a marquis in the street. This equality is what makes Paris so fine."[22] More conventional voices in eighteenth-century London sputtered in indignation at presumptuous plebeians who refused to "give the wall" to their obvious superiors when passing in the street. To take the street side and grant the more expensively dressed person greater protection from passing wheels had been an implicit prerogative that now appeared to be at risk. Additional uncertainty came with changing fashions. In 1780s Paris, Charles de Peyssonel claimed that "the most senior personages of the state walk the streets dressed like the least elevated of citizens. You think you are talking to an attorney's clerk, and it turns out to be a Prince of the Blood."[23]

Meanwhile, in the late eighteenth and early nineteenth centuries, Germany saw a lengthy controversy over hat-doffing. A 1750 etiquette guide warned that any visitor setting out to walk on a street needed to learn the local customs of "greeting and hat-doffing" in order to avoid being mocked.[24] The traditional male greeting to a social equal or superior, a bow accompanied by a sweep of the hat in hand, was coming under attack. The English were believed to be the trendsetters, having given up the custom because the London crowds made it impossible to get anywhere if one was expected to execute a full and formal greeting at every step. By the early eighteenth century, though, Johann Christoph Nemeitz explained in his guidebook that Parisians had already abandoned the awkward practice of greeting casual acquaintances on the street, preferring to carry their hats securely under their arms so as not to muss their wigs.[25] Germans, in their smaller cities, did not face the same pressures. Still, they had to worry about whether to remove their hats. Frequent grasping and doffing took a toll on an expensive felt hat, after all. Touching the hat, military style, was touted as a possible alternative.[26] Women were spared this particular dilemma, but they faced others, for example a possible "masculinization" of clothing and especially of shoes, a switch to low heels and sturdy construction for the kind of healthy walking increasingly recommended by physicians, at a cost to fashion and to a more distinctively feminine gait.[27] By the end of the eighteenth century, fashionable women did have the option of better walking shoes, but they remained at a clear disadvantage. A few decades later, Aurore Dupin made her notorious decision to dress as a man (and to adopt the pen name George Sand) because, she claimed, her feminine shoes and skirts prevented her from keeping up with her male companions on the rough and dirty Paris streets.[28]

In the era of the French Revolution, urban walking might display democratic sentiments—up to a point. The diverse crowds offered elite strollers an audience that could admire and emulate them. Their inferiors generally knew better than to interfere with the promenade; and if they failed to know their place, the forces of order could be counted on to intervene. At the same time, too much crowding posed a threat to upper-class display and to the deference that the elite expected from their inferiors. There developed a conflict in tempo, as unhurried strollers found themselves buffeted by commercial bustle. Crowding and jostling changed the character of streets once associated with leisure. The novelist Stendhal recalled his revulsion at the "fashionable and dusty" Grands Boulevards of the 1820s: "It was torture for me to be in that rendezvous of low-class swells, guard officers, high-class prostitutes, and their elegant bourgeois rivals."[29] One reaction was the insistent display of a slow pace, famously embodied by the apocryphal Parisian flâneur of the 1840s who strolled with a turtle on a leash in order to ostentatiously assert aristocratic values.

The transformation of the promenade can be seen in an 1840 story by a great observer of Parisian life, Honoré de Balzac, who called attention to a new and yet ephemeral type of fashionable lady. One character explains that this type is defined not by her invisible family name, the traditional marker of status, but rather by her grace in public, because she "knows the fine art of walking," setting her visibly apart from any lesser creatures. "This beautiful stranger does not jostle or shove; when she wishes to pass someone by, she waits with proud modesty for room to be made. . . . Her manner, at once serene and aloof, compels even the most insolent dandy to step aside for her." Her perfect posture and behavior complement her perfect dress, revealing "a woman who is confident but not smug, who looks at nothing and sees everything, whose vanity, jaded by ceaseless gratification, imbues her face with an indifference that arouses the interest of all who behold her. She knows she is being studied, she knows that nearly everyone, even the ladies, will turn around for a second look when she passes. Thus does she drift through Paris like gossamer, white and pure." Balzac proceeds to sketch a map of fashionable Parisian strolling, specifying just where such a lady will be found (the western reaches of the Grands Boulevards and certain stretches of the rues de Rivoli and du Faubourg Saint-Honoré) while noting that she will never be seen on "muddy, small, or commercial streets." Her hours, too, are restricted to between two and five in the afternoon: "These flowers of Paris bloom when the weather is Oriental; they perfume the promenades; and then, after five o'clock, close up like morning glories." An ordinary middle-class woman will never be mistaken for such a glorious creature, since the "bourgeoise" derogates herself with practical activities, bustling about, running errands in all weather, hitching up her skirts to step over a gutter, even dragging a child behind her.[30]

Balzac understood the distinctions of status and purpose that made a promenade unlike other uses of the same streets, even after the *promeneurs* had surrendered any exclusive claims to them. Indeed, the wide boulevards became a busy transportation artery during Balzac's time. Carriage traffic grew rapidly, and in 1828 Paris's first horse-drawn omnibus line began service along the arc of the boulevards. (For that matter, thirty-five years earlier, a cart bore Louis XVI along the same route on his way to the guillotine.) Balzac's lady embodied a style of pure display that replaced the certainties of aristocratic lineage with a relatively anonymous public spectacle, attracting the attention of a wider public but relying entirely on her majestic appearance to claim superiority over imitators or more mundane users of the street.

One of those mundane strollers, John Sanderson, visiting from Philadelphia in 1835, cast a skeptical eye on the ladies' command of the crowd (or perhaps the clumsy American simply lacked the discretion even of Balzac's "most insolent dandy"): "When a French lady walks out she always takes at one side her *caniche* by a string, and at the other, sometimes, her beau without a string. In either way she monopolizes the whole street, and you are continually getting between her and her puppy very much to your inconvenience; for if you offend the dog the mistress is of course implacable, and you very likely have to meet her gallant in the Forest of Bondy, next morning."[31] The Berlin humorist Adolf Glassbrenner also thought his city's "so-called elegant promenade" was ripe for ridicule. Appearances, after all, could be deceiving: "In order to get a breath of fresh air, every gift of nature, birth, good fortune, service, and the back stairs is put on display: rich clothes, innocent faces, lovely eyes, tiny feet, splendid heraldry and neighing horses, superb carriages, richly liveried servants, false locks, false rosy cheeks, and false medals. Perfectly ordinary people also stroll here."[32]

FIG. 30. Georg Emanuel Opitz, *Am Graben in Wien*, c. 1830, with elegant stroller (with dog), salami vendor, sedan chair carrier, and idlers.

The amalgamation of strolling and shopping forced a renegotiation of street space. Even at the time, shopping was often much more than practical drudgery. Although Balzac's grand lady might still have had her jeweler and dressmaker come to her house, many elegant women in Paris, and even more in London, soon became regular visitors to the finest shopping streets. Men, too, found a new spectacle there. The scientist Georg Christoph Lichtenberg confessed to missing an appointment in 1770 because he lingered too long on the Strand, looking at silver and at Native American crafts, among other treasures.[33] The composer Johann Friedrich Reichardt, visiting Vienna in 1809, was thrilled to call on the great Beethoven, and enjoyed the established promenade along the old city walls, but the highlight of his sojourn may have been the streets lined with the shops of jewelers and drapers. Even if you were enticed to stop and gaze at only a few of the goods on display, he explained, "you can have whiled away three or four hours without noticing. You find yourself in a ceaseless whirl of the liveliest commercial bustle, which reaches from here into Hungary, Turkey, Italy, the entire Empire and the Hanseatic cities."[34] The sights and smells of the pastry cook's art also brought passersby to a standstill. At the annual feast of the Epiphany, eighteenth-century London boys, often abetted by their elders, lay in wait for men and women who stopped to look at the "Twelfth cakes" on display at the finest pastry shops, and then pulled out hammers to nail the hapless shoppers' coattails to the shutters, vexing the victims while amusing perpetrators and onlookers.[35]

When strolling was combined with shopping, pedestrians' interactions with streets and buildings became more complex. Attention shifted from faces to shop windows, from the central promenade to the built edge. The tempo of the street changed, as Balzac intimates. The clustering of luxury shops also scrambled the hierarchy of streets. In 1821 Pierce Egan observed the rise of Bond Street in London, newly fashionable because of its luxury shops:

[It] is not one of the most elegant streets in the vicinity of London, but is the resort of the most fashionable people, and from about two o'clock till five, it is all bustle—all life—every species of fashionable vehicle is to be seen dashing along in gay and gallant pride. From two to five are the fashionable shopping-hours, for which purpose the first families resort to this well-known street—others, to shew their equipage, make an assignation, or kill a little time. . . . But to be seen in this street at a certain hour, is one of the essentials to the existence of *haut-ton*—it is the point of attraction for greetings in splendid equipages, from the haughty bend or familiar nod of arrogance, to the humble bow of servility. Here mimicry without money assumes the consequential air of independence: while modest merit creeps along unheeded through the glittering crowd. Here all the senses are tantalized with profusion, and the eye is dazzled with temptation, for no other reason than because it is the constant business of a fashionable life — not to live in, but out of self, to imitate the luxuries of the afflu- ent without a tithe of their income, and to sacrifice morality at the altar of notoriety.[36]

In Berlin, Unter den Linden may have remained the favorite prome- nade route, but by the end of the century it had yielded its com- mercial allure to Leipziger Strasse, where the department stores appeared, and then to the newly thriving boulevard of the wealthy western quarters, Tauentzienstrasse and its western extension, Kur- fürstendamm. Similarly, in Vienna, customers streamed to the big new department stores just outside the city center along Mariahilfer Strasse.

Paris remained the city best known for strolling and street enter- tainment in all forms, on the old boulevards and, after the mid- nineteenth century, the new ones through the city center. Rich and poor continued to brush sleeves routinely, their daily encounters gov- erned partly by customary deference, partly by the threat of police intervention, and partly by artful maneuvers executed by pedestri- ans or vehicles. It seemed idyllic to many visitors, such as the Ameri- can who thought the boulevard cafés offered "a true democracy — the only social equality to be seen in Christendom."[37] Radicals, however, commented on the social injustice on stark display when rich and poor crossed paths. So did more anxious observers. At Christmas- time in 1841, the German poet Heinrich Heine pondered the "sinis- ter contrast" between Paris's sparkling shop windows and the desti- tute crowds rushing past them: "These people might suddenly raise their clenched fists and smash all the bright and jingling toys of the elegant world along with that world itself!"[38]

Yet we have surprisingly few descriptions of these routine encoun- ters. A striking if fictional exception is Charles Baudelaire's 1864 poem "The Eyes of the Poor," set on one of Haussmann's new boule- vards. The poem's narrator is sitting with his beloved on the outdoor terrace of one of the luxurious new cafés when they are distracted by the appearance of a poor man and two ragged children, gazing wistfully at the glittering spectacle, so near to them and yet so out of reach. Their hungry eyes make the narrator "a little ashamed" of the injustice that puts him in front of a bounteous table in full view of a father who struggles to feed his children. When he looks to his companion to share his thoughts, he is shocked to discover how differently she reacts: she is angry that those six wide eyes are spoiling her pleasure and wants the head waiter to send them away.

The poem may be read as social commentary, but that is not its point, at least not directly. Baudelaire was anything but a political activist. Instead, the poor family serves to reveal to the narrator that he was deceived in his momentary belief that he and his beloved, gazing into each other's eyes, actually understood one another. While he indulged the guilt he felt, she did not think she should have to share the street with poor people. Her revulsion at the eyes of the poor turns his love abruptly into contempt. Out of this street scene, Baudelaire summons the kind of deeper truth prized by modern artists: that the sight of the anonymous poor reveals how little we understand even those closest to us—that we live in a world of strangers. This becomes both the poets' and the sociologists' standard reading of the nineteenth-century city street: as a fascinating and frightening site of alienation. Marxist revolutionaries agreed. So did conservatives who railed against the moral and political evils of city life.[39]

Shopping also changed the gender balance of street users.[40] Many luxury shops, and especially the grand department stores built after 1850, first in Paris and then in every city, catered primarily to upper-middle-class women. There was endless discussion about the propriety of unaccompanied ladies venturing out to shop, but they did so in growing numbers. Their presence further complicated the fears and frictions aroused by the crowded streets. Class plus gender demarcated the most worrisome dimension of bodily contact in public. The streets of every city continued to be filled with working-class women, doing their own kind of shopping, walking to and from their jobs, or, often, using the street as their place of work, selling wares of many kinds—even, as middle-class observers noted with a shudder, their bodies. But it was the bodies of well-to-do women—perhaps aristo-crats, but above all women of the newly prosperous commercial and professional classes—that obsessed many men and women. The fear that they were mingling with the morally corrupted women of the lower classes, and with the unfiltered torrent of men on the street, revealed itself in demands to shield middle-class women, to res-cue—or control—poor women, and to save men from temptation.

MEN AND WOMEN IN PUBLIC

Unwritten codes of many kinds governed interaction in the streets. The mere fact that a person was walking, rather than riding on a horse or in a vehicle, often sent a meaningful signal. Strolling in fashionable promenades or parks meant something different from walking in other streets. A walking style and pace broadcast signals about one's status and role—a saunter or a purposeful stride, head down or glancing about—as did the company one kept. Dress codes were losing the force of law by the seventeenth century, but cloth-ing might nonetheless speak eloquently if not definitively. Paris, the acknowledged capital of fashion, may have offered the clearest case where the style set at the royal court dictated every detail of proper dress for anyone who aspired to social acceptance, although Vienna's imperial court imposed similar standards. In the eighteenth century, visitors were immediately identifiable, unless they procured a com-plete set of new clothes upon arrival. Tobias Smollett observed in 1763 that London's fashions bore no resemblance to those of Paris. "What is the consequence? When an Englishman comes to Paris, he cannot appear until he has undergone a total metamorphosis. At his first arrival, he finds it necessary to send for the tailor, peru-quier, hatter, shoemaker, and every other tradesman concerned in the equipment of the human body." He added that "females are, if possible, still more subject to the caprices of fashion."[41] (Decades earlier, Joachim Christoph Nemeitz offered a more practical rea-son to dress fashionably in Paris—a step that he found the English particularly reluctant to take: if you are recognizably foreign, "beggars, coachmen, even shoeshine boys will not leave you in peace."[42] Meanwhile, numerous witnesses attested that the London mob was perhaps even more merciless to anyone they identified as French.) Needless to say, exposure of skin and hair was strictly limited, even if the rules varied, regarding, for example, the absolute necessity of men or women to wear hats. Sometimes a woman was expected to wear a veil in public, to shield her face from inappropriate attention. She might also choose to wear a veil, or even a mask, to enable her to look about without surrendering her modesty.[43] Everyone understood that these rules were class-specific: most men and women did not live by them, and as such they were immediately identifiable as people undeserving of their superiors' solicitude. The lower classes had their own codes of dress and behavior that recognized degrees of deprivation.

One way of evading the codes and rules, or of escaping one's prescribed role, was to walk the streets at night. The cover of darkness promised danger and uncertainty, but also, sometimes, excitement and liberation. For centuries the darkness was real and profound, and the authorities were suspicious of any moving shadows. Curfews enforced a general prohibition on the use of the streets at night, with exceptions only for a select few: night watchmen and priests, physicians and midwives, ragpickers and night-soil collectors. Anyone else wandering the pitch-dark streets was presumed to be up to no good. Things began to change, slowly, with the spread of municipal street lighting in the late seventeenth century. Even then it was often deemed advisable to hire a torchbearer to guide you home, although London's "linkboys" were rumored to conspire with the thieves lurking in the shadows. The brightness and spacing of the new lamps varied from city to city, as did their hours of use and even days of use (some cities left them unlit on moonlit nights), but they lent at least some streets a feeling of security far greater than had previously been imaginable. Where the lights of shop windows further brightened the narrow streets, nighttime shopping became a normal activity. A genre of "nightwalking" literature emerged by 1700 in London, catering to a public that wished to experience vicarious thrills and perhaps danger amid the illicit activities presumed to thrive in the dark.[44] A renewed impetus came in the early 1800s, when new lamps burning manufactured coal gas suddenly made the old oil and tallow lamps seem little better than darkness. Julien Lemer claimed that "since gas has reached into the narrowest lanes of the great city, it is never truly dark any more in Paris."[45] The same fate befell the gas lamps in the 1880s when electric lighting dazzled the nighttime crowds. Paris put on the first great display of electric streetlights in time for its 1878 world exposition. The Italian visitor Edmondo De Amicis was duly astounded: "It is not an illumination; it is a fire. The boulevards are ablaze. . . . The shops cast floods of brilliant light half-way across the street, and wrap the crowd in a golden dust. . . . There is not a trace of shadow on the sidewalk: you could find a pin there. Every face is illuminated."[46] In the course of the nineteenth century, exploration of the nighttime streets ceased to be the province of the rare urban explorer. In late-century London, groups of upper-class voyeurs went "slumming" in the East End, which served as a kind of exotic zoo. Bus tours even enabled them to keep their feet clean.[47] Around 1900 Berlin's notorious nightlife also made it a tourist destination, reputed to be even racier than Montmartre.

The thrill of the night, and the thrill of the street, was to a great extent that of illicit sex. Hopes and fears of urban public life have long been shaped by possibilities of homosexual and heterosexual contact. Across the centuries, therefore, the real or imagined dangers of the street have often been viewed through the lens of gender. Men set rules — explicitly as laws or implicitly as customs — to shield women as well as men from immoral or dangerous scenes. Women contributed to the making of these rules, but they also challenged or subverted them. Standards of acceptable behavior changed gradually and can never be dated with any precision. Beliefs about the need to control male sexuality varied, as did ideas about how (rarely if) to restrain female power and independence. In general, however, the policing of female sexuality has been one of the fundamental forces organizing street behavior.

In every city, in every century, fears of women were never far removed from facts and myths about prostitution. Because female sexuality loomed as a menace, the visible prostitute was a cause for worry. Up to the eighteenth century, it was masculine self-control that was typically understood to be under threat. Since public order was thought to depend on that male discipline, this was no small danger. By the nineteenth century, prevailing obsessions had changed, and the peril was defined differently. Female purity became the ideal that all men and women needed to protect. The threats to it took many forms. Worries about filth in the streets slipped easily and almost inevitably from visible dirt to invisible dangers of disease and on to notions of moral and sexual purity.

The reality of prostitution varied less than the legal responses to it, which in some times and places outlawed the practice entirely, without ever banishing it, but more typically regulated it in some manner, especially on the Continent. Many cities followed the Parisian model of licensed brothels, while Berlin closed them all in 1846. Although street solicitation might be banned, and prostitutes restricted to brothels, all such measures were doomed to fail. Street prostitutes were often required to register with the police and submit to regular medical examinations, as in Berlin, where they were forbidden to solicit on a long list of the city's busiest and most fashionable streets, a rule that failed on its own terms but did impose a certain discretion. Soliciting also might be legally limited to certain hours—in Paris, from seven in the evening until midnight. None of these rules had much effect. The American investigator Abraham Flexner concluded in 1914 that the appearance and behavior of streetwalkers varied little among European cities. "Public opinion objects to scandal without requiring complete suppression; to this attitude prostitution has everywhere accommodated itself. The streets of London, in which, as we shall see, no particular action is taken in reference to the prostitute, are not to be distinguished essentially from those of Paris and Berlin, in both of which minute specifications aim to exclude the evil from prominent thoroughfares; nor are Paris and Berlin distinguishable from Vienna, in which no such stipulations are made." The "general police attitude," he added, is "everywhere understood and everywhere much the same," in these capitals as well as in smaller cities.[48] The local constable often knew full well who the local street prostitutes were, even when they were unregistered or working illegally. Sometimes his enforcement was lax because of bribes or favors; sometimes he simply wished to keep peace with the women he encountered every night, as long as they avoided creating disturbances that caused complaints. Often it was enough to preserve the appearance of public order by asking the women to move along, in accordance with the accepted belief that the street was a place of circulation.

Male visitors to a city sometimes commented on the striking numbers and visibility of prostitutes—that is, women they confidently assumed to be prostitutes—while others fretted instead about the difficulty of knowing whether the well-dressed women they saw were in fact prostitutes or "respectable" ladies. The traits identified in the section "How to Know a Whore" of John Gay's 1716 poem *Trivia* were scarcely definitive, although they suggested that a discerning eye might recognize signs of desperate poverty concealed beneath gaudy dress: a visible lack of stays, "tawdry ribbons," "high-draggled petticoats," "hollow cheeks," and "a slattern air." The police might specify what a prostitute could or couldn't wear (hats, for example), or at least insist on modest dress, but they always faced a dilemma, as Alain Corbin put it in his study of French prostitution: "The independent prostitute who practiced soliciting had to refrain from any scandalous behavior that might reveal the nature of her activity to honest women, and especially to young females and children; at the same time she had to adopt behavior that clearly indicated to prospective customers that she was a prostitute."[49] In other words, she had to be invisible to children and other women, but unmistakable to men. This impossible standard left all prostitutes in legal limbo, and all women in danger of being mistaken for prostitutes. Nor could much be done for Parisian bourgeois men who complained that the prostitutes on the boulevards made it impossible for them to stroll with their wives and daughters.[50] The presence of prostitutes often drove out other women, for example from the buzzing social scene at

Paris's Palais-Royal gardens in the late eighteenth century. In many places, the arrival of evening marked the hour when the street was left to prostitutes. Respectable women had no place there, and all remaining men were understood to be potential customers.

The era we call Victorian saw the growth of missionary activities to rescue prostitutes from the street. Not that the practice was entirely new: in the 1690s John Dunton had scoured the nighttime streets of London for prostitutes in order to lecture them on their evil ways. But the Victorians were perhaps more hopeful that the fallen women might be redeemed. Sometimes these were individual initiatives, the most famous case being the pious politician William Ewart Gladstone, who as a young man began a habit of solitary night walks in London, where he accosted prostitutes (if not vice versa) and invited them home to share his and his wife's food and shelter. Even after serving as prime minister, Gladstone continued his sojourns. More typical, or at least better known, were organized street missions such as the London City Mission and later the Salvation Army as well as the Midnight Missions in Berlin and other German cities, organized through churches and fueled by the religious (usually Protestant) fervor of volunteers.[51] At the same time, nineteenth-century crusades against prostitution were often justified in the name of public health and led by physicians rather than clergy. Official restrictions, in fact, were always framed in part (but only in part) as medical regulations, the containment of venereal diseases being an obvious justification for medical intervention. However, the nearly universal conflation of medical and moral terminology guaranteed that unarticulated fears surrounding sexuality shaped rules as well as attitudes. There was little dissent from the generally employed language of cleansing and purification applied to the missionaries' work in the streets.

The desire to eradicate prostitution, or, more typically, to quarantine it, directly affected the behavior of and toward all women in public. Customary (rarely legal) restrictions on where or when an unaccompanied woman could appear on the streets, and how she should dress, were to a great extent guided by the fear that a respectable woman might be mistaken for a prostitute. At midcentury the historian Jules Michelet saw no place for her in public: "What difficulties a single woman faces! She can hardly go out at night: she would be taken for a prostitute [*fille*]. There are a thousand places where only men are to be seen, and if her affairs lead her there, they are astonished and laugh like fools. For example, if she finds herself delayed at the far end of Paris, and she is hungry, she dare not enter a restaurant. She would create a scene and be a spectacle. She would have every eye on her and would overhear bold and uncivil remarks."[52] Like most bourgeois men, Michelet thought the single woman's only escape from her seclusion was to marry and shut herself in with a husband and children. Where women made other choices, as in Victorian London, moral panic might ensue. In an 1868 article, Eliza Lynn Linton condemned the kind of "fast" young woman who "dyes her hair and paints her face" and "whose sole idea of life is plenty of fun and luxury."[53] In other words, such upper-middle-class women imitated the habits of courtesans and prostitutes, and on the street could easily be taken for them. By blurring the all-important line between virtuous and fallen women, they not only put their own reputations in peril, they endangered all respectable women and, not least, they left men uncertain how to treat any women they encountered.

Class distinctions further complicated the picture. At one extreme, Balzac's grand lady, keeping to prescribed streets and hours, probably did not have to worry about being molested. Michelet's middle-class woman was obliged to avoid the street in order not to be seen as a *fille*—a "girl," that is, a prostitute. The desire to draw a veil over public sexuality made it convenient to hold to the fiction that women on the streets were the euphemistic "public women" or "women of the streets" or "streetwalkers" (a synonym for "prostitutes" in English by the sixteenth century) and to preserve the gender order that used this language to stigmatize women in public. The reality was always more complicated. Lower-class women thronged the streets at most hours, going to work or shop or socialize even if their employment itself did not keep them outdoors all day or night. Their independence threatened the order of the streets because they were visible in so many places and so many roles. Regulations governing public markets, which teemed with women selling wares, sometimes grew out of a fear that any of them might be prostitutes—that is, women out of control.[54] Some did engage in prostitution at times, ensuring that the authorities would never be able to cleanly separate vice from virtue.

Many middle-class women guarded their reputations by going out only with a male relative or a servant, but there were always exceptions, increasingly so with the growth of shopping as a middle-class activity. Visitors to Paris in the seventeenth and eighteenth centuries, especially Italians, marveled at the visibility of women in the streets. By the nineteenth century, it was the independent women of middle-class London who attracted the most comment. Historians of Victorian London have led the way in puncturing myths about their supposed seclusion. Lynda Nead, for example, unearthed a revealing lithograph from the 1860s, featuring a fictional Gladstone-like clergyman's well-meaning efforts to limit the damage caused when the sexes mingled in the bustling streets.[55] He approaches a gaudily dressed young woman and offers her a religious tract: "I am sure it will benefit you." But this story has a twist: she is not a prostitute. "Bless me, Sir, you're mistaken. I am not a social evil, I am only waiting for a bus." No longer could a well-dressed woman standing alone on a London street be assumed to be a woman of ill repute. The joke is on him, but his cluelessness revealed a persistent problem. By late in the century, the general relaxation of restrictions on middle-class women's public behavior created uncertainty not only about the limits of what was acceptable but also, crucially, about appropriate male conduct on the streets.

Women knew the street was fraught with hazards far worse than nosy clerics. They had to worry about their safety, since thieves and harassers were always a threat. Many also agonized about their reputations. Etiquette guides show us the dos and don'ts—mostly don'ts—imposed on middle-class women. They were sternly reminded never to invite male attention by smiling at strangers, glancing about too much, or appearing to walk without purpose. An unaccompanied woman might be grateful for a policeman's intervention

FIG. 31. C. J. Culliford, *Scene in Regent Street*, c. 1865. Philanthropic Divine: "May I beg you to accept this good little book. Take it home and read it attentively. I am sure it will benefit you." Lady: "Bless me, Sir, you're mistaken. I am not a social evil, I am only waiting for a bus."

in an uncomfortable encounter, but she also had to fear that the constable might arrest her as a prostitute, or at least take the side of a well-dressed male harasser. Such a case of mistaken identity could imply that the woman dressed or behaved like a prostitute. The authorities, after all, wanted to be able to distinguish perpetrators from victims, and they could dismiss an unaccompanied woman on the street as unworthy of official protection. In Berlin as late as the 1870s, the police decreed that "any female who appears on the street after 10 p.m. without a male escort will be arrested." But they could no longer count on solid support for this policy: in the face of outraged protest, they hastily revoked the rule.[56] By 1903 the Berlin police had established a special plainclothes patrol in the central shopping streets, charged with protecting unaccompanied women, including working-class women, from male harassers.[57] However, it was left up to the police to decide which women deserved protection. In 1911 a Berlin newspaper reported with astonishment of a young woman who approached a policeman on Leipziger Strasse to complain that a man was following her. The officer looked her over and replied with a smirk, "Can't blame the gentleman."[58]

The typical scene of misunderstandings was an elegant shopping street such as Regent Street, the rue Saint-Honoré, or the Graben. A woman who lingered outside the fashionable shops might indeed be a prostitute exploiting the commercial atmosphere. Or she might be a working-class girl gazing hungrily at the unaffordable goods on display. Or she might be a middle-class daughter or wife with both the desire and the means to buy lace or a hat or a set of teacups. Complaints that respectable ladies risked their reputations by lingering in the street, or that working girls dressed too much like prostitutes, revealed the frustrations of men, and some women, who longed for a more visible order.

A few women, and some male allies, were willing to speak up for the rights of women to linger in the street, unmolested by constables, self-appointed moralists, or men seeking sex. But there was no simple way to identify harassers even if one wished to. Women, then as now, shared tips on ways to walk resolutely or look unapproachable in order to avoid misunderstandings and deter harassers, in view of the widely acknowledged fact that men "seem to find it difficult to rid themselves of the idea that every woman unaccompanied in public is in search of adventure."[59] Matters got even more complicated when women really were in search of adventure. The authorities might dismiss complaints of harassment with the insinuation that not all middle-class girls were as demure as their parents expected them to be. Even if it was a general rule that middle-class women did not wish to make men's acquaintance on the street, such was not always the case for young women of the working classes, who faced fewer restrictions on their public behavior and who sometimes happily engaged in public flirtation. They did not always welcome the intervention of policemen or other well-meaning bystanders.[60]

Part of the discomfort with street prostitution reflected an uneasy recognition that the sexual marketplace in its frankly commercial form could never be cleanly separated from other sexual transactions, on or off the street. The rules had been clearer when upper-class women stuck to the established rituals of the aristocratic promenade. The promenade functioned among other things as a marriage market, with families putting their eligible daughters on display and giving them carefully supervised opportunities to interact with the right sort of men. By the nineteenth century, these transactions were less likely to take place on the street, while opportunities for less ritualized looking and longing—and speaking and touching—multiplied in the crowded cities. Prostitutes could exploit men's uncertainties about the status or role of women visible on the street. Men nabbed with prostitutes sometimes protested that they were naive victims of entrapment or mistaken identity, while others took advantage of the uncertainty to defend their right to accost women on the street.

The anonymity of the street created new possibilities of social and sexual contact, sometimes with the aid of the new mass media. Tales of fortuitous encounters that led to love and marriage—mostly but not all fictional—appeared in mass-market newspapers. So did stories of missed connections. It was presumably a middle-class clientele that hit upon the idea of using newspaper advertisements to regain missed connections. The author of such an announcement always presented himself as a young man either too shy or too decorous to speak to the respectable young lady whose face he could not forget. Here are Berlin examples from the 1860s and 1870s: "The lady who lost her handkerchief on the Hercules bridge the day before yesterday, and was given it back by a gentleman, is asked by that same gentleman to appear in the Chestnut Wood at the same hour tomorrow."[61] "The gentleman who on the 18th at eight o'clock followed the dark-clad lady with the black, blue-trimmed hat, accompanied by a servant girl with a small child on her arm, on the left side of Friedrichstrasse from Behrenstrasse to Leipziger Strasse, and sadly lost sight of her before Leipziger Strasse, asks for a message that would give him the chance to see her again."[62] Bold or touching? Gallant or creepy? Most likely these stories ended here, but we cannot know. These passing glances happened in theaters or cafés as well as on the street, and not necessarily on foot: "The two elegant young ladies who in their own carriage, and at eight o'clock on Sunday evening, near Charlottenburg, passed by a young man in grey, who smiled to them, are begged to enter into private communication with him."[63] Such ads were not numerous—far outnumbered, in fact, by the more familiar kind of "marriage" ads that described the writer rather than any particular recipient. Those personal ads (as they were later known) cleanly separated visual contact from formal acquaintance. They were better suited to a particular conception of modern society, the kind that functioned apart from the promiscuous space of the street. It is in this sense that street prostitution felt unmodern: an uncomfortable and anachronistic relic in a middle-class world supposedly organized around private desires and private spaces.

LIFE IN PRIVATE AND IN PUBLIC

One of the hazy generalizations of nineteenth-century history is the growth of privacy, especially among the middle classes. We can certainly observe a tendency to withdraw from the street—in shopping, in entertainment, in transportation, in politics—with some trends dating back an additional century or more. Middle-class individuals and families found opportunities to spend more time and engage in more activities in enclosed or exclusive spaces. Their desire for physical separation from others also changed their behavior in the street. The quest for familial privacy is usually seen as working in conjunction with material forces of modernity—carriages and automobiles, central heating and plumbing, prosperity and suburbanization—to sweep people and activities off the street. The Whiggish or optimistic version of this history identifies street life as a vestige of poverty, happily left behind along with the filth, traffic, crime, and uncongenial people that drove us indoors. A competing, nostalgic view rejects this moralistically tinged history of progress by recalling the agreeable temptations of the street.

The street door often marked a crucial boundary, physically, symbolically, and legally. It separated the public space of the street from private spaces governed by different laws and customs.[64] Its role was most definitive where a continuous street wall sealed off the street, the typically European form that developed over many centuries. In the traditional houses of merchants and artisans, the door usually stood directly on the street, with it alone separating the public way from interior rooms open only to a select few: family members along with servants and apprentices. Lowlier workers might also boast a street door where they had their own private cottages—most typically in England, but less so in London than in smaller towns. Customs varied, and historical evidence is far from solid, on when or why these doors stood open to invite free talk or free passage.[65] In 1783 Friedrich Justinian von Günderrode found that practices differed sharply on either side of the English Channel: "In Paris all front doors stand open, while every room in the house is carefully locked. In London all the front doors are carefully locked, while every room in the house stands open."[66] Behavior around this threshold revealed class distinctions and invited moral judgments. Victorian reformers in England identified the most disreputable houses and streets as those in which residents left doors open, lingered on stairs, or leaned out windows.[67] This weak or absent distinction between public and private space was most apparent in the closed courts where many of the London poor lived. As nineteenth-century redevelopment replaced these courts with through streets, the street door assumed a more definitive role, and middle-class reformers saw an opportunity to protect children and families from the baleful influence of the street.[68]

Other structures might mediate between house and street, soft-

FIG. 32. Jacobus Vrel, *A Conversation in a Street*, c. 1660. Private Collection/Johnny Van Haeften Ltd., London/Bridgeman Images.

ening the transition marked by the door. Such were the outdoor benches of Renaissance Florence, attached to palazzo façades, which could serve the purpose of an entry hall but were accessible to anyone.[69] Arcades and loggias mediated between door and street in some places, with extensive networks maintained over centuries in a few cities such as Bologna and Bern. Although they sometimes functioned as entirely public spaces outside street doors, they might also be used as extensions of the adjoining houses. Other liminal spaces included porches, porticos, and vestibules of many kinds, which sometimes provided a socially acceptable site for outsiders to interact with women who were not supposed to be seen on the streets. Elsewhere, for example in Venice, balconies served a simi-lar purpose, offering women visual and aural but not tactile contact with the street.[70] Although the entry to the traditional Paris *hôtel* was mediated by a porte-cochère, balconies began to appear above the street by the seventeenth century. Open windows might serve the same purpose, but women were sometimes warned not to let them-selves be seen there. In fact, the nineteenth-century French expres-sion "faire la fenêtre" equated this behavior with prostitution. Rules that attempted to control prostitutes' behavior, for example in the Zurich of 1879, stipulated that they were forbidden "to lean out the windows of their rooms," to be visible at them, or to linger outside, at, or even behind the door of a known house of prostitution.[71]

The Georgian terraced houses of London marked a new archi-tectural relationship between house and street, whether they faced older streets or the new private squares laid out during the eigh-teenth and early nineteenth centuries. These new house designs in-cluded a raised basement usable as a kitchen and as servants' quar-ters. To bring light and air into it through large windows, a trench was excavated in front, typically two meters deep and at least a meter across. The result was to separate the house's doorway from the street both horizontally and vertically, with an iron railing en-closing the pit and defining the edge of the public street. The left-over space of the pit, neither street nor house nor garden, lacked an identity, a fact reflected in the peculiar name it acquired: "area." A stone stairway had to bridge it to provide access to the entrance door on the raised main floor.[72] This was a door to be approached only with forethought. Along with its raised and recessed position and its severe classical pediment, there developed a set of telegraphic con-ventions regarding knocks at the door and rings of the bell, with dif-ferent numbers and combinations of knocks and rings signaling a call to servants or to the kitchen (although a separate entry down to the lower floor eventually became standard), the arrival of the post-man or of a household member, or a guest of proper social stature calling on the family.[73] The existence of the code sent a clear message that the door was not to be opened promiscuously.

Architectural language developed differently on the Continent.

Unlike in England, single-family houses in the cities were mostly being supplanted by apartment buildings for the wealthier classes, with families moving into upper-story flats. Here the porte-cochère and porter's lodge, or perhaps the staircase or courtyard, sometimes played a mediating role, selectively extending public space behind the street wall. Even if ancient courts and alleys were gradually disappearing, as in England, poor people rarely had a street door to call their own. The proletarian districts of Berlin were an extreme case, with their deep lots and massive back buildings. Here most of the population lived in flats that faced courtyards rather than the street, and the courtyards became extensions of the street for many purposes.

Meanwhile, the street façade became a form of real-estate advertisement aimed at the better-off minority who could afford the larger apartments in front. Instead of the "area," the transition from public to private was boldly marked by façades that became increasingly ornate as the nineteenth century went on. Speculative builders and their architects drew on traditions of palace and villa design in their quest for an architectural language that might somehow lend an appropriately dignified, or at least conspicuous, public face to build-

Berlin-Wilmersdorf
Aschaffenburgerstr. — Prinzregentenstr. v. Pragerplatz

FIG. 34. Berlin-Wilmersdorf, Prager Platz. 1918 postcard.

ings that housed a varied and changing array of tenants. Most employed the forms of classical architecture, usually in its Renaissance and Baroque variants and sometimes drawing on local traditions, to present an eye-popping if often bewildering array of pilasters, pediments, and cornices rendered in stone, brick, or stucco. These robust façades reinforced the centuries-old visual emphasis given to the street wall, even as critics bewailed the architectural cacophony and muddled iconography of new apartment houses and office blocks. By the end of the century, these critics argued that the elaborate historicist architecture was a symptom of an excessive or even pathological emphasis on external display, at the expense of what should have been a healthy internal or family life in the neglected spaces behind the walls. In yearning for façades that called less attention to themselves, they pointed the way toward the eventual breakdown of the street wall.

The degree of class segregation varied within and between cities. In English towns of two-story terraces, street after street was lined with nothing but the tiny homes of the poor. The taller tenements of major continental cities might be nearly as segregated, but even a proletarian street often housed some middle-class residents in the street-facing apartments above the shops, while some poor residents, including servants, perched in the garrets above bourgeois apartments such as those on Haussmann's boulevards. Middle-class residents could usually lay claim to enclosed family dwellings, clearly marked by a door either on the street or off a courtyard or stairwell. They were less likely to linger on sidewalks or in doorways. By the late nineteenth century, the middle and upper classes limited their exposure to the street, and to the sort of people who lingered there.

What was visible in residential streets was an urban working-class culture. In the rapidly growing nineteenth-century cities, most poor workers and their families dwelt in extremely crowded conditions. Often an entire family lived in a single room, or in two rooms separated by a common corridor. Even where a family had its own apartment, it might share its space with lodgers who helped cover the rent. Middle-class ideals of family privacy were unattainable even if—as is not certain—they were sought after, and many facets of life spilled out into public spaces. These included cafés and pubs that offered a warm place for drink and companionship. In many configurations of metropolitan housing, courtyards played a major role as sites of work as well as leisure. Outside the pubs and courtyards lay the streets, which were often gloomy, filthy, and unsafe, but they could also become convivial places of conversation, leisure, and play, valued for their kaleidoscope of people, animals, vehicles, and goods rather than feared as cold or anonymous.

Although poor neighborhoods and side streets lacked the crush of vehicles and commerce found in the busiest (and most frequently described) thoroughfares, they could be unfailingly lively. Ellen Chase, an American social worker active in the London maritime district of Deptford during the 1880s, recalled the scene in the main street there:

There were tottering, grey-headed old pensioners with gilt buttons to their reefers; pinched, careworn women in rusty, ragged black; overdressed, boisterous girls amusing themselves by giggling and chaffing with strangers; smart young red-coats swinging along in couples;

FIG. 35. Heinrich Zille, Berlin courtyard, Ackerstrasse, c. 1910. Stiftung Stadtmuseum Berlin.

and groups of rough hearty sailors from the cattle-steamers, shoving and rollicking along the crowded sidewalks, carrying all before them. And there were generally peddlers and beggars of one kind and another, women selling jumping-jacks from trays hanging about their necks; and in their season, men hawking primrose-roots from baskets, or rabbits dangling from the end of a stick. Here would be a vendor of whirligigs, there a mender of old umbrellas, and perhaps a blind bugler, or a couple of gaily kerchiefed Italian women with cages of fortune-telling canaries set above their rattling hand-organs. To add to the din, the noisy salesmen of the rival butchers' shops, "touting" for customers, shout out at the top of their lungs, "What'll you buy, buy, buy? What do you want, my dears? Lovely steak! lovely chops! What'll you buy, buy, buy?"

Even in the side street where she worked, "there was always something going on": "So many of our people, young and old, passed their time leaning out of the windows, sitting on the steps, or swarming at play in the middle of the road, that the slightest provocation collected a crowd."[74]

An Austrian journalist, Otto von Leixner, recorded an unusually thorough description of such a scene in 1890. He set out to describe a typical day in one of the hundreds of new tenement streets that had recently sprung up on the rapidly expanding fringes of Berlin. Photographs and memoirs of similar streets confirm his observations, as do many of Heinrich Zille's popular sketches, but Leixner is the rare outsider who lingered to compile a detailed account. His unnamed and utterly typical side street in the Moabit district was lined with massive five-story apartment buildings whose ornate stucco façades rose up directly from the broad sidewalks. The street-facing ground floors housed shops: bakers, butchers, greengrocers, dairy shops, barbers, and, to Leixner's dismay, numerous pubs. Just above were the largest apartments, typically of three or four rooms, with the higher floors divided into three smaller units instead of two larger flats. Arched ground-floor passages gave access to each building's courtyard and from there to its other wings with their mostly small apartments facing the narrow court. Some courtyard wings might have housed workshops rather than residences, although Leixner does not mention any on his street. None of the residents were rich or extremely poor; they included municipal and postal officials, small-time merchants, and a few retired army officers, along with shop proprietors living next to their establishments. All these categories were outnumbered by skilled industrial workers and their families, drawn by the proximity to numerous factories, and mostly living in the small courtyard flats.

Children dominated the scene. From twelve to one o'clock, the street was notably quiet, after which the youthful hordes turned the street into a playground. Leixner counted 218 children at one time. The smallest ones squirmed all over the sidewalk "so that you must be careful not to step on a little hand or foot." Little girls barely old enough for school watched over even smaller children whom they set in doorways or on shop steps. Boys played ball games out in the roadway and managed to emit an astounding variety of noises. Along the curb the girls played school. So did boys, separately, but with them the main activity was the "teacher" hitting the pupils, which usually sparked a brawl. Children were also frequently tasked with errands, fetching food and milk from shops. Sometimes one of them carried an empty beer bottle to the spirits shop and secretly took a swig on the way home. After school on a warm day, many boys took off their socks and shoes and waited for the municipal spray wagons dispatched by the city in its persistent effort to control the clouds of street dust. Then the boys would roll up their trousers and run into the spray of water. The greatest excitement came when there was excavation work underway—a frequent event in this age of new sewer, water, gas, and electric lines as well as improved pavements. Boys and girls alike dug in the exposed earth, throwing dirt about, building and defending forts, or molding mud pies. At the lunch break, wives of street workers arrived with food, their children in tow, and the families ate together on the street.

The children's activities faced little interference from the sparse and entirely animal-powered traffic. Occasional freight wagons hauled vegetables or milk to the local shops. Coal dealers made their rounds with small wagons drawn by long-suffering dogs. Few taxis and even fewer private carriages disturbed the peace of a working-class street, while trams were restricted to busier thoroughfares. Leixner's description reminds us that even a street densely packed with residences and businesses, in a booming metropolis, could be almost tranquil, its peace destroyed only slowly during the twentieth century by the gradual increase in motor vehicles.[75]

Leixner found Berlin street commerce to be less lively on the street than in the courtyards of the deep tenement lots, where the coal dealers, ragpickers, and vegetable sellers uttered their distinctive cries for the benefit of everyone living above. Organ-grinders were regular visitors all day long, rousing the children to gather and dance. Itinerant boys' choirs also offered musical entertainment in the courtyards. As the day passed, street activity grew, with men and women gathering at doorways to chat. Those who had street-facing balconies settled there on warm days. Others, especially courtyard residents, brought chairs out to the sidewalk. Around nine in the evening, the children vanished, with the adults lingering for another hour or so. Then the street was quiet, with noise coming from an occasional wagon or pedestrian, but mostly escaping from the pubs. The only shop with light visible was an ironing business that kept its girls hard at work until midnight. Otherwise "you could almost believe you were in a small country town. Nothing betrays the metropolis."[76]

Well-to-do observers often deplored the culture of the streets, particularly the dirty and ragged children, and wished they could be led to parks or playgrounds, or given better homes to be kept inside, in order to avoid the filth and temptations outside their doors. Parts of Leixner's book are typically moralistic, especially his attempts to expose the thinly concealed sex trade in the city center. In this chapter, however, he offers little judgment. Instead, he puts human faces on the anonymous and perhaps frightening crowds that his middle-class readers might typically see. Certainly we can read his appealing picture as an attempt to make them understand and even cherish the city street along with the working class that inhabited it. In some ways his account resembles Jane Jacobs's 1961 description of the web of solidarity on her New York street, with her now-famous image of the intricate "sidewalk ballet" that wove routine encounters into a kind of social cohesion.[77] Unlike Jacobs, however, Leixner and other well-meaning contemporaries did not think they were capturing an endangered way of life. Yet by some measures, European reformers succeeded beyond their wildest dreams. Although many hoped that improved housing conditions would encourage families to renounce the filthy and wicked street, hardly anyone thought there would be a price to pay for doing so. Cars were not the only culprit, even if automotive traffic did eventually transform these quiet side streets more drastically than the already busy main thoroughfares. Twentieth-century prosperity, commerce, housing, planning, sanitation, and mobility all eroded the old ways of street life.

4

Out of the Muck

The Sanitary City

Twentieth-century anti-littering campaigns on the roadways were an attempt to crack down on what had been one of the liberating pleasures of automobile travel: the opportunity to treat the entire world as a garbage can. Motorists who tossed trash out the window did not linger to face the consequences of their convenience. Matters were quite different in premodern city streets. For centuries, one of their major functions was as a place to drain excess liquids and dispose of household and commercial refuse. Other uses of the street required a tolerance of this practice and its inescapable residues. The unending battle against filth vastly expanded municipal governments' intervention in the physical structure of streets and cities. Their enhanced authority in matters of engineering and design became the basis of modern urban planning during the nineteenth century. In much of Europe, the end of that century saw some remarkable victories over dirt and disease.

FILTHY STREETS

The squalor of the premodern street is at once legendary and perplexing. Lurid anecdotes about the bad old days can add spice to historical accounts. Yet it is often difficult to know just how contemporaries perceived their immediate environment. Although furious denunciations of sordid conditions in one's own or (more typically) a foreign city can often be found in the historical record, hardly anyone saw fit to leave us balanced descriptions of the typical street, however different it may have been from ours. Even a word like "mud" connoted peculiarly local textures and aromas that rarely merited description. To take another word, Charles Dickens's elaborate descriptions of Victorian London's "dust" employed the accepted term for the household waste of which coal residue was the largest component, but a passing acquaintance with northern European weather, or with Dickens's own descriptions of the London fog, suggests that these ash heaps were probably more dank and pungent than the word "dust" might imply.

Standards of cleanliness for crowded streets could not be very high. Although we find plenty of recorded complaints, it may be safe to assume that most citizens expected nothing better, and indeed that what long counted as a clean street might actually horrify most twenty-first-century Westerners. Surviving descriptions tell us something about the actual condition of the streets and perhaps even more about prevailing beliefs about propriety. So does the ceaseless trickle of official and often futile decrees to clean up streets.

Growing towns meant growing quantities of waste. Horses made their copious contributions, as did wandering or herded cows, pigs, and chickens, plus dogs and cats. Refuse from workshops was often dumped in the street as well. Sawdust and ash piled up or blew about, while butchers, tanners, and dyers discharged blood, grease, and other sticky or stinking liquids, which congealed in the gutters with food scraps from houses and street markets. In routine violation of centuries-old ordinances, cesspits and chamber pots were often emptied into the streets, most notoriously from upstairs windows, sometimes out of malice or mischief but usually for lack of any other convenient place to dispose of human urine and excrement.

Where did it all go? Before recycling was a fashion, it was a way of life. An impressive portion of this waste was scavenged either by pigs and dogs or by human ragpickers and dung collectors. The rest found its way into open gutters located in the center of the street or along each side. In dry weather the filth turned to dust and blew about in choking clouds. Wet weather might be even more unpleasant, with pedestrians stranded in ankle-deep muck. Even where a reasonably dry crossing was available, carriage wheels splashed pedestrians mercilessly. Only a torrential rain could effectively clear the gutters, and then they were likely to clog (dead dogs were often blamed) and overflow, flooding streets and houses. Waste was dumped into any accessible canal or stream, including those relied on for washing and drinking water. These open sewers reliably emitted noxious fumes.

In European villages and small towns, a typical house had its dung-heap, often out in front on the street. The dung had value as fertilizer to be used or sold. (Mark Twain quipped that Black Forest villagers appeared to measure a family's wealth by the size of its manure pile.[1]) Only slowly did growing towns crack down on dung-heaps, at least requiring that they not spill into the street.[2] Even in late eighteenth-century Berlin, they were still a common sight. From the fifteenth century, though, Vienna appointed knights as "dung judges" to supervise the clearing of streets.[3] Large cities sometimes required domestic dung-heaps to be underground and out of sight, but even there they remained a threat to health and safety, especially if the trapdoors in front of houses came open.[4]

During the seventeenth century and into the eighteenth, the foul condition of the streets seems mostly to have been taken for granted. Commentary was typically amused or resigned. Before he was executed for blasphemy in 1662, the obscene poet Claude Le Petit merrily offended good taste with his description of the

> Elixir of rotting feces,
> Accursed filth droppings of Paris,
> Dung of the abominable damned,
> Fecal matter of hell,
> Black droppings of the devil. . . .[5]

Although Jonathan Swift remained a clergyman in good standing, he, too, explored the outer limits of acceptable discourse. "A Description of a City Shower" (1710), one of his tamer efforts, concludes:

> Now from all parts the swelling kennels flow,
> And bear their trophies with them as they go:
> Filth of all hues and odors seem to tell
> What street they sailed from, by their sight and smell.
> They, as each torrent drives with rapid force,
> From Smithfield or St. Pulchre's shape their course,
> And in huge confluence joined at Snow Hill ridge,
> Fall from the conduit prone to Holborn Bridge.
> Sweepings from butchers' stalls, dung, guts, and blood,
> Drowned puppies, stinking sprats, all drenched in mud,
> Dead cats, and turnip tops, come tumbling down the flood.

By 1755 a poem printed in a Berlin newspaper at least pretended to call for action:

> I, a poor little pile of d—,
> lie here as ordered, since Monday,
> and no one hauls me away.
> Please, dear Mother Police,
> don't let me be trampled completely.
> I flow like porridge already;
> soon I'll be barely a pile.
> If another week goes by
> before your cart arrives
> I will melt completely away![6]

Filth did have its advocates. An article as late as 1787 in the *Encyclopédie méthodique* repeated the old belief that emanations from sewers could counteract the foul air causing the plague.[7] Even into the nineteenth century, Paris mud was sometimes said to have curative properties. Nevertheless, the philosopher Bernard de Mandeville knew he was trampling on conventional wisdom when the preface to his *Fable of the Bees* (1714) argued that dirty streets were a welcome sign of prosperity, "a necessary evil inseparable from the felicity of London." When people "come to consider, that what offends them is the result of the plenty, great traffic and opulency of that mighty city, if they have any concern in its welfare, they will hardly ever wish to see the streets of it less dirty." The German economist Paul Jacob Marperger likely had Mandeville in mind when his 1724 treatise on the merits of municipal street cleaning denounced the belief that "cities acquire prestige when riding, walking, and driving fill the streets with dung."[8] Viscount Tyrconnel also rejected Mandeville's view when he endorsed a paving bill in the House of Commons in 1741: "The filth, Sir, of some parts of the town, and the inequality and ruggedness of others, cannot but in the eyes of foreigners disgrace our nation, and incline them to imagine us a people, not only without delicacy, but without government, a herd of barbarians, or a colony of hottentots. The most disgusting part of the character given by travellers, of the most savage nations, is their neglect of cleanliness, of which, perhaps, no part of the world affords more proofs than the streets of the British capital; a city famous for wealth, and commerce, and plenty, and for every other kind of civility and politeness, but which abounds with such heaps of filth, as a savage would look on with amazement."[9]

Complaints about dirty streets mounted during the eighteenth century. Even more striking is the change in their tone and substance. Earlier, the eyes mattered more than the nose, as Lord Tyrconnel's words suggest. In the seventeenth century and into the eighteenth, upper-class pedestrians, who furnish most of our informants, bewailed the damage to their clothes and respectable appearance. They seem to have worried less about their experience in the street than about the impression they would make upon their arrival. In the seventeenth century, walking was unfashionable, at least in fashionable Paris, so street mud was a badge of shame.[10] Claude Le Petit wailed (in verse) that "my shoes, my socks, my coat, my collar, my gloves, my hat, have all taken on the same color and, in this state, I would take me to be a heap of rubbish, if I did not say to myself: That's me!"[11] Arthur Young, visiting Paris in 1787, claimed that the condition of the streets dictated Parisian fashion: "all persons of small or moderated fortune, are forced to dress in black, with black stockings," in order to hide the mud splashed by speeding carriages.[12] Meanwhile, a Frenchman traveling the other direction described the dreadful mud of the Strand but added that "the English are not afraid of this dirt, being defended from it by their wigs of a brownish curling hair, their black stockings, and their blue surtouts."[13]

For unspoken reasons, the bodies beneath the clothing, and especially the odors they emitted, were less worthy of comment. Descriptions of filth before the mid-eighteenth century seldom mentioned its stench, or that of the bodies covered with it.[14] This was, we should remember, an age in which bathing was infrequent and often deemed unhealthy, while strong perfumes, or at least nosegays, offered the acceptable antidote to bodily and environmental odors. An Italian visitor to Paris in the 1590s observed, "A stream of fetid water coursed through every street of the town, into which ran the dirty water from each house, and which tainted the air; consequently, it was essential to carry sweet-scented flowers in the hand to allay the smell."[15] Many of the recorded complaints came from medically astute outsiders. Daniel Defoe's *Due Preparations for the Plague* (1722), for example, urged London's leaders to clean up sources of pestilential stench. His fear of disease was not new. It was shared by Tuscan officials such as the one worried about the situation in Bientina in 1607, where the chamber pots spilled "through gaps in the walls and fall into certain narrow alleys between the houses in which [the inhabitants] throw all the dirt and rubbish from their houses. . . . The result is a stench and filth so awful that it is quite impossible to live there." A Florentine envoy reported from Vico in 1610 that "they tell me that in the heat of summer they can hardly bear to walk down the streets for the stink."[16]

We find surprisingly few of these vivid descriptions. People saw and smelled the same things we do, but they adjusted to them in ways we might find hard to fathom. (Perhaps it is true, as has been suggested, that they blocked out odors in the same way today's city dwellers ignore noise.) It is impossible to measure their tolerance of everyday filth, since those who were not moved to comment on the matter have, of course, left us no record of their silence. (We do have greater access to the millions who live in similar circumstances in twenty-first-century cities. Either they, too, don't much mind the various heaps and smells they encounter, or more typically they simply make their peace with the daily unpleasantness of street life.)

But sensibilities were changing. As the historian Georges Viga-rello has suggested, during the late eighteenth century the smell of the city ceased to be perceived as inevitable and instead became intolerable.[17] The Russian writer Nikolai Karamzin's disgust and astonishment were characteristic by 1790:

> Close by a glittering jewelry shop, a pile of rotten apples and herrings; everywhere filth and even blood streaming from the butchers' stalls. You must hold your nose and close your eyes. The picture of a splendid city grows dim in your thoughts, and it seems to you that the dirt and muck of all the cities in the world is flowing through the sewers of Paris. Take but one more step, and suddenly the fragrance of happy Arabia or, at least, Provence's flowering meadows, is wafted upon you, for you have come to one of the many shops where perfume and pomade are sold. In a word, every step means a new atmosphere, new objects of luxury or the most loathsome filth.[18]

The stench of Berlin was notorious by the late eighteenth century and remained so until the city built its sewer system in the 1870s, although we must read our sources with caution, since some visitors from rival kingdoms were eager to denigrate the upstart Prussian capital, while natives sometimes hoped to shame their countrymen into action. In 1808 the Prussian reformer Friedrich von Cölln joined the chorus of complaint by comparing Vienna favorably to Berlin, where the gutters emit an "insufferable stench" and you would never want to remove your handkerchief from your nose.[19] Their stench bewildered Karamzin: "Why are they not cleaned? Have the people of Berlin lost their sense of smell?"[20] In 1842 William Howitt also found it impossible to ignore the stagnant gutters, a "stinking festering kennel, rank with bubbles of a putrid effervescence. So accustomed are the inhabitants to this, that they do not even cover it over. There it is, open to the day. Children roll into it as they play in the streets, and the whole city has the odor of a great sink. Yet again, so insensible has custom made the inhabitants to this nuisance, that when we spoke of it they said, O, was that anything uncommon? They thought that was the smell of all cities!"[21] We should mistrust the Englishman's prejudices—after all, covering gutters was not a choice available to individual citizens—but he is the rare observer who paused to ask how people adapted to their circumstances.

Howitt did not state his case in explicitly moral terms, but the slippage between sanitary and moral language was nearly universal. In 1835 Frances Trollope used the odor of Paris to illustrate the general want of delicacy in France (and, actually, the entire Continent) when compared to England, although she hastened to explain that the French moral defects had environmental and therefore remediable causes, above all the lack of sewers: "That people who from their first breath of life have been obliged to accustom their senses and submit without a struggle to the sufferings this evil entails upon them,—that people so circumstanced should have less refinement in their thoughts and words than ourselves, I hold to be natural and inevitable." In other words, "the indelicacy which so often offends us in France does not arise from any natural coarseness of mind, but is the unavoidable result of circumstances, which may, and doubtless will change."[22] While the English were particularly keen to proclaim their fastidiousness, the self-evident connection between cleanliness and morality was international. The influential French sanitary reformer Alexandre-Jean-Baptiste Parent-Duchâtelet put it this way: "Prostitutes are just as inevitable in an urban district as are sewers, dumps, and refuse heaps. The authorities should take the same approach to each."[23]

In 1771 Tobias Smollett put blunt words into the mouth of a fictional visitor to London: "I breathe the steams of endless putrefaction; and these would, undoubtedly, produce a pestilence, if they were not qualified by the gross acid of sea-coal, which is itself a pernicious nuisance to lungs of any delicacy of texture. . . . Human excrement is the least offensive part of the concrete, which is composed of all the drugs, minerals, and poisons, used in mechanics and manufacture, enriched with the putrefying carcasses of beasts and men; and mixed with the scourings of all the wash-tubs, kennels, and common sewers."[24] Still, most visitors preferred London's streets to those of Paris, which were narrower, more crowded, hemmed in by taller buildings, and notorious for their *boue*, a sticky brew of food scraps, animal fat, and human and horse excrement. In 1782 Jacques-Hippolyte Ronesse offered a dispassionate visual—not olfactory—taxonomy:

> Dirt and debris scattered by rubbish-carters, saltpeter-makers and plasterers; construction debris; horse dung, which by itself makes up a large portion in busy streets; finally the dust, cinders, soot, and other fine sweepings from houses, which are spread along the walls, scattered by carriages, by the feet of passersby, and by ragpickers and chimney sweeps. All this ordure mixes with gutter water and especially with the greasy liquid that issues from kitchens, forming this foul mud [*boue*], filled with dissolved iron that makes it a black and potent stain, and which covers the streets of Paris nearly all year, harms the salubrity of the air, and causes so much unpleasantness for pedestrians.[25]

Louis-Sébastian Mercier claimed that his city's mud was so laden with sulphuric and nitric acid that a spot of it would eat through fabric. He declared that its smell was "intolerable to foreigners."[26]

In 1797 Pierre Chauvet, writing anonymously as a "French citizen" on "the cleanliness of Paris," lamented:

> It is humiliating that I am unable to walk through the metropolis, the seat of our Senate, without coming across sewers, piles of filth, heaps of rubbish, smashed bottles that seem to have been thrown down like traps in order to injure men and horses; by seeing scat-

tered limbs of dead animals; by meeting stray dogs that make me fear
rabies; by goats and pigs even along public promenades; by having to
walk on uneven pavement covered with greasy mud that makes me
slip if I want to move quickly and fall if I stand too long; to see women
who are the models of taste for all of Europe obliged to run about in
this mire, and often, in order to cross a street, forced to balance on
a wobbly plank that makes them fear falling into a muddy ditch; by
carts supposed to clean the city but themselves spreading stinking
filth; finally, to see, against all decency and good manners, men and
women relieving themselves in public.[27]

Chauvet was humiliated because, like many educated Europeans, he
had come to see dirty and reeking cities as backward and shameful.

Such a fundamental shift in sensibilities is likely to have had multiple causes. Crucial among them was a broad revival of interest in
miasmatic theories of disease. According to these widely dissemi-
nated medical teachings, foul-smelling air, particularly from de-
caying organic matter, was not merely unpleasant and not merely
evidence of disease: the air was itself diseased. It was the source
of plague and typhoid and the other fevers that seemed to rise directly from fetid cesspits and gutters. This heightened attention to
urban health is apparent in the emergence of a new genre of books,
the "medical topography," churned out by physicians around 1800.
Each of these volumes surveyed the dangers to health found in a city,
compiling statistics of endemic diseases, but also surveying bodies
of water, the disposal of household and bodily waste, the purity of
food in the markets, and the cleanliness of streets, all with an eye to
threats to public health. The fear of foul smells, and of streets and
cities themselves, became even more acute after 1830 when cholera
swept across Europe for the first time, bringing sudden death to
thousands in city after city.

Although awareness of these medical theories spread far beyond
the medical professions into the educated populace and beyond, it
would be a mistake to cite them as the sole cause of new sensibilities
about smell and new efforts to clean up cities. Something as primal

as a smell does not lend itself to rational control, so we must look at other influences on perceptions and beliefs.

Like distinctions between attractive and repellent odors, beliefs about beauty and visual order defy rational explanation. Gradual changes in urban aesthetics accompanied the growing attention to public health. A belief that the most attractive streets were wide and straight can be traced back to the Renaissance. Even then it may have seemed new only because medieval European rulers had rarely possessed the power and wealth to rebuild cities. It is nevertheless striking that the seventeenth-century philosopher René Descartes, in his *Discourse on Method*, uses the image of tangled streets to illustrate his distaste for cluttered minds and argues that a logically ordered city would be built with straight streets and right angles. By the eighteenth century, Enlightenment intellectuals' advocacy of rational governance gave wider currency to the belief that broad, straight streets were the most beautiful kind, and to a determination to build many more of them.[28]

Neither the medical nor the aesthetic views stood independently of moral principles, which, in turn, can expose psychological roots and perhaps also political fears. The queasiness apparent in the new sensitivity to smells expressed a barely conscious aversion to bodily contact that may not have been entirely new but was certainly becoming more apparent. Then, as now, medical beliefs and unspoken convictions reinforced each other. Theories of disease justified not only clean bodies but also an aversion to people who were thought not to smell right. Beneath these expressions of dread sometimes lay a revulsion at promiscuous sexuality. The darkest and most unspoken fear may have been that of incest. A deeply rooted discomfort with massed bodies became most apparent in growing worries about overcrowded urban housing, but it also influenced etiquette and behavior on the street.

Medical, aesthetic, and moral sensibilities promoted a desire for "light and air" that became the mantra of sanitary reform and of urban planning throughout the nineteenth century and beyond. It had roots in the miasmatic theories that traced disease to stagnant water, air, and odors, but it survived the late-century triumph of the germ theory, with which it proved broadly compatible.[29] Engineers, architects, and civic leaders followed the lead of activist physicians in promoting the circulation of air and water, of traffic, and of bodies. This new sensibility also had political implications and perhaps had political causes as well. No one can fail to notice that it arose alongside the French Revolution of 1789 and a new political order in which the unwashed masses (as English snobs called them) grasped at the reins of power. The wide, straight streets that brought light and air into the city also made the upper classes feel more secure there— most famously in Haussmann's Paris—and offered the authorities either the reality or the illusion of surveillance and control.

It is easy to recognize the repulsive power of an odor. It is more difficult to know what associations such a smell might trigger. A stinking city was not merely unpleasant. It was dangerous, and it was backward. For example, Cologne, still confined within its once-capacious medieval walls, attracted far fewer visitors than Paris or Berlin but may have rivaled them in olfactory notoriety around 1800. Its economic stagnation and its reputation for intolerant Catholicism may have done as much as its miasmas to shape the responses of visitors like Samuel Taylor Coleridge, who dedicated one of his lesser poems to an unhappy visit in 1828:

> In Köhln, a town of monks and bones,
> And pavements fang'd with murderous stones
> And rags, and hags, and hideous wenches;
> I counted two and seventy stenches. . . .

James Fenimore Cooper was one of many visitors in this era whose thoughts turned to the city's most famous product, eau de cologne: "I do not know that there is a necessary connection between foul smells and Cologne water, but this place is the dirtiest and most offensive we have yet seen, or rather smelt, in Europe. It would really seem that the people wish to drive their visitors into the purchase of their great antidote."[30]

One possible impetus for a new sensitivity was the fact that the upper and middle classes were bathing more frequently, thereby removing certain odors from their own bodies and making them more aware of smells emanating from others, especially from poor people who had fewer opportunities or less inclination to bathe.[31] This olfactory divergence culminated in the attitudes George Orwell identified in a trenchant taxonomy of the English class system in his 1937 book *The Road to Wigan Pier*. According to him, the middle class firmly believed that "the lower classes smell." Reflecting on his own Edwardian upbringing, he added, "Very early in life you acquired the idea that there was something subtly repulsive about a working-class body; you would not get nearer to it than you could help." The potential implications for interaction on the street, or lack of it, were profound.

Both a decreased tolerance for organic odors and a broader change in attitudes toward privacy and bodily exposure became apparent in judgments about basic bodily functions. Customs and laws governing eating in the streets, for example, have varied across time and space, revealing aversions and taboos. Prohibitions on spitting were never entirely about public health or cleanliness. The royal ban on smoking in Berlin's streets during the early nineteenth century made cigars into tokens of rebellion.[32] Most revealing, however, was the distress Chauvet and many others expressed at the sight as well as the smell of public urination and defecation. Here we gain insight into beliefs about the proper display or concealment of bodily functions, which are difficult to trace except when they are violated.

In the eighteenth century, and long before, riverbanks, walls, and alleys served as public toilets. The sight of men urinating against walls was routine. They can even be spotted in old paintings, prints, and (later) photographs. By the nineteenth century on London's teeming streets, a preferred target was a wagon wheel at the edge of the gutter.[33] Earlier, medieval towns often had an acknowledged dead end or "pissing alley" for excremental use; sometimes these were also the location of brothels.[34] Inhabitants of larger cities followed other customs that were little discussed and seldom recorded. There

were formally and informally designated sites where the display of
natural functions was politely ignored. Taverns and playhouses in
Elizabethan London put up "pissing posts" or directed men to particular corners and away from other walls and entrances.[35] Jonathan
Swift was merely making use of readily available evidence when he
featured excrement in his satirical attack on overwrought political passions, "An Examination of Certain Abuses, Corruptions and
Enormities in the City of Dublin" (1732): "Every person who walks
the streets, must needs observe the immense number of human ex-
crements at the doors and steps of waste houses, and at the sides
of every dead wall." He proceeded to spin a tale of paranoid British
Whigs declaring that the excrement lying in abundance on Dublin
streets was identifiably and exclusively Irish in origin, a claim they
made in order to refute an imaginary Catholic conspiracy spreading
the rumor "that these heaps were laid there privately by British fun-
daments, to make the world believe, that our Irish vulgar do daily eat
and drink; and, consequently, that the clamour of poverty among us,
must be false, proceeding only from Jacobites and Papists."[36] Swift
concluded his convoluted pseudo-conspiracy with a graphic account
of the medical expertise supposedly necessary to prove that British
and Irish shit, and thus humanity, were indistinguishable.

His frankness was deliberately shocking. A century later, it was
unimaginable. This change in sensibilities is the kind of profound
historical transformation that is hard to document with any precision. Amid a growing search for individual and family privacy, however, there seem to have been mounting objections to the sight—and
discussion—of urination and defecation. The typical traveler's report
couched its complaints in hints and euphemisms. From the London
of 1808, James Peller Malcolm lamented that "beer houses render
our streets unpleasant in summer; and delicacy forbids my adding
more on the subject."[37] Frances Trollope warned her readers in 1835
that "at every step" in the Paris streets they would endure "sights
and smells that may not be described," and in fact she declined to
offer any description of "the perpetual outrage of common decency
in their streets."[38] Henri Gisquet, prefect of police at the time, was

no more explicit: the most popular promenades, the most sanctified monuments, every grand and glorious place in Paris "bears the imprint of this destructive habit, of these vile profanations."[39] Paris was particularly bad, agreed Johann Friedrich Reichardt in 1802: "The shamelessness with which even well-dressed people, soldiers, and uniformed guardsmen defile the streets: you don't see such things even in the poorest little German town."[40] Not all his countrymen shared his patriotic claims of German superiority, as is obvious from their complaints of precisely the same problem in their own towns.[41]

Individual property owners tried to deter miscreants by, for example, installing horizontally grooved walls "to conduct the stream into the shoes,"[42] a distant ancestor of recent experiments with repelling paint in Hamburg. Citizens hoped mostly in vain for effective police intervention. Instead there was broad international agreement with Pierre Chauvet's plea that "manners must change." And they did. We might question his belief that things had once been better: "There was a time when a Frenchman was disgraced for revealing his backside in public."[43] An anonymous 1824 pamphlet by a "Parisian pedestrian" chose instead to predict the future, and it did so presciently: "Perhaps one day we will be ashamed of having lived for so long in the mire."[44] Chauvet's golden age of the past may have been imaginary, but it arrived during the nineteenth century.

CLEANING THE STREETS

A shrinking tolerance for filth is apparent in the many initiatives to cleanse the streets during the late eighteenth and nineteenth centuries. More active municipal governments played a role, as did new technology. The moral revolution is harder to trace, but the organizational and technological improvements are clear, if gradual. Among the major reforms were more systematic street cleaning, better paving, sewers, piped water, and public toilets.

Throughout the eighteenth and nineteenth centuries, cities' reputations for cleanliness, or lack of it, fell and rose, as deteriorating conditions prompted most of them to undertake ambitious pub-

lic works. Visitors' expectations rose accordingly, and local patri-
ots across Europe became keenly aware that laggards could count
on a bad press. From time to time, visitors showered praise on a
city for its visible—or sniffable—progress. The various Paving Acts
of the 1760s quickly improved conditions for London pedestrians,
and London soon gained a reputation as the best-paved and best-lit
city in Europe, with the possible exception of Vienna, although many
visitors on the Grand Tour reserved special praise for the streets of
Florence, and Dutch towns were also acquiring their salubrious
reputation. For the next half-century, English visitors were consis-
tently appalled by the streets of Paris: the filth, the obstacles, and
the rough paving shared by vehicles and pedestrians alike. William
Hazlitt, in 1824, even concluded that Parisians' distinctive gait was
merely their way of making the best of a bad situation: "The very
walk of the Parisians, that light, jerking, fidgeting trip on which they
pride themselves, and think it grace and spirit, is the effect of the
awkward construction of their streets, or of the round, flat, slippery
stones, over which you are obliged to make your way on tiptoe, and
where natural ease and steadiness are out of the question."[45] A few
decades later, though, it was post-Haussmann Paris that drew ac-
claim for its broad, well-paved, and well-drained boulevards. By 1900
German cities impressed visitors with the sheer orderliness of their
explosive growth.

Improved paving was sometimes intended to speed up traffic, but
before the late nineteenth century its more important purpose was
to make cleaner streets possible, by creating a smooth surface and
by sealing the miasmas emanating from below. Although suburban
streets typically remained unpaved in 1800, by then most major city
thoroughfares had been paved with stones of some kind, and some
cities had laid down hewn stone blocks to replace the old rounded or
pointed cobbles that left large gaps between them. Sidewalks, newly
raised or marked off in many streets, were often given distinctive
flagstone paving, which was smoother and easier to clean, especially
since horses were mostly kept off it. Crushed stone macadam came
into wide use during the early nineteenth century, offering better

footing for horses and a quieter ride for wagons, but it was dustier—
or muddier—than stone blocks and did not hold up well in heavy
wheeled traffic, so that Baudelaire could write of the poet who has
lost his halo in "the mire of the macadam" while crossing a Parisian
boulevard. Wooden block paving had its day in some places, provid-
ing a smooth and quiet surface that, however, did not always hold
up well, could become slippery when greasy, and had an unfortunate
propensity to absorb horse urine. Increasingly the favored material
was asphalt, at first from natural deposits where they were available
(especially in France) and more widely as a petroleum-based industrial product at the end of the century. Its smooth and impermeable
surface was quieter than stone and offered the promise of greater
cleanliness, although progress proved more elusive than Balzac
thought in 1837, when the sight of the new material inspired him
to predict that the notorious Paris mud would vanish within a decade.[46] The smooth surfaces incidentally expanded the prospects of
an already established entrepreneurial niche, that of pavement chalk
artists.

The eighteenth century was a golden age of street-cleaning regulations. German towns were particularly assiduous in issuing "Gassen-
ordnungen" as templates for orderly streets. These ordinances
banned dung-heaps and codified the traditional rule that home-
owners or shopkeepers were responsible for cleaning the pavement
and removing snow in front of their properties, out to the center of
the street. In some towns, civic pride and neighborhood pressure inspired residents to keep up appearances for generations thereafter.
Enforcement was difficult, however, and in major cities clean streets
remained more the exception than the rule. In fact, many of these
regulations had already been reissued countless times over the centuries. In Paris, for example, they can be documented back to the
twelfth-century King Philip Augustus. By the fifteenth century, they
threatened violators with imprisonment, the pillory, or even death.[47]
To little avail, it seems. By 1800 the sheer quantity of waste threatened to overwhelm the growing cities.

Animals were major contributors to the waste problem as well as to traffic jams, but most cities were slow to divert the herds of live-stock on their way to market. Only in the course of the nineteenth century did they crack down on cattle drives through their streets. Henry Mayhew tells us that in 1848, 1.8 million cattle, sheep, and pigs—that would be five thousand per day—were driven into Lon-don's central livestock market at Smithfield.[48] Mischievous boys sometimes managed to lure a bull away from its herd and send it on a wild chase through the busy streets.[49] To Max Schlesinger, Smith-field was not only "the dirtiest of all the dirty spots which disgrace the fair face of the capital of England"; it was also "an inexhaustible source of accidents. Men are run down, women are tossed, children are trampled to death. But these men, women, and children, belong to the lower classes. Persons of rank or wealth do not generally come to Smithfield early in the morning, if, indeed, they ever come there at all."[50] Only in 1855 did London convert it to a market for butchered meat, with live animals diverted to the Caledonian Market in Isling-ton. Even then, livestock remained a common sight on its way to the many private slaughterhouses.

Meanwhile, horse-drawn vehicles were crowding the commercial thoroughfares. The density of traffic was most astonishing in central London, at London Bridge and Cheapside, where traffic counts in the 1850s tallied more than a thousand wagons passing every day-time hour—as many as twenty per minute.[51] James Grant claimed that "so great is the number of vehicles to be seen at one time in Cheapside, that could a person scramble along horses' backs as well as over the top of coaches, cabs, carts, omnibuses, etc., he might almost pass from one end of that street to the other, though more than a third of a mile in length, without once putting his foot on the ground."[52] The earliest London street films, decades later, show the commotion, but rarely zoom in to the street surface under the horses' hooves. Mayhew somehow calculated London's annual street dung deposits at 40,000 tons: more than a hundred tons per day.[53]

Dung, both human and animal, could be put to good use in gar-dens and fields, so it had value as long as the supply did not over-whelm the local demand. While serving as the American consul in

Liverpool, Nathaniel Hawthorne loved to walk the streets but saw "nothing more disgusting than the women and girls here in Liverpool, who pick up horsedung in the streets—rushing upon the treasure, the moment it is dropt, taking it up by the handsfull and putting it in their baskets. Some are old women; some marriageable girls, and not uncomely girls, were they well dressed and clean. What a business this is!"[54] Goethe displayed an older mentality, or perhaps a postmodern one, when in 1787 he expressed his joy at seeing the old and young people of Naples operate a "cycle of vegetation" by loading the street sweepings onto donkeys to haul out to vegetable gardens beyond the city. These eager and industrious "collectors of horse and mule dung" recognized what a "rich vein of treasure" the city was.[55] By the nineteenth century, though, the old dung economy was breaking down. The distances to farm fields became too great in the big cities, and the quantities far outstripped demand, especially in the face of competition from imported guano and new chemical fertilizers. It became obvious that cities could not rely on the initiative of individual women wishing to fertilize their gardens, or even on the more systematic efforts of the rag-and-bone men.

Despite all the rules and procedures to keep streets clean—either by requiring property owners to clean or, later, with impressive municipal sanitation departments—crossing the street remained a messy ordeal. One had to watch for traffic but also keep an eye out for threats from below. Women had a particularly hard time, since they were universally expected to wear skirts that kept their ankles safely out of view. How did they cope? Edward Tilt, a physician critical of Victorian fashions, divided London's female pedestrians into three types:

(1)   Those who never raise the dress, but walk through thick and thin, with real or affected indifference to mud. These are generally country ladies, who have never been abroad and but little in town.

(2)   Those who raise the dress, but allow the mass of underclothes, like the mud-carts in Regent Street, to collect the mud and beat it up to the middle of the leg. This class is the most common.

(3)   Those chosen few, who, without offending the rules of modesty, which of course must take precedence of all others, know how to raise both dress and petticoats, so as to protect both.[56]

Lady F. W. Harberton, a London dress reformer, claimed to have inventoried the debris swept up by one woman's dress along Piccadilly: "two cigar ends, nine cigarette ends, a portion of pork pie, four toothpicks, two hairpins, one stem of a clay pipe, three fragments of orange peel, one slice of cat's meat, half a sole of a boot, and one plug of tobacco, chewed; straw, mud, scraps of paper, miscellaneous street refuse."[57] In 1851 the English humor magazine *Punch* offered sardonic praise of the women whose skirts "assist in sweeping the London streets": "We know of none, among the numerous acts of utility performed by ladies in the present day, involving so much self-sacrifice, as the practice adopted by our fashionably-dressed women, of cleansing the public thoroughfares."[58] *Punch* thought its readers could find humor in the obvious distress suffered by these ladies (and their laundresses). Other men saw skirts as a menace to their own health. A petition presented to the Berlin authorities in 1878 complained that in dry weather the fashionable dresses with trains stirred up clouds of choking dust on the city's walkways.[59]

London's answer to the pedestrian's woes was the designation of crosswalks to ease the perilous passage across the filthy roadways and frightening streams of wheeled traffic. They were typically constructed with distinctive stone paving and raised above the level of the street. Even within the crosswalks, though, the enormous growth of traffic made it impossible to keep pace with the fresh horse manure deposited atop animal and vegetable grease and all the other debris. The services of the shoeblack—sometimes a boy, sometimes a man, often wielding a discarded wig—remained in high demand. And even a clean-swept crosswalk did not always suffice. In 1821 the raconteur Pierce Egan recorded tales (possibly real) that will ring true to pedestrians of the automotive age, instances of elegant carriages blocking a busy crosswalk, with coachmen or owners who refused to budge. One of Egan's heroes seized the horses' reins and led

them forward out of the way. In another case, a posse of sailors declared and then exercised their right to climb through the offending
carriage to effect their passage.[60]

Entrepreneurial crossing sweepers were mostly a London phe-
nomenon, a familiar sight during the eighteenth and nineteenth centuries. These smallest of small-time entrepreneurs worked their way
back and forth at a crosswalk all day long, sparing ladies and gentlemen the need to step in deep mud. There was but one tool of the trade,
a broom, and no guaranteed income. In some eyes they were little
more than beggars, like the squeegee men of the late automotive era,
pretending to offer a service as an excuse to accost passersby. Other
Londoners, however, valued their efforts. Many sweepers were children, both boys and girls. Others were men and women driven out
of other trades by unemployment or disability. Mayhew interviewed
many, and they were a popular subject of late Georgian and Victorian
art, treated both satirically and sentimentally, although here they
nearly always appeared as boys, most famously Dickens's fictional
Jo in *Bleak House*.[61] Arthur Munby, Victorian London's great admirer
of female workers, spoke with a fourteen-year-old girl who worked
a territory at Charing Cross. "She plies her daring broom under the
wheels, which bespatter her with mire as they fly; she dodges under
the horses' heads, and is ever ready to conduct the timid lady or nervous old gentleman through the perils of the crossing; she is wet
through her thin clothing when it rains; she is in the street all day,
the lowest and least protected of that roaring buffeting crowd."[62]

Each established sweeper claimed his or her own corner or crossing and generally held it by unwritten rules, probably enforced at
times by the local constable, despite the absence of any legal authority to do so. Nor, it seems, were sweepers ever prosecuted as
beggars.[63] Their familiar presence did bring them some solicitude.
Already in 1716, John Gay's poem *Trivia* urges the walker to be liberal
with his purse. Some sweepers reported that prosperous neighbors
gave them a regular sixpence or shilling, with others receiving only
the occasional small coin. West End or City crossings frequented by
lords or bankers were the most lucrative, while sweepers in poorer

FIG. 36. "The Crossing-Sweeper Nuisance," *Punch*, 26 January 1856.

FIG. 37. London crossing sweeper, c. 1900. From George R. Sims, ed., *Living London* (London: Cassell, 1902), 2:199.

neighborhoods could expect very little remuneration. Mayhew suggested that they hoped their status as neighborhood fixtures would ultimately pay off, that "the benefits arising from being constantly seen in the same place, and thus exciting the sympathy of the neighbouring householders" might ultimately win them "small weekly allowances or 'pensions.'"[64] One explained to Mayhew that the sum of his tips "ain't worth mentioning. . . . I'll tell you the use of a crossing to such as me and my likes. It's our shop, and it ain't what we gets a-sweeping, but it's a place like for us to stand, and then people as wants us, comes and fetches us" to act as a messenger or deliveryman.[65] Dickens's Jo, we might note, serves to connect characters and plot threads across the sprawling novel.

Rumor and legend swirled around these familiar figures. Some who benefited from their services may have taken comfort in the dubious belief that they were not at all destitute. Mayhew's informants denied knowing of any sweepers who had stashed away fortunes thanks to wealthy patrons. Nor had they ever heard of a retiring sweeper selling his or her post to a successor. (Similar tales were told about Parisian ragpickers.[66]) *Punch* repeated the common accusation that sweepers extorted their tips by flicking mud in the faces of those who failed to pay. It also claimed that sweepers finished their day by sweeping the mud back into place, in order to generate a need for and appreciation of their labors. The American journalist Elizabeth Banks, who as a publicity stunt worked half a day as a sweeper, claimed to have been taught the method of flicking mud on nonpayers.[67] Mayhew, however, found no one to confirm that such things ever happened. Nor did sweepers need to exert themselves in order to create a demand for their services. In London especially, the sweeper's task appeared either heroic or futile. Indeed, *Punch* concluded its snark with a tribute to "the unwearied exertions of a woman in the Quadrant, who is continually sweeping without any effect; for as soon as the slightest clearance is made it is covered over by the enormous traffic of vehicles. We have always venerated this person as the Sisyphus of crossing-sweepers."[68]

The obvious inadequacy of private efforts inspired many

eighteenth-century schemes for municipal street cleaning. From midcentury the Paris police supervised private contractors who engaged laborers, carts, and horses to gather and haul away street rubbish.[69] In 1780 they removed 270,000 cubic meters of mud.[70] An entrepreneur obtained a similar contract from the Berlin authorities in 1777.[71] Emperor Joseph II set beggars and prisoners to work sweeping Vienna's streets, although they were soon replaced by regular day laborers.[72] The presence of London's many crossing sweepers attested to the fact that less was accomplished amid the fragmented local government there, despite schemes put forward by, among others, the enterprising colonial agent Benjamin Franklin. Elsewhere, the broom and shovel brigades were increasingly accompanied by wagons spraying the streets with water to keep down the plague of dust, a practice adopted by many cities during the nineteenth century.

Municipal trash collection was another nineteenth-century innovation. Along with the old dung economy, the established ways of removing other refuse were also in crisis. Long after the indispensable wandering pigs of village life had been banished from the major cities, ragpickers sifted and recycled street refuse, extracting everything of the most minimal value. They practiced an astonishing degree of specialization: sorting cigar ends, dog dung ("pure," used by tanners), rags, bones, old wood, scraps of metal, and ash. The American Israel Potter, stranded in London after the American Revolution and reduced to street work that did not suffice to feed his family, recalled that "while crying 'old chairs to mend,' I collected all the old rags, bits of paper, nails and broken glass which I could find in the streets, and which I deposited in a bag" for sale to dealers in these various goods.[73] These collectors and dealers crop up in Dickens's novels, notably the wealthy "dust" magnate John Harmon in *Our Mutual Friend*. Sometimes they were even honored like other street hawkers in dignified artistic portrayals.[74]

Ragpickers were widely despised, however: shadowy figures who loomed large in the collective imagination.[75] They often worked at night, sifting through the debris in the streets with their hooks and pointed sticks, which looked like the tools of criminals and only

FIG. 38. Eugène Atget, *Chiffonier* (ragpicker), 1899–1901. Digital image courtesy of the Getty's Open Content Program.

deepened the mistrust they aroused. Suspicion of these ragged, stinking, often Jewish figures reinforced a growing belief that their efforts no longer sufficed. By the nineteenth century, gratitude for their recycling efforts was outweighed by accusations that they merely strewed garbage about. A French investigator summed up the official view of them: "Matters of hygiene are totally alien to these people; the very word terrifies them. They see it as a malevolent goddess who has chosen to persecute the poor ragpickers. . . . In the course of my investigations, I have often heard the exclamation: 'You see, hygiene is our worst enemy.'"[76] When cities established municipal trash collection services, ragpickers were sometimes banned from the streets, depriving them of their livelihood. In 1828 Paris restricted their numbers by requiring them to be licensed, and in 1883 it forbade the overnight placement of rubbish bins on the street.[77]

Hawkers, too, were sometimes targeted on ostensible grounds of public health. Many street stands and markets were shut down for the same reason: after all, they did produce organic waste in profusion. In reducing the load of refuse in the streets, the authorities removed other things—people and commerce—as well. By the twentieth century, many street workers were uniformed public employees rather than shadowy scavengers. By the same token, where government services broke down, entrepreneurs saw an opportunity. In twenty-first-century Rome, for example, freelance immigrant street sweepers appeared after the collapse of municipal sanitation left the city awash in litter.[78] To call their presence "Dickensian" might serve as a lament for the failure of government but also as praise for the revival of a community bound by informal ties.

<h2 style="text-align:center">SEWERS AND WATER</h2>

The most dramatic improvements in hygiene came with the creation of citywide sewer systems. Along with paving, drainage was the other crucial component of street design and construction. In 1800 Londoners looked down on Paris, and Viennese on Berlin, because the latter pair, like most cities, still drained most streets through open gutters. Whether a single central gutter (as in the narrow lanes of Paris) or one on each side (as in Berlin), they posed an unsavory challenge to pedestrians and vehicles. Very small-time Parisian entrepreneurs seized the opportunity to appear on wet days with a plank and charge the fastidious a sou or so for the privilege of using it to cross the gutter (see fig. 6, p. 33).

Human waste was mostly if far from entirely kept out of the gutters. Where possible, it was dumped directly into available sewers, canals, or streams, such as London's River Fleet, whose stench had been a source of complaint as early as the thirteenth century. (Ben Jonson's mock-heroic 1616 poem "On the Famous Voyage" sends his classical heroes on a sordid and perilous trip up that putrid water-

FIG. 39. Charles Marville, Passage du Dragon, Paris, c. 1860. State Library of Victoria.

course.) Otherwise, cesspits were nearly universal before the late nineteenth century. Although they were usually invisible, under cellars and courtyards, their odors escaped all too frequently. And sooner or later they filled up. The job of emptying them was an established trade. Crews shoveled or siphoned the foul matter into barrels and hauled it away. In most places the work was strictly limited to the overnight hours, so the workers themselves were not usually familiar presences, although their noise and odors were a frequent cause of complaint. Medieval Vienna called them "night kings" or "shit kings." Eighteenth-century Berlin hired crews of women to lug buckets nightly down to the Spree River. This was a nightlife that bore no resemblance to the celebrated Berlin of a century later. One night in the 1770s the visiting physician Johann Friedrich Grimm was disagreeably surprised to encounter "the caravan of old dirty women who were carrying the human filth to the Spree," although he couldn't help but laugh at their coarse remarks.[79] Friedrich Schulz, a few years later, was not at all amused: "Since witnessing this revolting operation I can no longer enjoy my food in Berlin. I can't suppress the thought that our cook may have used Spree water."[80]

Other big cities did a slightly better job. Until 1848 London maintained "night-yards," where the waste was collected for transportation out of town.[81] Paris relied on similar facilities for a few decades after it prohibited dumping in the Seine by the 1720s. After 1761 all barrels had to be hauled outside the city to a central dump at Montfaucon (once the site of the royal gibbet, now Buttes-Chaumont park). After it was closed in 1849, a new site, farther out in the forest of Bondy, remained in use until 1890.[82] A similar arrangement in Vienna dated to the sixteenth century.[83] Ordinances generally forbade the dumping of human waste into gutters or sewers, rules widely flouted and hard to enforce. In the Paris of 1697, for example, a report lamented that residents "are accustomed to throwing into the streets, from the windows of their houses, day and night, all their water, rubbish, dirt, urine, and feces," although the practice had been prohibited, repeatedly, for centuries.[84] The city of Amsterdam built wooden sheds for cobblers in the 1660s, stipulating that in return the cobblers working in them were expected to prevent people from throwing trash into the streets or canals.[85]

Stringent enforcement was never going to solve the problem. The fastidious moral sensibilities of the nineteenth century may have been more effective. Whereas earlier writers like Swift frankly accepted the fundamental grossness of the human body, the Victorians (not to mention their descendants) wished to hold bodies as well as minds to a higher standard. Urban life would be tolerable for them

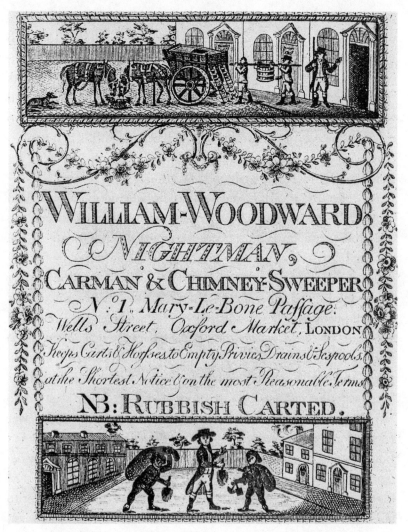

FIG. 40. Trade card of "Nightman," eighteenth century. Wellcome Images.

only if the baser traits of humanity could be banished. Far more than their ancestors, they promoted systematic municipal refuse collection and above all the construction of citywide sewer systems, a daunting and expensive task that major cities carried out after the middle of the nineteenth century. Before that, ancient sewers and piecemeal modern extensions drained parts of cities. Vienna was unusual in having built covered sewers through most of its inner city by the early nineteenth century. Elsewhere (including Vienna's sub-urbs, where the city's sewers emptied into canals and the little Wien River), open gutters and foul streams were the rule. Eighteenth-century London did construct many sewers, notably covering its rank River Fleet to build Fleet Market (later Farringdon Street) and New Bridge Street. (The same had been done to the Walbrook two centuries before.) The notoriously foul Bièvre on Paris's Left Bank—lined with tanneries, dye works, and the famous Gobelins factory—lasted much longer, until the end of the nineteenth century.

No doubt the growing sensitivity to organic odors helped build support for the massive sewer projects across Europe and beyond. The immediate impetus, however, came from adherents of the miasmatic theory of disease, whose cause was bolstered by the ter-ror spread by recurrent cholera pandemics after 1830. The leading figure, lionized in many histories of public health, was the tireless English bureaucrat Edwin Chadwick, who produced the influential *Report on the Sanitary Condition of the Labouring Population* (1842) along with subsequent recommendations to build sewers that would propel the stench of disease out of the cities. One pioneer was Ham-burg, which seized the opportunity created by a terrible 1842 fire to hire a Chadwick disciple who incorporated a comprehensive sewer network into its reconstruction. The Paris sewer system was one of Haussmann's proudest achievements, although he successfully de-fended the position that human solid waste should be kept out of it and hauled away separately. (This salient fact makes it easier to understand the popularity of underground tours of the new sewers.) Only in 1894 did Paris begin the onerous process of replacing its cesspits with sewer connections: in his memoir of the 1920s, Ernest Hemingway recalled the nightly noise and odor of the horse-drawn cesspit pumps.[86] In the 1860s London began its own massive project. A turning point in public opinion there had been the "Great Stink" of 1858, when a hot and dry summer left the Thames nearly dry except for the outflow from the growing number of new water closets, trick-ling into the river from various old sewers and buried streams like the Fleet. The curtains of river-facing rooms in the Houses of Parliament were soaked in lime chloride in a vain attempt to keep the building usable, and the MPs suddenly proved eager to expedite the construction of a comprehensive sewer system. Berlin built its impressive system during the 1870s, about the same time as most other major German cities. Vienna, which had long since banished open sewers from the inner city, waited until the 1890s to pipe its sewage into the Danube below the city.

An effective sewer system required an ample supply of municipal piped water (and vice versa: abundant water had to drain out of the city somehow). Vienna's admired early nineteenth-century sewers, for example, were flushed only by rain, so they clogged and stank during dry spells. Water mains rivaled sewers as the great infrastructure projects of the nineteenth century. A key difference was that private entrepreneurs saw money-making opportunities in piped water, whereas sewers threatened to eliminate a lucrative supply of dung. London had led the way in granting franchises to private companies that piped water into the houses of customers willing and able to pay. Their efforts, coupled with the growing popularity of water closets, contributed to the Great Stink, and thus indirectly to the demand for sewers. However, piped water into houses was still a luxury in 1850. Most people obtained their water from private wells in courtyards or from public pumps or fountains in the streets, from which someone had to carry it home and up the stairs. Many citizens bought theirs from mobile water carriers.

The private water companies had little interest in unprofitable extensions to poor neighborhoods, and disputes over the extension or control of water supplies eventually led most municipal governments to buy out the private concerns and expand them into citywide networks. In addition to sanitation, the benefits to firefighting helped build support for the projects. Hamburg was again a pioneer after its 1842 fire—although, ironically, its failure to filter its water was responsible for its 1892 cholera epidemic, the last such outbreak in western Europe and one successfully averted nearly everywhere else. Vienna, too, was relatively progressive, with an aqueduct that conveyed water to public fountains by 1565. A project in 1803 extended pipes to some parts of the city, and after the arrival of cholera, a major aqueduct built between 1836 and 1841 supplied much of it. An even larger project followed during the 1860s and 1870s, at about the same time as most large European cities (including Paris and Berlin) built citywide systems.

Earlier water projects enhanced street life, if they piped water to public fountains and no farther. The fountains themselves could be both elegant civic monuments and neighborhood gathering places, as is still visible in such cities as Basel and Rome. When pipes and water pressure were sufficient to carry water up into residential buildings, the fountains became mere decorations. At that point, piped water and sewers facilitated a dramatic transformation of the streets, most obviously by removing sewage from the street gutters. The stinking bucket brigades ceased to haunt the overnight hours. But so did the enterprising water carriers who had long been a welcome sight in city streets. And neighborhood gossip networks atrophied when every wife or servant who obtained piped water at home no longer made the trip to the local pump or fountain.

PUBLIC TOILETS

Complaints about public urination and defecation typically blamed the perpetrators for their shamelessness. Wiser heads made the obvious point that many people who lived or worked on the streets had no alternative. Public toilets, whether provided by government or private enterprise, were a rarity in every city in 1800. London probably had the most, in the form of makeshift urinals offered by private businesses such as taverns, or by a few parishes. Some were just the old "pissing posts" with a minimum of concealment added. During the more fastidious nineteenth century, most of these disappeared. Evidence of a new sensibility, but not of a lasting solution, can also be found in a new trade that flourished briefly in several cities around 1800, that of the portable toilet carrier who charged a small fee to use his mobile facility, consisting of a bucket and a large cape that offered the user a modicum of privacy in the open street.[87] Early nineteenth-century Vienna designated "urination stones" as a "symbolic invitation" (as one contemporary put it) to direct men toward the quieter corners of its streets. The mess they created made them unpopular, but the city's subsequent decision to get rid of them merely spread the problem more widely.[88]

Later proposals for public toilets may have been motivated by sheer crowding in the streets, but mainly they responded to new standards of privacy and public hygiene. Their presence was mostly but not entirely unprecedented; those in Paris were nicknamed "vespasiennes" on the mistaken belief that the Roman emperor Vespasian had promoted them. London's lack of a strong municipal government helps explain why crowded Paris was the pioneer. Demands for public toilets were heard already in the late eighteenth century, and by the early nineteenth, individual Parisian proprietors had constructed a few. The city began to erect a few "urinoirs" in 1830 and then put up hundreds after 1841.[89] In 1847 Adolf Schmidl lamented that his Vienna lacked the facilities found not only in Paris but by the mosque of every poor Turkish village: "The lowliest Turk would consider shameless and intolerable" what was accepted on the streets of Vienna.[90] Vienna had built two public urinals in 1846 but in the face of public unease with their presence failed to add more until the 1860s.[91] In 1841 the Berlin city council also declined to follow the Paris example, fearing improprieties that no one dared describe. Only in 1863 did municipal pissoirs appear in Berlin. Soon they were widely accepted, although their placement in particular locations often raised objections. In 1871 a new one erected in a central square, Molkenmarkt, was removed almost immediately amid the outcry of upper-story residents of surrounding buildings, who were treated to more sights than they could endure. (As usual, the records are silent on the nature of the offense.) By 1874 city council members were pleading with the Prussian government to place pissoirs in the royal Tiergarten, Berlin's central park. They referred urgently but obliquely to "incidents that insult the eye and injure one's sense of propriety"—a scandal they had only recently banished from their streets. The 1870s and 1880s finally saw major municipal initiatives in Vienna and London as well.[92]

As urinals proliferated, it was time to crack down on men who persisted in the old ways. After 1843 the Paris police prohibited public urination anywhere outside "urinoirs" in the streets that were equipped with them. By 1850, in the face of "frequent, well-founded complaints," streets without them also faced some restrictions: no urination on sidewalks or against public monuments, shopfronts, or doors.[93] Three decades earlier, Vienna had prohibited public urination anywhere except at its "urination stones," to little effect. It tried again in 1862 as it began to build public urinals in large numbers.[94]

In many countries, public toilets have long been notorious places of gay male sexual encounters. Some of the resulting fears sprang entirely from the imagination of men infected by anti-gay hysteria, but scholars who have combed through nineteenth-century police records confirm that the nexus was a real one.[95] Some facilities were closed to suppress gay sex, others were subjected to police inspection, and some were redesigned either to permit more surveillance or to isolate users in separate compartments.

The early Parisian models took the form of tall, dual-use kiosks, a urinal enclosed within a cylindrical column suitable for posting placards. The possibility of confusion or embarrassment furnished an opportunity for humor, as in a contemporary lithograph that shows one man asking another what "these little monuments" are, "where I can step inside and read the little posters?" His flustered companion stammers that "these are new, well, literary cabinets, that satisfy a very great need."[96] Berlin briefly tried the same combination of urinal and message kiosk, but both cities discontinued them by the 1860s. Paris's Morris columns and Berlin's Litfass columns assumed the job of disseminating announcements, while newer urinal designs attempted to assuage worries about privacy and decency, not always successfully. Paris's new multi-stall urinals, like the older ones, typically shielded users from public view with only a narrow horizontal strip of metal. A few years later Berlin settled on an eight-sided shape for its more substantial green cast-iron urinals. They acquired the nickname Café Octagon and remained a familiar sight throughout the next century. The simplest public urinals were built without any plumbing, simply draining into the ground or onto the street, which

FIG. 41. Combined urinal-column, Paris, 1860. Watercolor by Charles Hoguet.

FIG. 42. Charles Marville, Paris urinal, c. 1865. Also note the curb, bench, and tree grates, all typical of Haussmann's streets. State Library of Victoria, Gift; Government of France; 1880.

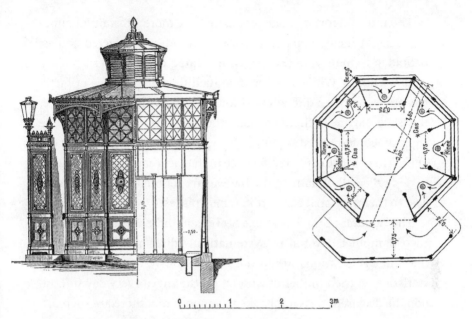

FIG. 43. Berlin, design of street urinal. *Berlin und seine Bauten* (1896).

was assumed to be already soaked with the urine of multiple species. The spread of piped water made upgrades possible. The first full-fledged public toilets with plumbing may have been those installed at the Crystal Palace in Hyde Park for London's Great Exhibition of 1851. They proved to be popular with visitors from many lands.

Late in the century, many cities built more robust public toilets. They were connected to municipal water and sewer pipes and typically required patrons to pay. Most were put up by private entrepreneurs who obtained municipal franchises. Often they included first- and second-class toilets, with the former offering more space or finer materials, or merely a wash basin. A modicum of architectural elegance became expected. They were often built of iron or even stone and at least minimally ornamented. A few gestures of classical architecture, such as pilasters, served to ennoble their intrusive presence on the street. Some became quite sumptuous in appearance, with orientalist details added to suggest a kind of luxurious domestic comfort. A Jugendstil facility under Vienna's Graben remains in use to this day.

The most important change was that the more substantial buildings usually included facilities for women. All-male elected bodies, beholden to male voters, engaged in heated debates over women's sanitary needs. While some men argued that the absence of facilities put women in a difficult position, others seemed eager to deflect the issue. No one bothered to voice the unquestioned belief that the sight of women urinating in public was utterly intolerable. Nor did any of them make explicit reference to the fact that girls were taught to deny the call of nature, at what was undoubtedly a considerable cost to their personal comfort in public places.

The London physician James Stevenson did point this out in an 1879 pamphlet devoted to systematically dismantling arguments that later generations would not take seriously. After marshalling statistics on the number of women on the move every day in London, he declared, "It is a mistake to suppose that there are such differences in the female organization, that these primal requirements of physical being can be disregarded by women with less suffering than by men."[97]

Some men argued that ladies would be shocked at the very sight of sanitary facilities, and certainly would be ashamed to enter them. In fact, feminine fastidiousness had already been raised as an objection to the combined pissoir-columns of Paris in 1860: knowing what was behind them, "the posters cannot be looked at by a woman, even on the arm of her husband."[98] In 1874 Berlin's elected city council voted to build public toilets for women. The professional administration exercised its veto, however, arguing that "the natural modesty of the female sex would prevent women from using facilities on public squares."[99] In Paris, where things moved even more slowly, members of the municipal assembly introduced a resolution in 1891 to provide free facilities for women, raising the obvious point that the 1850 prohibition on urination in streets equipped with pissoirs simply ignored women. An opponent objected that "in these narrow spaces the two sexes jostle each other with unavoidable rumpling that cannot fail to shock the natural and proper sentiments of feminine modesty."[100] Others argued that the only proper place for women's toilets was out of sight inside public buildings. But these facilities were few, hard to find, and little used. Male proponents of women's toilets proposed new designs with separate entrances for men and women, on opposite sides, as one way of making women feel more secure. Underground structures were also long debated in all the capitals. London, Vienna, and Berlin finally authorized and built facilities for both sexes in the 1880s (Paris waited until after 1900), and women's innate delicacy proved no hindrance to the frequent use of them.[101]

CLEAN STREETS, HEALTHY BODIES

The late nineteenth century marked the triumph of the sanitary city across much of Europe. The accomplishments of the age were impressive: waterworks, sewer systems, municipal street cleaning and refuse collection, better paving, and the thoroughgoing removal of unpleasant sights and smells. All these projects were carried out, and celebrated, in the name of public health, and with good reason. The incidence of many infectious diseases plunged, as did urban death rates.

Yet this achievement conceals a more complicated legacy. It was not simply a triumph of medical science, because the embrace of new medical theories did not occur, and probably could not have, in isolation from moral, aesthetic, and political beliefs. Few nineteenth-century advocates of sanitation doubted that cleaner streets and houses, and greater access to "light and air," would raise the moral standards of their inhabitants. Political motives, too, lurked in the background. Everyone's favorite example of a nineteenth-century urban reformer remained Haussmann of Paris, because his comprehensive sanitary reforms came packaged with new boulevards, autocratic government, and military repression, thus satisfying his supporters that all these measures belonged together, while his critics could categorize them all as repressive measures.

The hygienic achievements were the least contested of all, and their measurable success makes it difficult to argue that the sanitary city was an ominous project of social control or social engineering by a ruling class determined to keep the unruly masses in their place. In obvious ways, late nineteenth- and twentieth-century European streets became pleasanter places than they had been. The removal of mud and stench certainly drew people onto the streets to stroll, play, and linger in sidewalk cafés.

That change may have not been long-lasting, however. The process of making streets antiseptic and deodorized places often entailed not only eradicating germs and smells but also removing the people and activities blamed for the contamination. Even as citizens had less cause to fear the streets, they had fewer reasons to gather there. Work had mostly moved indoors, along with commerce, recreation, and politics. Loss of the freedom to befoul the streets accompanied the decline of neighborhood socializing, street commerce, street politics, and perhaps an alluring, if also frightening, aura of mystery. Across most streets and most cities, the crowds eventually dispersed, as the charm and excitement of city streets, including hawkers and street markets, was largely banished in the name of sanitation. Increasingly, people who did use the streets merely passed through them, if possible while sealed inside vehicles. The successful campaign to banish bodily functions and bodily odors managed in the end to banish bodies.

5

Transportation

The Acceleration of the Street

Things move more quickly than they used to. At least we expect them to. When they don't, we grumble about clogged roads. Complaints about slow traffic are not new, however: the history of urban congestion is a litany of vexation. The greater change has been in the expectation of improvement.

Streets have always been intended for circulation. Over time they acquired many other uses, along with the inevitable conflicts that ensued. The nineteenth century brought technological innovations that made travel possible at previously unimaginable speeds. To a great extent, however, the acceleration of the street has been driven by culture and politics — by impatience and changing expectations — more than technology. In other words, the nineteenth century enshrined rapid transportation, in whatever form was available, as the street's main purpose, meaning that the fastest vehicles were granted priority over people working, playing, or walking. Those other users were pushed aside. The street was no place to linger.

WALKING AND RIDING

The proliferation of new transport technologies made it possible to leave behind the old "walking city." European towns of the Middle Ages and Renaissance were fairly pure examples of this type. Even the largest were not too vast to walk across in less than an hour, and few streets were wide or well-paved enough to handle rapid transport, whether galloping horses or wheeled carriages. The shift away from this urban scale was long, gradual, and never quite complete. In post-medieval streets, especially those of the largest, most crowded, and dirtiest cities, wealthier citizens increasingly found ways to separate themselves from the mass of ordinary pedestrians. Sedan chairs came into wide use during the seventeenth and eighteenth centuries, offering protection from the mud and the rabble. Private carriages appeared in the sixteenth century, as freight wagons were modified for use by passengers. At first they were the privilege of kings and queens—mainly queens—but during the seventeenth century many aristocrats in major cities acquired them. Where street conditions permitted, they offered their privileged passengers a quick and sometimes comfortable ride through town, shielded from dung and beggars.

Among the great variety of Parisian carriages in the seventeenth and eighteenth centuries was the brouette or vinaigrette, effectively a sedan chair on two wheels, pulled by a man and usually also pushed by a boy or woman, according to the English scientist Martin Lister, who found their presence shameful.[1] Otherwise the carriages were horse-drawn, with new designs appearing frequently. By the late eighteenth century, improved suspension enabled the light new cabriolets to combine speed and comfort as never before, where street conditions permitted. Although visitors admired the firm, smooth, and relatively clean new stone paving of Paris and Vienna, they were often startled by the carriages flying through the narrow streets at alarming speed. The carriages of Parisian aristocrats notoriously terrorized pedestrians, while Viennese coachmen were alternately praised or damned for the deft way they threaded through the crowds.

Visitors to eighteenth-century London sometimes claimed that nobody walked there—"an entire city at a full trot," in the words of the Prince de Ligne.[2] Long before that, John Taylor was guilty of even broader exaggeration in the title of his 1623 pamphlet, *The World*

Runs on Wheels. As a Thames boatman, the "water-poet" Taylor may have feared competition from the new carriages, but he was far from the last to discover that a coach ride "made me think myself better than my betters that went on foot."[3] In the Vienna of 1785, Joseph Richter thought that "the many narrow streets offer proof that they [our ancestors] built their cities for people and not for horses. . . . How their astonishment would grow when they heard that . . . in many capitals there are now nearly as many horses as people, and that walking is seen as almost disreputable."[4] At about the same time, Louis-Sébastian Mercier lamented that the desire to own a carriage meant that his fellow Parisians were coming to see the pedestrian as an ignoble figure. He claimed, with obvious hyperbole, that people seemed to be losing the use of their legs.[5]

This overblown rhetoric found an audience because the 1780s were in fact a time when walking came into fashion among the upper classes. No one who claimed that "nobody walks" could fail to see that carriages were far outnumbered by poor people on foot. The speeding coaches in the streets came to signify the physical, psychological, and political gulf between rich and poor in pre-revolutionary Paris. Mercier was insistent on this point, but we owe many of these reports to British visitors who offered them as evidence of their own kingdom's moral superiority. In 1779 the Scottish physician John Moore blamed France's rulers for the fact that Parisian pedestrians must "grope their way as they best can, and skulk behind pillars, or run into shops, to avoid being crushed by the coaches, which are driven as near the wall as the coachman pleases; dispersing the people on foot at their approach, like chaff before the wind." Better street lighting and the recent construction of sidewalks in London "seem to indicate that the body of the people, as well as the rich and the great, are counted of some importance in the eye of government."[6] The infamous heedlessness of Parisian aristocrats and their drivers in the narrow, crowded, sidewalk-less streets often had deadly results, as we know from many reports of horrified bystanders such as Sir James Edward Smith in 1787, who was appalled to see someone run down by a coach and then be told that there would be no consequences "because it is a nobleman's carriage."[7] Two generations later, Dickens drew on these descriptions for his novel of revolutionary Paris, *A Tale of Two Cities*, where he establishes the smoldering atmosphere of the 1780s with a shocking scene of an aristocrat's cold indifference to the fate of a child killed by his speeding coach.

Stendhal bought himself a cabriolet in 1810 but had no illusions about it. The next year he wrote, "Every pedestrian who looks at a carriage, however mean, views it with hatred."[8] George Sand obviously thought along similar lines. Visiting Venice in 1834, she believed she saw an admirable republican spirit there, since "the absence of horses and carriages in the streets, and everyone's need to travel by water, contribute greatly to the equality of manners."[9] When the Goncourt brothers claimed in 1857 that "everyone has a carriage today," for them it was the clearest evidence of conspicuous, extravagant, and ruinous consumption.[10] In St. Petersburg, a city notorious for its strict social hierarchy, the carriage loomed large as an instrument of class consciousness in, for example, Dostoyevsky's novel *The Double*.[11] A late and vivid fictional example, set on the same street, is a character in Andrey Biely's 1913 novel *St. Petersburg* whom we meet as he prizes the privilege of being driven down Nevsky Prospekt in his closed carriage, safe from the rabble.

Carriages were also available for hire, although for a long time these were few in number. London's hackney coaches date to 1620, about the same time as their counterparts in Paris. The latter came to be called "fiacres," apparently because they were first rented from a building named after St. Fiacre. Later in the century, Vienna borrowed the name and germanicized it to Fiaker. Only in 1740 were they licensed on the streets of Berlin, which later borrowed its style of wagon and a name, Droschke, from Warsaw.[12] By the nineteenth century, the short-term hire—the taxicab—became indispensable to men and women of the burgeoning middle classes. Many of them simply welcomed the respite from the crush of bodies on the street. Others found that it furnished just enough of a carapace to make the street pleasantly exciting. The hansom, a cabriolet with an exter-

FIG. 44. London street with hansom. Drawing by Sidney Paget. *The Strand Magazine*, September 1901.

nal driver's seat raised above and behind the partly enclosed passenger compartment, quickly became a fixture of London life after its introduction in the 1830s. The memoirs of the novelist Mary Augusta (Mrs. Humphry) Ward, looking back to 1885, evoked the pleasure of a ride:

I can recall one summer afternoon, in particular, when as I was in a hansom driving idly westward towards Hyde Park Gate, thinking of a hundred things at once, this consciousness of *intensification*, of a heightened meaning in everything—the broad street, the crowd of moving figures and carriages, the houses looking down upon it—seized upon me with a rush. "Yes, it is good—the mere living!" Joy in the infinite variety of the great city as compared with the "cloistered virtue" of Oxford; the sheer pleasure of novelty, of the kind new faces, and the social discoveries one felt opening on many sides; the delight of new perceptions, new powers in oneself;—all this seemed to flower for me in those few minutes of reverie—if one can apply such a word to an experience so vivid.[13]

Although this proper Victorian lady might not have tolerated the jostling of costermongers and beggars, or the crowded bench of an omnibus, she craved the stimulation of the street, if only from the sheltered space of her cab.

Men, too, could appreciate a protective shield that permitted them to feed on the energy of strangers. Another Victorian writer, Arthur Munby, was an inveterate city walker; nevertheless, "If a man want to meditate in and on London streets, let him take a hansom. Like a hero of old with his cloud and his guiding deity, he is in the midst of the roar and the conflict, but he is safe and quiet: it is an excitement that does but breed and colour reflections. Reflections on the crowd of hard isolated men, intent on gain or on duty, each one, in spite of himself, the centre of some little circle of loves and interests; and on the crowd of women, frivolous and flaunting, or honest and singly self reliant, and womanly."[14] Later in the century, Henry James found that the view from a hansom softened London's image, turning the street into a theater:

The edifices are mean, but the social stream itself is monumental, and to an observer not positively stolid there is more excitement and suggestion than I can give a reason for in the long, distributed waves of traffic, with the steady policemen marking their rhythm, which roll together and apart for so many hours. Then the great, dim city becomes bright and kind, the pall of smoke turns into a veil of haze carelessly worn, the air is colored and almost scented by the presence

of the biggest society in the world, and most of the things that meet
the eye . . . present themselves as "well appointed." Everything shines
more or less, from the window-panes to the dog-collars. So it all looks,
with its myriad variations and qualifications, to one who surveys it
over the apron of a hansom, while that vehicle of vantage, better than
any box at the opera, spurts and slackens with the current.[15]

Early automobiles offered the same kind of view, but soon their
speed robbed motorists of any real intimacy with the streets, just as
railroads had earlier transformed the stagecoach rider's rural tour
into a formless blur.[16]

PUBLIC TRANSIT

Public transportation, by contrast, coupled protection from the street
with prolonged exposure to strangers. For many people it offered an
affordable convenience along with a corporeal challenge. It began
nearly everywhere as a private enterprise, but in offering rides to the
public, on the streets, it brought together—physically, intimately,
and on an equal footing—individuals who would otherwise have encountered one another only in prescribed roles of haughtiness and
deference. It was one of the new experiences of urban life, sometimes exciting, often unsettling.

Urban public transit was almost entirely a nineteenth-century development. There had been one notable precedent, a Parisian bus
service established in 1662. Louis XIV approved a scheme by, among
others, the philosopher Blaise Pascal to deploy eight-passenger carriages open to all, women as well as men, along fixed routes and
schedules. The prospect of mingling socially diverse bodies was apparently too much for the Parlement of Paris, which amended the
royal order to ban soldiers, servants, and manual laborers. For other
Parisians, the service seems to have quickly become a great success,
attracting many riders for whom a private carriage remained out of
reach. Despite the initial excitement, however, it proved not to be a
long-term success, lasting only a few years.[17]

Intercity coaches served as a more direct model for nineteenth-century city buses. Here travelers of a middling sort (the rich owned or hired private carriages; the poor walked from town to town) learned to share cramped quarters with strangers. This was a growing business in the late eighteenth century after the introduction of tightly scheduled post coaches.[18] City dwellers also became familiar with short-stage coaches that carried passengers out from the city to nearby destinations. In 1825 a Berlin entrepreneur began scheduled service from the Brandenburg Gate to the nearby royal town of Charlottenburg. After 1815 *Stellwagen* plied fixed routes between Vienna and its suburbs. They also began to serve some inner-city routes, making them pioneers of "omnibus" service, a name they adopted after 1840.

Schedules, frequent service, and fixed routes made the omnibus different from its rural predecessors. The Latin name, meaning "for all," proclaimed its democratic ambition. A French entrepreneur introduced omnibus service to Paris in 1828, following a brief experiment in Nantes, and several competing companies quickly followed suit. The first London line began operating the following year from Paddington to the City (the same route taken by the first underground line some thirty years later). Service began in New York around the same time, and in many other cities soon thereafter. Rural stagecoaches furnished models for the design of the vehicles. Two or three horses pulled a wagon that typically carried twenty or more passengers along with a conductor and a driver.

Meanwhile, the success of the railroads prompted entrepreneurs to adapt rail technology to intra-urban use. Street railways developed slowly, however, as lumbering steam engines proved ill-suited to urban transit. Instead, horse-drawn trams on rails emerged as a more efficient alternative to buses, since the reduced friction of rails made it possible for a pair of horses to pull more passengers. Although regular service had begun in New York by 1832, the installation of rails in city streets met with resistance in much of Europe, where they spread rapidly only after 1860. London, notably, never permitted street railways in the city center (nor did Vienna inside its Ringstrasse), so they remained confined to outer districts and be-

FIG. 45. A.-P. Martial, *Omnibus de l'Odéon*, 1877. Bibliothèque nationale de France.

came mainly lower-class conveyances, unlike the buses that plied the centers of commerce and government. In Berlin the roles were reversed: trams dominated in the city center, while horse-drawn buses were seen as the domain of suburban workers.

For the more or less privileged minority who rode instead of walking, horsecars and buses offered a chance to travel without being exposed to the full range of people, activities, and filth of the streets—a choice that private carriages and cabs had already made available to the wealthiest citizens. This was reason enough to entice many people to climb aboard and pay the fare, even at the cost of enduring the literal press of strangers and the associated moral perils. The enforced confinement was both physically intimate and often more diverse than riders were likely to find in any other confined space. Prince Hermann von Pückler-Muskau, who liked to travel incognito, discovered the Parisian bus immediately. "It's a delight to take such a bus ride in the evening, without a destination in mind, because of the extraordinary caricatures you encounter and the remarkable conversations you overhear. It's easy to believe you are at a show of the variety theater."[19] Soon after, the poet Ernest Fouinet ruminated at greater length on the bus ride as a theater for which every spectator paid a mere thirty centimes. Possible plot lines abounded. Imagine, he wrote, if a debtor stepped on board and came face-to-face with the creditor who had been pursuing him for a year. What might ensue?[20]

A more typical reaction seems to have been distress at physical and social discomfort, real or imagined. For the Italian tourist Edmondo De Amicis, the contact atop a London bus was rather more intimate than he had expected: "I had many occasions to marvel at the familiarity with which my neighbors made use of my shoulder as a support in order to pass from one section of the seats to another, making me feel for a moment their whole weight, and then while removing their hands giving me a vigorous shove, like an athlete who flings away his pole after vaulting the rope."[21] The German visitor Max Schlesinger described the omnibus more ironically as "among the few places in England where you come into immediate contact with Englishmen without the formality of a previous introduction."[22] In theory, the ride was available to anyone, although conductors sometimes refused entrance to men or women because of their rude dress. What excluded the lower class more generally was the fare, but the jumble of diverse bodies was still remarkable in these stratified societies. The railroad was exposing long-distance travelers to a similar experience at the same time: by greatly expanding intercity travel, it gave many people the new experience of traveling while confined with strangers.[23] Unlike most omnibuses, however, the railway companies quickly segregated their passengers into three or four classes.

A bus or tram ride offered a variation on the mingling of bodies in a crowded street: less promiscuous, since the poorest people rarely rode them, yet more intimate, since the contact was not momentary but rather lingering, with passengers at leisure to ruminate on the sensations they felt as well as the etiquette choices they faced: to look or to avert one's gaze; to protest objectionable behavior or to keep silent; to attempt awkward conversation with strangers or to maintain an embarrassed silence.

Reinforcing the omnibus's reputation were artists in search of genre scenes, who found a wealth of material in the motley array of passengers facing each other across the tightly packed benches. Stories and memoirs recalled the uneasy interaction, or lack thereof, among strangers confined in extreme proximity, hip to hip and knee to knee, and eye to eye across the benches, and forced to endure the even more ungainly tangle of bodies during the climb in or out of the bus, a particular hardship for women. The bus, and later the tram, could be proclaimed either the apotheosis or the nightmare of urban life. In 1895 Paul Lindenberg saw democracy in action: "The horsecar is among modern Berlin's most populist institutions. It brings the principle of equality to its complete fulfillment, since it recognizes neither privileged seats nor special prices. The poor old woman from the most remote working-class quarter in the north, condemned to toil until her final days, has the same rights for her nickel as the young countess from the fashionable west in her stylish spring dress. Rich and poor, old and young, grand and humble: they all have their daily rendezvous in the horsecar."[24] The art historian Eduard Kolloff made the same observation in Paris: "Apart from coffeehouses and churchyards, it is the only place on earth where all people are completely equal." Nor was that all:

An omnibus ride has a deep philosophical meaning: it resembles human life. Like bus passengers, we all arrive from who knows where;

FIG. 46. Honoré Daumier, *Intérieur d'un omnibus*, 1839. National Gallery of Art, Ailsa Mellon Bruce Fund.

we take our places next to each other and make fleeting acquaintance with people on the same journey as us. When they depart along the way, the memory of them soon fades, since other travelers take their places. In the bus, as in the whole world, we step on each other's feet, because all the rows are packed full and each of us seeks to go our own way without a thought for our neighbor. . . . When, finally, the bus reaches its inevitable terminus, the travelers disperse without knowing where the others come from or where they are going. Thus we recommend the Paris omnibus to genre painters, novel writers, dramatists, vaudevillians, moralists, sensitive souls, the melancholy, indeed everyone.[25]

Other commentators made more modest attempts to elucidate the ephemeral community of the bus. Young Charles Dickens saw the peculiar formation of a fleeting social solidarity: "It is rather remarkable, that the people already in an omnibus, always look at newcomers, as if they entertained some undefined idea that they have no business to come in at all."[26] By the 1920s, after the motor bus had retired the horses, Joseph Roth offered an even darker vision: "The passengers on a bus make up a community of a kind. But they don't see it that way, not even in a moment of danger. As they see it, they are bound always to be the others' enemy: for political, social, all sorts of reasons."[27] Decades earlier, Gustave Flaubert satisfied himself with a laconic observation about the social class he professed to despise: "Since the invention of the omnibus, the bourgeoisie is dead. There it sits, on the common bench, and there it stays, now the equal of the rabble, in spirit, in bearing, and even in apparel."[28] Neither Flaubert nor Roth would have been surprised to see bourgeois passengers fleeing the bus for their private automobiles.

The mixture of classes on the bus and the tram accentuated the proximity of unrelated men and women. In most places, women were permitted to ride the buses and trams from the very beginning, and it was their presence that attracted the most comment. It took no great imaginative effort for Fouinet to conjure an imagined sexual frisson in the mind of a male passenger who found himself seated next to a beautiful woman. Meanwhile, women worried, or at least were told to worry, about the touches and glances that threatened their well-concealed bodies. Men discussed their duty, and that of the conductor, to protect the dignity of ladies in their midst and wondered where they should direct their eyes and place their limbs. Young ladies were usually expected to have an escort—a male relative or an older woman—and to be anything but bold in their words and gestures. Opinion was divided on whether an unescorted young woman should ride the bus at all, and to what extremes she should go to avoid exchanging words or glances with any man. Certainly she was led to understand that any solicitous word or glance might put her in danger of being mistaken for a prostitute: at least in Paris, they were said to use buses to solicit clients.[29] Only gradually did these fears fade. In her 1925 novel *Mrs. Dalloway*, Virginia Woolf showed the independent spirit of seventeen-year-old Elizabeth Dalloway, wealthy Clarissa's daughter, by having her spring onto a London bus and climb to the upper deck.

Many big-city buses offered extra seats on the roof, accessible by a ladder or steep stair. London double-deckers date to the late 1840s,

the Parisian "impériale" to 1853. Because the upper perch was open
to the weather and sometimes precarious as well, it could typically
be had for a reduced fare. It attracted urban adventurers, writers like
Victor Hugo and even bankers like Péreire and Rothschild.[30] Guidebooks declared that the best way to see London was from the top of a
bus. A character in a Guy de Maupassant story makes a regular practice of climbing up to his "theater": "it's as if I'm taking a trip around
the world, the people are so different from one street to the next,"
all to be observed at the pace of two trotting horses.[31] In Paris and
Berlin, women were long forbidden to climb to the upper deck. Paris
lifted its prohibition in 1879, after buses had replaced their ladders
with stairs modeled after those of the newer trams, which were subject to no such ban.[32] Berlin's prohibition was lifted in 1896—at first,
the police warned, as a temporary experiment, to see if everyone
behaved themselves. Berlin followed English models, covering the
back side of ladders to prevent immodest viewing.[33] London never
banned women from the top deck, but before 1890 only an adventur-
ous few ventured up there, for example the energetic social reformer
Olive Schreiner and the young poet Amy Levy, who extolled the view
from her favorite perch in the "Ballade of an Omnibus" (1889):

> The scene whereof I cannot tire,
> The human tale of love and hate,
> The city pageant, early and late
> Unfolds itself, rolls by, to be
> A pleasure deep and delicate.
> An omnibus suffices me.

A few years later, young Virginia Stephen (later Woolf) was herself
an enthusiastic denizen of the upper deck, at about the same time
as the exiled Vladimir Lenin, who had an eye for the crass inequities
visible around him, while also (according to his wife) observing that
the most abject poverty remained hidden in courts and alleys, out of
the comfortable bus passenger's sight.[34]

Buses, trams, and taxis increased mobility. They also increased speed in the streets, although not drastically. The decisive break with the pace of the walking city came later, when horses were replaced by electrical and petroleum traction. This brought real speed, and true mass transit, with vehicle capacities and fares enabling the working class to ride. Experiments with mechanically powered street railways had continued throughout the century, mostly with limited success. In the largest cities, the need for greater transport capacity was obvious to anyone forced to negotiate streets jammed with pedestrians and wagons. Neither steam engines nor cable cars proved sufficiently reliable, but practical forms of electric traction were perfected during the 1880s. Most were powered via overhead wires attached to the cars by a "trolley" pole. Wires buried in a street trench were an alternate type, mostly employed in places where municipal rules banned the unsightly overhead wires. After 1890, electric trams spread rapidly, bringing a new dimension of speed to city streets. Even faster were the underground railways, from the 1860s in London and after the turn of the century in a few other cities. They removed people from the street, of course, but funneled enormous crowds through their street-level entrances. Noisy and smoky elevated steam railways were less of a technological challenge but more of a blight, and were rarely permitted a major role in European intra-urban transport, apart from one major line across central Berlin.

THE ACCELERATION OF THE STREET

The 1890s also saw the bicycle craze. After several decades of experiments, the bicycle had assumed its modern form and spread far beyond a small circle of fanatics. It was something really new. Its speed and silence made it a startling new factor in street traffic, especially when steered by ruthless commercial messengers or newspaper deliverymen. Its only precedent as a fast individual vehicle was the horse and rider, but its size and maneuverability made it practical to ride in busy streets where a galloping horse was unimaginable. Urban bicycling may not have promoted social contact, collisions apart. It did, however, increase the visibility of riders, notably the middle-class women who provoked controversy about the acceptable appearance and vigor of women's bodies. Bicycling permitted women to experiment with mobility and with clothing in unprecedented ways, but at a price. As one Englishwoman wrote in 1897, "It's awful—one wants nerves of iron. . . . The shouts and yells of the children deafen one, the women shriek with laughter or groan and hiss and all sorts of remarks are shouted at one, occasionally some not fit for publication. One needs to be very brave to stand all that."[35]

During the same decade, the first automobiles appeared on city streets, and after 1900 their numbers grew rapidly. It is often argued that cars radically transformed city streets, making them raceways rather than sites of public encounter. For the twentieth century as a whole, that is largely true, but the first automobiles merely added one more ingredient to the strudel of the streets. (Their immediate impact was more dramatic on rural roads and quiet residential lanes.) The desire for speed came first, and the various technical innovations responded to it. Electric trams were far more important—for two decades in the United States, and for longer in most of Europe. Only gradually did automobiles push aside tram and pedestrian alike. In some ways they completed a long-term trend. Already in 1831, Ernest Fouinet claimed that Paris's first omnibus line along the Grands Boulevards had led cobblers, umbrella vendors, and shopkeepers to bewail the loss of business, and that "flânerie"—a word just coming into use—was already dead.[36] Little could he imagine what was coming, decades later.

Urban mass transit sped up movement in the streets, changed the mix of uses there, and confounded established standards of propriety. To understand how it changed behavior and relationships in the nineteenth-century street, we might return to the 1860s London lithograph of the nosy clergyman (see fig. 31, p. 126). The young lady mistaken for a prostitute explains that she is "waiting for a bus," which is visible coming around the corner. The omnibus and its successors made it possible for a respectably dressed woman to linger on the street without violating any proprieties. Here the respectable woman is standing, alone, and not as part of a promenade, and therefore, in traditional terms, inappropriately. Etiquette guides invariably insisted that ladies never loiter in the street. But of course this woman is waiting only in order to be removed from the street and whisked away in the bus. The bus has made possible a measurable acceleration of her movement. Merely to measure the speed, however, is to miss the dimensions of class and gender. This speed was not entirely dependent on new technologies: earlier in the century, elites could set themselves apart by promenading on horseback or in carriages. What mattered was who raced through the streets, and who did not. In general, nineteenth-century elites sped up their movement through the street, reduced their exposure to it, and, with the new vehicles, withdrew from it to some extent. But not everyone joined them.

This is the crucial and easily overlooked shift in the time and speed of nineteenth-century streets: a change in attitudes and in behavior reversed old roles. Early in the century, the elite moved slowly through the streets and their inferiors rushed around—or at least were believed to. This set of attitudes and behaviors flourished in the era of the aristocratic promenade, but it had deep roots. In ancient Rome, for example, dignitaries moved slowly (and surely "dignity" has never connoted haste); slaves and commoners hurried.[37] The apotheosis of the flâneur in the mid-nineteenth century was among other things a last-ditch attempt to reclaim the ostentatious display of leisure in the street. Roles soon reversed: idleness in the street became increasingly associated with the poor and unrespectable, while the elites were less likely to linger there. Instead, they rushed through it, and increasingly did so inside vehicles of one kind or another. Idlers in the street were, from the elite perspective, either obvious reprobates such as beggars or the unemployed, or lowly street vendors; or, more insidiously, they were morally dubious people not easily distinguished from respectable folk, except by their idleness— notably prostitutes. Those people did not count when intellectuals mourned the decline of urban leisure. By 1911 a Berlin journalist lamented that "the art of walking" and "the art of strolling" had been lost in the rush of modern life, and that any woman who appeared to be enjoying a stroll immediately attracted a policeman's suspicion.[38] The apparently idle may even have outnumbered the busy few, but despite—or perhaps even because of—that fact, proper behavior now meant rushing through the street. So, by 1900, an emerging ideal associated the street with speed, not leisure—that is, with a desire to reduce time spent on the street. The very haste that had startled visitors to eighteenth-century London was now the way of the world.

Increased speed went hand in hand with urban growth. Greater distances to cover, especially between home and work, were both an impetus for faster transit and a result of it. In other words, the century of the railroad saw the birth of a more mobile society, and that society built railroads along with other tools of speed. Of course, it is possible to explain this transition in more abstract, economic terms: the rise of capitalism created a new bourgeois elite that measured its worth by the acceleration of capital—and, more visibly, of goods and workers and customers. People who lived by the belief that "time is money" spurned the aristocratic display of leisure in public, just as they bewailed the lack of industriousness among the poor. In *The Wealth of Nations* (1776), Adam Smith famously deplored workmen's "habit of sauntering" from one task to another, a defect to be remedied by the division of labor—and indeed by 1848 John Stuart Mill declared that the rise of industry had set laborers moving at a salubrious tempo.[39] The highly industrialized and reputedly ultramodern Berlin of 1900 was heralded for its relentless haste: the city's watchword was said to be "tempo." Whether seen as an impediment to commerce or as an ominously idle horde, congested streets were a growing cause for worry. Among the many expressions of anxiety, perhaps the most often cited is the Berlin sociologist Georg Simmel's 1903 essay, "The Metropolis and Mental Life," in which he described the psychological armor necessary to avoid being overwhelmed by the sensory overload of the urban crowd. Some of Simmel's readers shared his fascination with the crowd, others shared his trepidation—and most were probably of two minds. Usually, however, the crowd was a problem to be solved, and speed seemed to offer a solution.

FIG. 47. Thomas Rowlandson, *Miseries of London*, 1807. Text from James Beresford's *Miseries of Human Life* (1806), who quotes Virgil's *Aeneid*: "In going out to dinner (already too late) your carriage delayed by a jam of coaches—which choke up the whole street and allow you at least an hour or more than you require to sharpen your wits for table talk. 'Breast against breast with ruinous assault. / And deafning shock they came—'" Metropolitan Museum of Art, The Elisha Whittelsey Collection, The Elisha Whittelsey Fund, 1956.

The crush of traffic was the chief obstacle to speed. In the great metropolises of London and Paris, traffic jams had long been frequent events. For centuries, the markets of central Paris suffered from daily gridlock. The enormous numbers of wagons carrying all kinds of goods, along with the business carried out in the narrow streets, made passage difficult. Often the Seine, like the Thames, was acknowledged to be the more reliable traffic artery. When growing numbers of private carriages were added to the mix in the seventeenth and eighteenth centuries, traffic jams became all too common. Samuel Pepys recorded an unpleasant but far from extraordinary event in the London of 1661, when his carriage was stuck in traffic for an hour and a half.[40] On one fateful occasion in 1610, Henry IV's royal coach became trapped in Paris traffic long enough for the fanatical François Ravaillac to leap aboard and stab the king to death. (A similar scenario played out, now with an automobile, a pistol, and far graver consequences, when the Austrian Archduke Franz Ferdinand's driver lost his way in Sarajevo in 1914.)

Worries about traffic flow and about the breakdown of social order were closely intertwined, as we know from literary and artistic treatments of chaos in the streets. A vigorous seventeenth-century literary genre of satires, in the classical Roman tradition, described "les embarras de Paris," the most famous of which was Nicolas Boileau's 1665 poem on these "obstructions."[41] John Gay's 1716 poem *Trivia* described the "Oaths," "Fists," "Blows," and "Blood" amid the "Rage" sparked by a blockage in the Strand.[42] Traffic jams created a kind of democracy in the streets, with everyone forced to wait his or her turn. This equality proved intolerable to some aristocrats, and perhaps even more to their lackeys. Early cases of road rage seem to reflect an outraged sense of injured privilege. In 1660 another traffic jam not only stranded Pepys but also provoked a fight among servants in which one of Lord Chesterfield's footmen was killed.[43] In 1722, when the carriages of the duke of Châtillon and the count of Charolais came face-to-face at the Palais-Royal, neither would back up, and the count's men proceeded to cane the duke's coachman and horses.[44] The sad fate of another innocent victim was reported by the *London Post* in 1702: "Yesterday a Gentleman's coach meeting a hackney in Long-Acre, and the latter refusing to make way for him upon a stop, the Gentleman jumpt out of his coach in fury, and killed one of the hackney-horses."[45] In an earlier case from Paris in 1655, a guards captain was slain by servants of another nobleman after their coaches became entangled and the captain sprang to the defense of his coachman. King Louis XIV responded with a decree forbidding servants to carry swords or firearms in Paris.[46] It seems that the danger of mixing driving and weapons is not unique to the automotive age.

Freight wagons and laborers' carts fed the ever-larger cities' insatiable demands for food, fuel, building materials, and all the goods for sale in markets and shops. The lumbering vehicles came in

FIG. 48. *L'embaras de Paris*, 1715, engraving of the Pont Neuf by Nicolas Guérard. The verse captions reads: "Be watchful while walking in Paris, and keep your ears open, so that you won't tumble or suffer a blow—for if you don't listen amid the hubbub, and heed the calls to look out, you're sure to be crushed." Bibliothèque nationale de France.

many sizes and shapes. Most were horse-drawn, but there were also humble carts pulled by pairs of dogs (not to be confused with the English "dog-cart," a light horse-drawn carriage originally designed to carry hunters and their dogs). Before the nineteenth century, London and Paris had banned carts drawn by dogs, but in Berlin and Vienna they long remained a familiar if pathetic sight. Handcarts and wheelbarrows were also major contributors to the maelstrom of the streets. Weaving their way through these obstacles were the main antagonists, pedestrians and horse-drawn passenger vehicles. As the Connecticut pastor Nathaniel Wheaton wrote of London in 1830, "Were a coach to pull up till an opening was made in the throng of foot passengers, it would be in the predicament of the clown, who waited for the river to run by before he attempted to cross."[47]

In 1800 vehicles for passenger transport were mainly limited to the relatively few private carriages and taxis plus rural stagecoaches on their way to and from city depots. Soon their numbers grew

FIG. 49. London traffic and policeman at Mansion House, 1890s.

rapidly, while human-powered passenger transport largely vanished. Enclosed sedan chairs, fashionable during the eighteenth century, mostly disappeared soon after 1800. They offered protection from the elements and an extra degree of privacy, since they could be carried directly into entrance halls. Their ambiguous status also lent them an advantage amid the largely unregulated flow of traffic: they could be carried amid pedestrians on the sidewalk or out with the wagons and carriages. In the ever-larger cities, however, especially London, two strong men could no longer compete with a horse and carriage. As Horace Walpole observed in 1791, "The town is so extended, that the breed of chairs is almost lost; for Hercules and Atlas could not carry anybody from one end of this enormous capital to the other."[48]

By the nineteenth century, municipal authorities were at work on many initiatives to clear the streets: improved paving and drainage, sidewalks, crackdowns on street commerce, and parking restrictions.[49] They also recognized the urgent need to acquire the legal powers, and the financing, to straighten street walls on busy thoroughfares like the Strand and the Graben, whose general breadth merely guaranteed larger traffic jams when their narrow chokepoints became blocked. The desire to improve traffic flow went hand in hand with the clamor for sanitation. The emerging ideal of urban circulation encompassed the movement of goods and people along with the circulation of fresh air and clean water. It was a policy defined by a biological metaphor, derived from a more or less explicit belief that cities were organisms, with streets as their "arteries."

The separation of vehicles and pedestrians promised to improve both safety and traffic flow. Visitors, especially Parisians, praised London's provisions for pedestrians: after the Great Fire of 1666, many streets were equipped with smooth flagstone sidewalks, protected from vehicles by stout wooden posts. Early eighteenth-century Vienna also installed wooden and stone bollards on the few streets wide enough for them. After the 1760s, London began to replace its posts with curbstones, which had the additional advantage of channeling water into the gutters. Similar measures in other cities were rare before 1800. Visitors to late eighteenth-century Berlin almost invariably complained about the raised driveways and stairs that repeatedly forced pedestrians into the center of the muddy streets.

Although most of Paris was equipped with sidewalks after 1820, its narrow streets remained treacherous. Francis Hervé's 1842 Paris guidebook immersed its readers in "the confusion of so many people bustling along upon a little bit of pavement not two feet wide":

> When, compelled to give place to some lady, you descend from the narrow flags into the road, and whilst you are maneuvering to escape a cart you see coming towards you, "*Gare*" is bawled out with stunning roar; you look round and find the pole of a coach within an inch of your shoulder, you scramble out of the way as fast as you can through mud and puddle, and are glad to clap your back against a house to make room for some lumbering vehicle, . . . happy to congratulate yourself that there is just room enough for it to pass without jamming you quite flat, and that you are quit of the danger at the expense of being smeared with a little mud from the wheel.[50]

Perhaps Hervé felt compelled to play the gentleman, but the American John Sanderson did not see Frenchmen doing the same: "If a lady meets a gentleman upon the little side walk, which French cour-

tesy calls a '*trottoir*,' it is the lady who always *trots* into the mud. The
French women seem used to this submission and yield to it instinc-
tively."[51] Certainly the Parisian writer Delphine de Girardin found
no respect on her streets. She could no longer enjoy a stroll, as she
bewailed in 1837:

> The journey is a struggle, the road itself a battlefield: walking is com-
> bat. A thousand obstacles surround you, a thousand traps have been
> set for you. The people around you are your enemies. Every step you
> take is a hard-fought victory. The streets are no longer open thorough-
> fares, public ways that take you where your heart desires. Streets today
> are bazaars where everyone spreads out merchandise. They are work-
> shops where everyone carries on his trade in broad daylight. The side-
> walks, already so narrow, have been invaded by a permanent exhibi-
> tion.

She proceeds to describe a walk in which she, the lady, is forced off
the sidewalk again and again: by water poured from a window; by
work spread out on the pavement; by a toothpick vendor settled in a
chair; by a hanging slab of beef. Finally she blunders into a horse and
taxi, and, with a sigh of relief, accepts the offer of a ride.[52]

Her eagerness to escape from the street was typical for men and
women of her class. Indeed, Hervé added a note of reassurance to
his British audience: "Happily for my readers, it is not very probable
that many of them will ever be called into those neighbourhoods, or
if they be, it will probably be in a carriage, when they will not stand
near the same chance of being crushed to death; but as I explore all
parts and am thereby the better enabled to give a faithful picture of
Paris, I consider it incumbent on me to inform my country people
that there are such streets that they may better know how to enjoy
Paris by keeping out of the way of them."[53] A few years later, Haussmann's new boulevards would make it even easier to avoid these
plebeian lanes.

As congestion grew, official policies and prevailing attitudes endorsed the principle that circulation trumped other uses of the street,

and that traffic should move as quickly as possible. There was nothing sudden about this change, especially in London, where judicial enforcement of traffic flow can be traced back to the seventeenth century. By the late eighteenth century, the difficulty in getting through Paris in a carriage, or even on foot, spurred the authorities to regulate street vendors, while new ideas about both commerce and hygiene encouraged the belief that, as one French observer wrote, "circulation is the prosperity of nations."[54] However, the 1830s and 1840s seem to have been the time when, in the historian Nicholas Papayanis's phrase, "the ideology of circulation" came to dominate thinking about Paris streets.[55] Delphine de Girardin, for example, concluded her lament about the difficulty of taking a stroll by declaring that "the street is a road, not a refuge. It belongs to those who are moving along it, not to those who dwell on it."[56] By the early nineteenth century, Paris police ordinances cited "the freedom of circulation" to justify restrictions on the use of streets for labor and the display of merchandise, and they declared that "the public way is intended particularly for traffic."[57] The fact that such rules were reissued throughout the century suggests that they may not have been very effective. A similar frustration may explain the Vienna regional government's 1863 decree forbidding pedestrians to venture into the roadway.[58]

In both French and English, the medical term "congestion" came to denote the clogged circulation of city traffic as well as bodily fluids. Policy remedies were slower to arrive in London, even though the change in attitude may have come earlier. Perhaps the need for police intervention was somewhat less pressing thanks to some combination of wider streets, better sidewalks, and drivers as well as pedestrians who were more willing to fall into line. Already in 1782 Carl Philipp Moritz found it striking that "you seldom see a sensible person walking in the middle of the street in London."[59] In 1843 César Daly still saw a sharp contrast between Paris and London, where pedestrians stayed out of traffic.[60]

Jammed roads compelled governments to impose new traffic regulations. The English practice of driving on the left (but walking on the right) was a long-standing custom, eventually enshrined in law. An orderly system came later to the Continent, where right-driving and left-driving customs variously prevailed, even within a single kingdom. Confusion and erratic compliance were guaranteed in Vienna, for example. The city mandated driving on the right in 1819, but after 1824 a coachman who reached the suburbs was immediately subject to the Austrian monarchy's left-hand-drive rule. Vienna gave in and switched to the left in 1852 (switching back only when annexed by Nazi Germany in 1938).[61] Driving on the right became the law in crowded Paris during the early nineteenth century. Berlin did not follow suit until the 1860s, and even then commercial drivers protested against the rule. They argued that their informal methods worked better to keep travel moving. Speeding coachmen, for example, might utter a distinctive cry to warn their colleagues to clear the way.[62]

The twentieth century accustomed us to thinking of traffic as a matter of engineering, with the biological metaphor of circulation supplanted by a physical one of hydrology to describe the flow of traffic. In the nineteenth century, the political implications of "circulation" were clearer, if still usually veiled. What made traffic controversial was its class dimension—rich and poor used the streets differently—against the backdrop of growing fears of revolution rising from the streets. The understandable wish to clear the way for carriages and wagons also served as a pretext to separate classes or to privilege carriage riders at the expense of walkers, hawkers, and talkers. It would be a mistake to interpret traffic in purely political terms, but it is worth noting that the 1830s and 1840s, when the leaders of Paris demanded "circulation," were the heyday of revolutionary barricade-building across Parisian streets at times of political unrest, as Hugo's "misérables" employed such readily available materials as paving stones and overturned wagons (including the new omnibuses) for the opposite of their intended purpose. During these same years the authorities, notably the prefect Rambuteau, sliced a few new and wider streets through the dense inner city. Then, after 1850, Napoleon III and Haussmann systematically opened the city to the circulation of vehicles, air, water, and soldiers.

At times the connection between traffic flow and political repression became explicit. Amid the revolutionary uprising of March 1848 in Berlin, the beleaguered royal police decreed that "the events of recent days make it necessary to ensure that free movement in the streets not be impeded anywhere. Therefore it is forbidden to traverse the streets in groups or to gather in the streets and squares. If any order to disperse is resisted or not immediately obeyed, those who are recalcitrant will be forcefully dispersed or arrested."[63] Two days later, their worst fears came to pass as barricades sprang up across the city. Later in the century, when the English artist and social reformer William Morris decried police crackdowns on socialist assemblies in the name of traffic flow, he acknowledged that any political motives were rooted in deeper class tensions. Although Morris accepted "the natural wish to keep the streets as clear as may be," he feared its abuse:

> I have noted of late years a growing impatience on the part of the more luxurious portion of society of the amusements and habits of the workers, when they in any way interfere with the calm of their luxury; or to put it in plainer language, a tendency on their part to arrogant petty tyranny in these matters. They would, if they could, clear the streets of everything that may injure their delicate susceptibilities. . . . They would clear the streets of costermongers, organs, processions, and lecturers of all kinds and make them a sort of decent prison corridors, with people just trudging to and from their work. It is impossible but, that this feeling should influence the police, who are their immediate servants.[64]

Another telling example comes from the explosively growing Berlin of 1910: an official notice mounted on Litfass columns by order of the royal police chief, Traugott von Jagow, and including the proclamation "the street is exclusively for traffic." This sign is well-known among labor historians. The notoriously reactionary Jagow had it posted in an effort to suppress socialist street demonstrations. The next line read, "Resistance against the authorities will be met with the use of weapons." Historians have interpreted this claim to the street in political terms—correctly—as a transparent excuse to repress the socialists. The clear implication was that all uses of the street were to be dictated by the state.[65] But that implication was cloaked in an assertion about traffic, declaring in the face of all evidence that the street had no other legitimate uses. Why did Jagow make this transparently absurd claim? It was immediately mocked by commentators who pointed out that parading soldiers and royal processions frequently clogged the streets of Berlin. A mass-market magazine printed Jagow's proclamation as a derisive caption to a picture of a typical Berlin military parade.[66] In order to understand why Jagow might have considered it credible to assert that "the street is exclusively for traffic," we need to recognize that the rumblings of revolution were playing out amid changing patterns of mobility. Socialist demonstrations could plausibly be prohibited on the pretext that streets were for speed—because, increasingly, they were, just not for everyone.

It is ultimately impossible to separate a desire for faster movement from a fear of the unruly masses in the street. In Paris since 1789, and sooner or later in every metropolis, the visible crowds of poor workers in the streets aroused unease if not terror among the wealthier and ruling classes. Fear of crime, fear of dirt and disease, fear of moral contamination, and fear of revolution: all helped make the street a place to avoid.

THE MODERN STREET

During the nineteenth century, the street acquired a new, simplified identity. By 1890 Josef Stübben's authoritative textbook of urban planning declared that city streets "are primarily traffic routes; only secondarily do they support the construction of buildings."[67] In elevating movement over place and structure, Stübben was ratifying a consensus that had been building for decades, choosing one aspect of Antoine Furetière's seventeenth-century definition—"passage"—over the other, "space between houses." The equation of streets with transportation was not unknown to previous centuries, but it had rarely described the reality of the cities. The more crowded and mobile world of 1900 seemed to demand that clear priorities be set.

Circulation, the faster the better, became the reigning ideal of the street. Forward motion meant progress and improvement: in commerce, in health, and in morality. The prevailing logic implied that what poor people lacked was circulation and speed. Amid early Victorian London street improvements, for example, the desire to speed up the movement of freight wagons, carriages, and omnibuses could be justified as a boon to the slums that would be ripped open. The report of an 1838 parliamentary committee pointed to districts of London through which "no great thoroughfares at present pass, and which being wholly occupied by a dense population, composed of the lowest class of labourers, entirely secluded from the observation and influence of better educated neighbors, exhibit a state of moral and physical degradation deeply to be deplored." New streets, that is, "great streams of public intercourse," offered the solution to this "lamentable evil," because "the introduction at the same time of improved habits and a freer circulation of air" would be certain to wipe out dangerous diseases and "the moral condition of these poorer occupants must necessarily be improved by immediate communication with a more respectable inhabitancy."[68] Decades later, the dedicated London social worker Octavia Hill displayed an even greater faith that literal light and air could be transmuted into enlightenment. As she explained to a parliamentary committee in 1882, "A great deal of the degradation of these courts is because no public opinion reaches them; if you hear anybody talk about a cul de sac, and contrast it with any place that is a thoroughfare, you feel at once that it is the public opinion that affects the character of a court more than police or anything else."[69] In Paris, Haussmann claimed that the archbishop endorsed his projects with the words, "Your mission assists mine. . . . In wide, straight, bright, odorless streets, people do not behave in the same negligent way as in narrow, crooked, gloomy streets. To bring light, air, and water into the dwellings of the poor does not merely restore physical health. It also encourages good housekeeping and personal cleanliness, which gradually improves morality."[70]

The quest for speed in city streets decisively shaped urban design in the twentieth century. After streets had been redefined as transportation corridors, visionary planners decided that it was not enough merely to restrict other uses of them. Instead, radical new designs would reorganize cities around new and efficient roadways. The twentieth century downplayed Victorian moral language in favor of a technocratic emphasis on measurable efficiency. Large-scale redevelopment projects sacrificed the street itself in the interest of light and air, decongestion and mobility. At its most ambitious, this "urban renewal" replaced densely packed streets with generously spaced tower blocks, automobile highways, parking lots, and unbounded open spaces.

General acceptance of the belief that "the street is exclusively for traffic" ensured that other uses, and other users, would be ignored. With a figure like Jagow, the desire to move the masses off the streets was undeniably political and repressive. By no means was that the case everywhere. Indeed, many leading modernists were socialists or liberal reformers committed to improving the miserable living conditions of industrial workers. For them, Victorian morality re-emerged in the languages of biology and social science. Reformers envisioned a radical transformation of urban form that banished old hierarchies. Slum neighborhoods and teeming tenement streets would disappear. Street peddlers would acquire indoor facilities, and in a sanitized city there would be no need for bootblacks, ragpickers, or crossing sweepers. The poor would no longer have any need or desire to socialize in the noisy, filthy street, thanks to spacious new homes and parks. Rapid transportation would enable the poor to live in these greener, cleaner places. In this better world, aristocrats and workers could share the public park instead of fighting for supremacy on the street. With public space no longer limited to the narrow confines of the street, mobility would not be at war with immobility, and conflicts could be diffused. The politics, feasibility, and aesthetics of these radical plans were often challenged, but for decades their assumptions about streets were rarely questioned.

In retrospect, the automobile seems to have been the crucial force that reshaped streets and cities, either from the pressure of their sheer numbers (as in the United States in the 1910s and 1920s) or through its promise of a thrilling new future, as in the minds and plans of such influential enthusiasts as Daniel Burnham and Le Corbusier. The historian Peter Norton, for example, makes a compelling case that the concerted efforts of automotive interests were decisive in redefining and redesigning American city streets during the 1920s.[71] But the auto manufacturers and their allies were able to capitalize on decades-old beliefs in Europe as well as the United States. Long before cars came along, users of carriages and trams had sought to clear the way for their speedy vehicles. Later, as popular enthusiasm, economic pressures, and government regulations combined to hand over streets to automobiles, they became synonymous with the long-standing desire for rapid mobility. Other uses of the street, even trams, became associated with pedestrians, and these uses came to seem illegitimate. Soon the cycle was complete: the very presence of cars, with their noise, stench, and dangerous speed, sealed the fate of streets as genteel promenades, even where earlier problems of dung, trams, and proletarian crowds had been vanquished. By the 1950s, a Berlin planning document exuded confidence that the matter was all but settled: "And the pedestrian? The new street has no place for unreconstructed Neanderthals. Anyone who has a destination should be sitting in a car. Anyone who doesn't is on a stroll and should proceed immediately to the nearest park."[72] The promenade could enjoy a suitable revival, as long as it was pushed off the streets and back into the parks where it had been born.

This way of thinking also shaped the ideology of the twentieth-century traffic engineer. The firm link between streets and speed governed the rating of streets strictly in terms of their efficient movement of motor vehicles. Implicit in this logic was the belief that any time spent on the street was wasted time. The fact that so many contemporary streets offer pedestrians an alienating or even a terrifying experience is, in the language of software, a feature, not a bug: the transportation program produces its desired result.

6

Public Order and Public Space

Control and Design

Streets acquire identities over time, through use and through events. These historical processes are usually beyond anyone's control, the result of thousands of individual choices. However, when rulers seek to impose their authority on urban populations, one of their tools is the manipulation of urban space. They can exert power over the populace through their very presence; in their laws and the enforcement of them; or by rebuilding the city.

Whether the prince lived in a castle at the top of the town, or somewhere far away, he sometimes needed to rally support from the townspeople, while they had to demonstrate their allegiance from time to time. A noble procession was a momentous occasion — a symbolic conquest of the town for all to see. Town leaders staged the event carefully, decorating the procession route and perhaps holding a formal ceremony at the town hall. They knew it was their duty to display heartfelt gratitude for the protection the prince offered, even when their real motivation was merely to ensure that the prince would feel sufficiently flattered to refrain from seizing more of the town's treasure or liberties. The townspeople were expected to turn out to watch from windows or to line the streets, and no doubt many of them were thrilled to see the rich costumes and royal standards or to glimpse the exalted person of the ruler. Others were enticed by the promise of a fair or a feast. This is a scene that played out often

FIG. 50. Antoine Sallaert, *L'Ommegang de Bruxelles le 31 mai 1615*. Archduchess Isabella at procession of crossbowmen's guild, Brussels.

in the later Middle Ages and, in many places, long after, as compliant crowds endorsed the existing municipal and royal order of things.[1] Even the French revolutionaries of the 1790s thought it necessary to stage desacralized republican ceremonies in order to ratify their usurpation of royal privileges.

Before 1789, and even after, these demonstrations of power were suffused with religious authority. Every procession invoked the sanction of God to claim legitimate secular power. More than politics, in fact, Christianity long gave European streets their identity. Religious processions, held on saints' days, hewed to prescribed routes through the town. Stops along the way might venerate corners or niches that had been ceremonially consecrated and marked by permanent shrines. Annual fairs also had religious origins, usually as patron saints' celebrations or pre-Lenten carnivals, although they often became raucous festivals dedicated to street entertainment, music, dancing, and a toxic combination of drinking and brawling. In their sacred or profane form, many processions and ceremonies endured for centuries, their visible or invisible imprint conferring a durable identity on their paths through town. This meaning was shaped, and changed over time, by those who organized the traditional rituals: religious confraternities, guilds, town governments, or church authorities. By the nineteenth century, though, official religious rites might be outshone by private ones, notably funeral processions but also weddings and christenings, spectacles that nonparticipants were free to ignore.

In the vastly enlarged cities of the nineteenth century, working-class neighborhoods sometimes clung to the anchor of their parishes, but increasingly their residents' mental maps revolved around different reference points, old and new: markets, fountains, factories, or pubs. Most of the time, people's daily routines knit the invisible patterns that bound a city together. When politics or labor disputes drew crowds into the streets, familiar landmarks acquired a more charged identity. Politics often still took a traditional form, though, with an orderly crowd flattering its ruler, to the dismay of restless souls who hoped to shake the masses out of their torpor. On the eve of World War I, Maximilian Rapsilber lamented that Berliners lined the street "like rigid walls" for imperial parades, standing "rather stupidly in order to catch a fleeting glimpse of the empress's hat or of the emperor and crown prince as they ride by."[2]

Outsiders were sometimes astonished by the order that emerged from the apparent chaos of the streets, especially in London. Streams of pedestrian traffic kept flowing thanks to body language and barely detectable signals that averted collisions every second. Conflicting claims to a smidgen of pavement occasionally erupted into shouting matches or brawls, but hawkers and other regulars usually parceled out street space according to invisible rules. Disputes might be adjudicated on the spot by an acknowledged but entirely unofficial authority figure. When crowds threatened to get out of hand, visible authority could step in, in the form of either the police or, more radically, of redesigned streets.

CRIME AND PUNISHMENT

Informal order has always been essential to the functioning of crowded cities, even as mechanisms of enforcement have varied. Before the growth of urban police forces in the nineteenth century, authority was invariably present if often invisible to outsiders. During the seventeenth and eighteenth centuries, the French (later also English) word "police" and the German "Policey" or "Polizei" meant "governance" and did not refer to any specific institution or body of uniformed men. Louis XIV's royal order formalizing his administrative authority over Paris in 1667 explained that "the police consists in assuring the tranquility of the public and of individuals, of ridding the city of everything that causes disorder, of procuring plenty, and of ensuring that everyone lives according to his condition and his state."[3] Learned treatises and administrative practices enumerated "police powers" that encompassed most of the matters discussed in the previous chapters: commerce and sanitation as much as traffic and crowd control. Policing entailed responsibility for public works (including the paving, lighting, and cleaning of streets), fire prevention and firefighting, medical facilities, and market regulations dictating who could sell what, where they could sell it, and when. Eventually the enforcement of these rules was put into the hands of a uniformed force, as the word "police" acquired a more urban emphasis and it became possible to identify *the* police as the visible guardians of authority in the streets.

Meanwhile, authority was visible in other forms, at least from time to time, notably in the infliction of punishment. Until the nineteenth century, kings and their officials believed that they needed to feed the public's bloodlust now and then. Judges sentenced evildoers to various forms of public humiliation. The stocks or the pillory were long a prominent sight at, for example, Charing Cross in London, the Place des Halles in Paris, and in front of the Berlin town hall. Petty criminals were clapped into the boards, typically for just a few hours, to be subjected to discomfort and disgrace. Crowds gathered to gawk, jeer, and perhaps beat the condemned or pelt them with dung or rotten food. Public whipping, another spectacle intended to humiliate and deter criminals, was still practiced in eighteenth-century streets. Reckless drivers in Vienna might receive up to fifty strokes.[4]

Above all, executions were a major public entertainment, whatever their moral value, and whatever their method: mainly the rope in England, the guillotine in post-revolutionary France, and the ax or the wheel in much of Germany. Excited crowds followed the condemned's journey from prison to the gallows, usually to hurl abuse although sometimes to celebrate the notoriety of a famous outlaw. The processions typically began in the center of town, while the gallows usually stood at its edge, beyond the walls, for example outside the Scottish Gate (Schottentor) in Vienna and the Oranienburg gate north of Berlin. In Paris, though, until 1830 the crowds followed the prisoner into the central Place de Grève, after the brief era of the Revolution's guillotine in the Place de la Concorde. Before those notorious beheadings, the most celebrated route led from London's Newgate prison out Oxford Street to the gallows at Tyburn, where criminals were hanged until 1783. A large and spirited crowd escorted the prisoner's open cart and stayed to watch the spectacle, accompanied by sellers of food and drink and broadsheets, by entertainers and by pickpockets.[5] A macabre form of urban decoration came after the execution of ordinary criminals in some places but more often with the beheading of traitors: as late as the eighteenth century, their severed heads were displayed on conspicuous town gates such as Temple Bar and London Bridge—sinister reminders of the fate of those who defied authority, or perhaps just a gratuitous display of official cruelty. More common, until the early nineteenth century, was the practice of leaving executed corpses on display at the suburban scaffold.

Within a few years in the mid-nineteenth century, these public punishments disappeared from the streets of most European cities. Deterrence from crime was now believed to operate in less visible ways, or else was present in the form of the uniformed policeman.

FIG. 51. *An Execution Scene at Newgate*, after Thomas Rowlandson, early 1800s. Yale Center for British Art, Paul Mellon Collection.

The stocks and pillory were dismantled. Capital punishment continued, but for fewer crimes, with executions mostly held behind prison walls, where crowds could not gather. Authorities no longer valued the spectacle of official cruelty, for reasons that remain in dispute, historians having questioned the self-serving explanations of contemporaries who congratulated themselves on their moral progress. It was feared that public punishments stimulated bloodlust and popular disorder more than they served as a sobering reminder of divinely ordained justice. The sight of unruly crowds, whether reveling in the spectacle or disparaging it, also seems to have made the ruling classes increasingly uneasy. In other words, they may have been motivated less by considerations of humanity—after all, the executions continued behind prison walls—than by delicacy.[6]

The desire to conceal the destruction of criminals' bodies accompanied broader initiatives to clear the streets. The same squeamishness about frail human bodies was apparent in the quest to avoid the sight of bodily functions, of sexual activity, and of disfigured beggars and the poor. In praising the advance of "civilization" in 1836, for example, John Stuart Mill declared that "the spectacle, and even the very idea, of pain, is kept more and more out of the sight of those classes who enjoy in their fulness the benefits of civilization," freeing those enlightened classes from "the spectacle of harshness, rudeness, and violence."[7] The removal of punishment from the street was also consistent with the growing priority given to mobility. The growth of eighteenth-century London made the Tyburn processions an affront to Oxford Street commerce and traffic, and half a century later the prefect of the Seine cited "the difficulty of traffic circulation" as one reason to move executions away from the central Place de Grève after 1830.[8]

Fear of street crime rose and fell over the centuries. A lack of reliable crime statistics makes it impossible to know if changing perceptions of the threat corresponded to reality. One source of fear was certainly the presence of bands of rowdy young men. Early eighteenth-century London trembled at the menace of the "Mohocks," thought to be an organized gang of young upper-class men who terrorized random victims in the streets. By the nineteenth century, belief in the connection between poverty and crime—or poverty and revolution—was more typical, as was a fear that the poor were abandoning their deference to their social and economic superiors. In late nineteenth-century Paris, the preferred American Indian name, supposed to evoke merciless ferocity, was "les apaches." Elsewhere, vaguer references to hooligans or rowdies were used to stigmatize the unfathomable enemies in the streets.[9]

Politics infused everyday policing, often in subtle ways. Perceived injustices, including cases of notorious criminals who somehow escaped the noose, were among the grievances that could stir urban unrest. But riots could erupt at any time, for many reasons: resentment at the abuse of privileges; rumors of treason or blasphemy; anger at bread prices or gin taxes; and, especially as the scale of industrial employment grew, the loss of work or wages. When matters got out of hand, soldiers might be called out, or else the embers of rage were left to die down on their own. Smaller disturbances were common. Simmering resentment at the authorities sometimes boiled over when the police made arrests or otherwise flaunted their authority in the streets. Officers of the law knew they had to be prepared for shouts of abuse or a rain of stones, which they sometimes chose to ignore for fear of sparking a greater conflagration.[10]

During the eighteenth century, neighborhood order was often preserved by truly local authority. Neighborhood notables—aristocratic or bourgeois property owners—frequently commanded enough respect to settle disputes and quell disturbances. Trade guilds in many towns retained legal authority, visibly embodied by the masters in their shops. In pre-revolutionary Paris, "les dames de la Halle," the women vendors of the central markets, also possessed corporate privileges. Their organizational strength, visibility, and daily interaction with nearly everyone enabled them to arbitrate routine disputes, to be received as the voice of the people of Paris, and to play a prominent role in the French Revolution as well, famously in the women's march to Versailles on October 5, 1789.[11] After the Revolution, the European ruling classes' fear of the crowd became existential. Masses of poor people on the street, a normal sight in big cities, became a specter of revolutionary upheaval. (Most historians who write about "the crowd" mean only the kind that posed a political threat.) The revolutionaries' dream was that the crowd would overthrow the old order by seizing control of the streets around the palace or other centers of power. In 1848 that dream came true, if only briefly, in most European capitals, and memories of the sites and events of 1848 shaped hopes and fears for the rest of the century. The fear that the masses might rise up and seize power meant that the constable on the street now upheld the visible order of the state in much the same way as the king's own procession once had.

Yet the nineteenth century also saw more orderly urban crowds in their daily routines, less prone to random violence and bloodshed in the streets. Historians continue to debate the reasons for the changing character of the crowd. Certainly the authorities across much of Europe became less tolerant of rowdy and violent behavior, in part because of the fear of revolution but also because of changing standards of decorum. More professional policing also played a role. Urban police forces, patrolling the streets by day and by night, were largely a product of the nineteenth century. The most lauded innovation was the creation of the London Metropolitan Police in 1829 (the "bobbies," headquartered at Scotland Yard), which served as a model for many cities, although improved policing was in fact a gradual process that reached far back into the eighteenth century.[12] Before the nineteenth century, continental countries displayed a more visible police presence than England, because the army typically assumed law-enforcement duties. Daytime street patrols were a rarity, however. The role we associate with the beat cop was filled either by local notables, organized into militias watching over their neighborhoods, or by soldiers. A handful of night watchmen patrolled the dark streets from dusk to dawn. Often they were untrained citizens not known for their acumen, their dubious reputation personified in figures like Shakespeare's bumbling constables Dogberry and Elbow. Improved street lighting probably made a greater contribution to citizens' sense of nocturnal security.

The professionalized nineteenth-century police forces set out to be more visible than their predecessors. Regular patrols through the streets made them a presence in daily life and put them in a position to prevent crime rather than merely investigate it. In many places they cracked down on long-established forms of popular recreation that were now deemed too violent or simply immoral. The likes of dogfighting, cockfighting, and bull-baiting, as well as organized fistfights, were among the sports driven off the street, although they often continued a clandestine existence at less visible sites. Children's street games, too, might be broken up. The police's presence enabled them to function as arbiters of morality and behavior, most visibly in sweeping up drunks and beggars, whose very presence was an embarrassment, an affront to commerce, hygiene, and traffic, and often illegal as well. Many of the urban poor resented the police for their imposition of middle-class morality, especially when they cracked down on drinking and public intoxication.[13] Whether they commanded fear or respect, they modeled acceptable public behavior. They employed an even broader brush with the demand to "move along," which conveyed a fear of revolutionary crowds, a distaste for the sight of poor people lingering on the street, and also a growing conviction that traffic flow took precedence over all other uses of the streets. In short, the nineteenth-century beat cop embodied official authority in a newly visible way.[14]

Imperatives of sanitation, mobility, and morality justified these efforts to impose order on the street. Beneath them lay deeper fears about social and political order. Rumblings of rebellion might bring forth a show of force, or even an explosion of official brutality, but invisible rules, more than visible authority, ordinarily guided daily routines. An undercurrent of fear occasionally broke out into panic, fueled by rumors but sometimes also by real events, perhaps most famously in the East End of London in 1888 when a series of unsolved murders was blamed on the mysterious and terrifying Jack the Ripper. Even with a more visible police presence during the nineteenth century, though, the streets usually remained lightly regulated spaces in the ever larger and more anonymous cities.

DESIGN AND CONQUER

In the nineteenth century, and even more in the twentieth, urban form became an instrument of urban order. Rulers with growing architectural ambitions began to shape buildings and streets not only to make their cities magnificent but also to keep their people healthy and happy or at least orderly and docile. Modern urban planning, as an academic discipline and a practice, emerged during the nineteenth century as rulers' showcase projects became enmeshed in broader initiatives to guide rapid growth while improving sanitation, transportation, and street design.[15]

Eighteenth-century rulers' ambitions drew them both to Baroque grandeur and to new theories of rational governance. Advisers steeped in the doctrines of the Enlightenment sought to employ princely power to make cities more orderly and manageable. Although streets had long borne names, for example, they were mostly traditional rather than official, given from within rather than bestowed from above. Names might be drawn from geographical features (Hill Street), nearby landmarks (Church Walk, St. Mary's Lane), trades (Butchers' Alley), or some tidbit of neighborhood lore lost in the mists of time (Bollocks Terrace). During the seventeenth century, the French monarchy began to give royal names to streets. Later, especially after the French Revolution, the custom of using street names as propaganda came into wide use, honoring kings, generals, battles, and politicians.[16] Only in the eighteenth century did most towns mount signs to label streets for the benefit of strangers from other lands or other neighborhoods. (The same purpose was served by street maps that became less decorative and more geometric.) After midcentury, all the major cities took the additional step of numbering houses as well. Until then, strangers knew they had to stop and ask locals for directions, or else they needed more elaborate instructions, such as those provided by the Parisian artist who presumably hoped to drum up business by signing his engravings "J.-B. Greuze, painter to the King, rue Pavée, first porte-cochère on the left as you enter from rue Saint-André-des-Arts."[17] Mercier agreed that "it would be much easier and more convenient to go directly to see Mr. So-and-so at number 87 than to find Mr. So-and-so at the 'Blue Ribbon' or the 'Silver Beard,' the fifteenth doorway to the left or to the right after such-and-such a street." With sequential numbering, locating an address became a more rational process, less dependent on local knowledge. It also established a kind of notional equality of all houses, and Mercier suspected that resistance to numbering could be traced to the same sense of aristocratic privilege that had been outraged by traffic jams, any number other than Number One being an unpardonable insult.[18]

Names and numbers could only do so much to make sense of a warren of twisted lanes. Reformers lamented the scarcity of broad and straight streets. Voltaire himself, the epitome of Enlightenment, shuddered at the "dark, confined, hideous" center of Paris, a product of "the age of the most shameful barbarism," and declared that "we must widen the narrow and unhealthy streets."[19] Johann Georg Krünitz's late-Enlightenment encyclopedia agreed, observing that past generations had paid little attention to the design and construction of proper streets, since they were concerned too exclusively with their monumental palaces, churches, and town halls. Only in his enlightened age would it be possible to make up the deficits in paving, cleaning, and widening streets.[20] Voltaire and Krünitz were entirely typical of their era in deploring the narrow, winding lanes of the towns they knew. Nearly all their educated contemporaries shared the view that the grand avenues of the finest royal capitals were without doubt the most beautiful streets of all. Enlightenment intellectuals may have understood well enough that most princes built these streets in the pursuit of glory, not of the general welfare, but they did not doubt that broad, straight streets offered visible evidence of rational rule, a well-governed city, and even a morally upright populace.

Wide streets had indisputable advantages: they were cleaner and brighter and better suited to traffic. They held out the promise of an orderly solution to very tangible dangers. In the old lanes, pedestrians faced an unhappy choice between dodging traffic in the middle of the street or stumbling over obstacles at its edge. Krünitz's encyclopedia echoed many a traveler's account: "In well-populated quarters you must always be careful to avoid being bumped, or trod upon, or ridden or driven over, when you choose to walk in the roadway; or else to avoid bumping your nose or some other body part on protruding cornerstones, stairs, or doors. In short: narrow streets always place you in danger, if not of losing your life, then certainly of being injured, to say nothing of being sprayed with dung or dirt." The encyclopedia also, however, sought to explain the deficiencies of old streets in scientific terms: "No one bothers to notice that narrow streets, which are crooked as well, letting few rays of sunlight pass between the tall houses with their projecting gables, must be harmful to the health of their inhabitants, especially as a result of the many devilish emanations, partly from street muck, partly from cesspits and all the animal, vegetable, and mineral matter that the air is incapable of carrying away, because the wind cannot penetrate the narrow streets."[21]

Underlying the practical and the medical rationale for new streets was a deeper aesthetic or moral disgust. Many a later reformer echoed

Jean-Jacques Rousseau's sentiments from the 1760s, as he recalled his arrival in Paris in 1732, eager to find Baroque magnificence surpassing what he had previously seen in Turin: "I had imagined a city of a most imposing appearance, as beautiful as it was large, where nothing was to be seen but splendid streets and palaces of marble or gold. As I entered through the Faubourg Saint-Marceau, I saw nothing but dirty, stinking little streets, ugly black houses, a general air of squalor and poverty, beggars, carters, menders of clothes, sellers of herb-drinks and old hats. All this so affected me at the outset that all the magnificence I have since seen in Paris has not been sufficient to efface my first impression."[22] Rousseau's memories were colored by his long-standing abhorrence of an overly refined urban civilization. Others who did not share his hatred of cities nevertheless agreed that something needed to be done about their degraded conditions.

Although nineteenth-century rulers continued to pursue grand urban gestures in the Baroque tradition, they usually lacked the power to impose radical changes, partly because of modern constraints on their political and economic authority, partly because their cities had grown so vast. But the most ambitious of them sought to do more than carve out a solitary monument somewhere in their burgeoning cities. They hired architects to design broad streets that embodied beauty and grandeur, improved sanitation and transportation, and enabled police or armies to maintain order. Their ambitions, however self-serving, were welcomed by dedicated social reformers who agreed that disorderly cities needed a firm hand to lift them out of filth and misery. Improved streets and drainage opened the way for a broad vision of urban transparency and decongestion. Wide streets brought "light and air," which banished damp and disease along with its associated stench. Not only tuberculosis and typhoid, but also mental, moral, and criminal disorders fled from the light: the language of reform in all these endeavors was suffused with images of light and darkness. Modern streets, broad and straight, opened the way for health and virtue along with sunlight and traffic. These associations were so ingrained that they were seldom made explicit.

In typically English fashion, London resisted any grand plans. Lacking a metropolitan government for most of the century, it was poorly positioned to act boldly, but Parliament authorized one piece-meal street project after another during the course of the nineteenth century, even earlier in the case of the New Road bypass from the 1750s. Taken together, they reshaped the arteries of the metropolis while leaving many dark corners untouched—not unlike the more systematic reconstruction of Paris. The most ambitious was Regent Street (1816–24), which neatly separated the slums of Soho from the elegant West End. Later, New Oxford Street (1843–47) sliced through the notorious "Little Dublin" rookery in St. Giles. Then came Victoria Street (1845–51), Holborn Viaduct (1863–69), Queen Victoria Street (1867–71), Charing Cross Road and Shaftesbury Avenue (1884–87, knocking down more of St. Giles), and the Aldwych-Kingsway proj-ect (1899–1920). Vienna eased inner-city traffic with a few new and widened streets while also undertaking a grand project, the redevel-opment of its former fortification belt, which after 1858 was turned into the Ringstrasse quarter, centered on a spacious ring boulevard that gave the city a new center of activity as well as a striking con-trast to the dense core it surrounded. Other cities dismantling an-cient fortifications, notably Cologne, also seized the opportunity to encircle the crowded old town with wide streets. An even sharper contrast between an old city and its new extension was the vast grid designed by Ildefons Cerdà for Barcelona in the 1850s. Berlin pierced its small medieval core with the new Kaiser-Wilhelm-Strasse (now Karl-Liebknecht-Strasse) in the 1880s, and widened other streets, but most of its explosive late-century growth sprang up on vacant land. It was guided by a plan drawn up in 1862 by the young engi-neer James Hobrecht, who projected a network of wide streets far into the countryside that was rapidly being swallowed up by the city. To his dismay, the generous midblock spaces quickly filled up with densely packed tenement blocks (just as happened in Cerdà's Barce-lona). When combined with the new and widened streets through the old center, the result was a city of wide streets but with a large fraction of the population crowded into apartments that faced dim

FIG. 52. Vienna, Kärtnerring, 1890s. Library of Congress.

FIG. 53. Berlin-Friedrichshain, 1933. Aerial photograph by Walter Mittelholzer. ETH-Bibliothek Zürich, Bildarchiv.

courtyards. Vienna grew in a similar pattern, except that its streets were narrower.

The most celebrated and influential project of the century was the rebuilding of Paris by Emperor Napoleon III and his prefect Georges-Eugène Haussmann. It also offers the most striking evidence of the tangle of medical, moral, economic, technological, and political motives that converged in nineteenth-century street plans. The centerpiece of Haussmann's scheme was the network of broad, straight boulevards that pierced the dense inner city within the old boulevard ring. Previous regimes had sliced a few new streets through the inner city, but with the emperor's enthusiastic backing Haussmann was able to demolish and build on an unprecedented scale. His firm control of reconstruction also gave Paris its unmistakable look. In an era of private real estate development, he could not build the continuous and uniform façades that Bourbon kings had decreed at the Place Royale (now Place des Vosges), the Place Louis XIV (now Place Vendôme), and rue Royale. However, he constrained builders with strict codes that ensured a remarkably uniform appearance for the stately apartment buildings lining his new boulevards. Standardized building heights, alignment of stories and windows, carved stone façades, and iron balconies complemented his rigorous design rules for the boulevards' trees, sidewalks, and street furniture to define the city's look ever since. The wide streets also visibly fulfilled the era's goals of speedier traffic and abundant light and air, while the hygienic achievements were less visibly but no less crucially enhanced by new sewer and water systems that made the new boulevards, and also the narrow old streets, drier and less pungent places to walk.

Nineteenth-century urban planning has often been interpreted in narrowly political terms, especially in Paris. It was no accident that the broad, arrow-straight boulevards of Napoleon III's Paris proved well suited to marching soldiers and to cannon fire directed at insurrectionary workers. It has been a frequent mistake, however, to single out the political motive as the decisive one. From the eighteenth century onward, wide and straight streets promised to solve problems of sanitation, crowd control, transportation, and aesthetic

FIG. 54. Charles Marville, boulevard Saint-Germain, c. 1860.

order. The urban upper classes believed that the poor masses did, or soon would, appreciate the blessings of visible and rational order. The air in windswept boulevards seemed sweeter than in fetid lanes; sunlight enhanced hygiene, security, and splendor; the boulevards made it possible to move goods and passengers more rapidly; and the hygienists' demand for "light and air" became inseparable from prevailing ideals of architectural grandeur.

FROM THE STREET TO "PUBLIC SPACE"

Contemporaries praised Haussmann for revitalizing street life. George Sand, for one, found renewed pleasure in strolling, because the new boulevards "permit us to walk on and on, hands in pockets, without getting lost and without being forced at every moment to consult the affable grocer or the porter on the corner."[23] Their cafés, shops, and promenades drew the bourgeoisie onto the streets of central Paris, even as they also, by some accounts, obliterated the neighborhood street life of poor Parisians. The carefully regulated order of the boulevards—with their neat paving, curbs, walkways, benches, lampposts, kiosks, and disciplined trees—called to mind a

genteel bourgeois interior, suggesting to some observers that Haussmann had reversed the growing separation of private and public
life.[24] The new atmosphere of the bourgeois street was most striking in crowded Paris but not unique to it. Vienna's Ringstrasse and
broad new streets in London and Berlin also attracted theaters, department stores, cafés, and other nodes of activity that encouraged
well-heeled residents and visitors to stroll and linger. Well into the
twentieth century, Haussmann's boulevards inspired ambitious civic
leaders around the world. The combined traffic artery and tree-lined
promenade—punctuated by benches, kiosks, and sidewalk cafés—
became the iconic image of thriving metropolitan life in the years
around 1900.

The Viennese and Parisian boulevards inserted the Baroque avenue and the aristocratic promenade into the crowded nineteenth-
century city. Part of their appeal came from the addition of shopping
to the traditional promenade. Also important was, presumably, the
removal of odors, thanks to sewer construction and efficient street
cleaning—although the absence of smells, unlike their presence,
almost never merited notice in contemporary accounts. Like the
earlier promenades, but often more centrally located, the new boulevards served as magnificent showcases for the wealthy and powerful,
with everyone else permitted to come and watch. The sidewalk café,
already known from earlier promenades like the Grands Boulevards
and the Graben, invited spectators to linger and watch the crowds.
This enduring image of Parisian leisure was widely imitated from
Bucharest to Buenos Aires (although not so much across the English
Channel).

But the bourgeois boulevard carried the seeds of its own destruction, proving to be more of a transitional phase than an enduring
model for street design and use. One persistent problem was apparent in the uneasy class and gender relations that shaped the
nineteenth-century street and hastened the withdrawal from it. The
political uncertainties of the age reinforced the visceral discomfort
aroused by promiscuous street crowds. A suggestive anecdote is
offered by Heinrich Heine's 1831 description of the newly crowned

French King Louis-Philippe's attempts to appear as a man of the people: "He used to shake hands with every spice dealer and artisan, and it is said that he wore a special dirty glove for the purpose, which he took off and exchanged with a cleaner kid glove when he returned to the more elevated company of his old aristocrats, banker-ministers, and crimson lackeys."[25] (This was decades before the acceptance of the germ theory of disease.) Not that all fears of moral contamination were imaginary: consider the female shoppers on Regent Street and Oxford Street who wished to avoid the distress of being harassed by men who mistook them for prostitutes or merely pretended to do so, because their presence on the street made them fair game.

More pressing was the demand for speedy transportation in the rapidly expanding cities. The post-Haussmann transformation of street design can be seen in the career of the Viennese architect Otto Wagner, who established his reputation as a designer of buildings for the Ringstrasse quarter. He later became a pioneer in the simplification of street façades, changing his style from the ornate historicism of the early Ringstrasse era to Secession or Jugendstil elegance at the end of the century and ultimately to buildings nearly devoid of traditional ornament. Late in his career, in 1911, he wrote a pamphlet envisioning his city's future growth along wide radial boulevards that extended far into the countryside. Rapid transportation would coexist with strolling and shopping as "the uninterrupted profile of a thoroughfare adorned with elegant shops that display the finest products of city and country to the crowds rushing by" was complemented by "other streets suitable for a promenade where strollers may gaze at one another to their hearts' content."[26] The boulevard would continue to thrive, as long as rapid transport permitted access to the fresh air and open space of the country.

But the priority given to speedy movement threatened the leisurely atmosphere that attracted crowds. When efficient streets could offer shoppers a quick escape to more distant and exclusive precincts, the allure of display windows no longer guaranteed the vitality of the boulevards. The arcades of the early nineteenth century had already shown how to move shoppers off streets that were not pleasant places to linger. They were the precursors of Victor Gruen's mid-twentieth-century suburban malls: just as the arcade permitted the nineteenth-century bourgeois to shop in peace, undisturbed by speeding carriages and piles of dung, the immigrant American Gruen sought to recapture the appeal of streets from his native Vienna by separating cars from enclosed shopping corridors. The mall was a restored city street for the automotive age: a street without vehicular traffic, but also without the odors and filth—and, not incidentally, the beggars, hawkers, and political agitators—of its nineteenth-century ancestor.[27] By turning the "street" over to real estate developers and retail behemoths, the move to the mall revived old questions about who was or was not welcome in the places where people gather.

The mall and the automobile were twentieth-century developments, but shopping and traffic were already in conflict before 1900. What justified expensive street projects above all was the need for circulation: of air above, water and sewers below, and especially the wheeled traffic that increasingly dominated sight, sound, and space. The defining characteristic of the new streets was speed. After all, modern people were in a hurry, even pedestrians. During their day they expected to cover more territory than earlier aristocrats or merchants ever had. Their streets were transportation corridors, increasingly designed less for pedestrians than for carriages. The vectors of motion gave the city its dynamism, its modern appearance, and its practical justification. Architects like Wagner designed building façades with streamlined features and horizontal lines, to be taken in at a glance. Pedestrians felt out of place. The "Loss of a Halo" in Baudelaire's poem of that name happens when the poet crosses one of Haussmann's boulevards "in the midst of seething chaos, with death galloping at me from every side." The great caricaturist Honoré Daumier also captured the experience of the pedestrian in an 1862 drawing. In the foreground a stout bourgeois on a crowded sidewalk examines his watch and exclaims, "How fortunate it is for busy people that they have widened the thoroughfares!" Behind him we see a hapless figure risking life and limb to dance across the lanes

FIG. 55. Honoré Daumier, *Le Nouveau Paris: Comme c'est heureux pour les gens pressés qu'on ait élargi les voies de communication*, 1862. The Phillips Collection.

of speeding carriages, while an immobile crowd on the sidewalk watches and waits. Daumier's traffic-choked boulevard offers the pedestrian neither speed nor leisure, and its value as a promenade was increasingly in doubt, long before the onslaught of automobiles brought the crisis to a head.

The idea of abolishing the street arose even earlier in the nineteenth century. It can be found in the works of post-Enlightenment visionaries who dreamed of a revolutionary social order with entirely new cities. These utopian schemers have received far more attention from historians than they did from their contemporaries, in part be-

FIG. 56. Claude-Nicolas Ledoux, Royal Saltworks at Arc-et-Senans. Photograph by Zairon.

cause their elaborate but impractical schemes lay bare some of the deepest fears and aspirations of the age. The most audacious of them imagined a world without streets. The street was too uncomfortably diverse and exposed, a place of conflict and difference at odds with their visions of harmony and community. Claude-Nicolas Ledoux's ideal city from the 1770s dissolved the street into nature, leaving only the portico as a place to gather. A few decades later, Charles Fourier described a city that replaced streets with galleries like those of the Palais-Royal, while the visionary industrialist Robert Owen's plans offered cloisters in place of streets. The motives for and implications of these designs can be better understood with reference to the contemporaneous writings of Jeremy Bentham, whose model of the Panopticon envisaged perfectly ordered workshops and other establishments where no one could hide from view—a prototype that proved particularly well suited to the design of prisons. Bentham's "utilitarian" philosophy (as he called it) fused authority and surveillance to forge a social order that left nothing to chance.[28] For believers in the possibility of a rationally ordered society, the unplanned cacophony of the street was a mistake that could be corrected, with its many functions sorted out and supplanted. Their detailed schemes promised to organize and simplify urban life, starting with the street.

The scale and grandeur of the Baroque, the crowd control of the nineteenth century, and these utopian schemes, along with Bentham's ideal of perfect surveillance, all promised an urban order and clarity that appealed to twentieth-century autocrats. The everyday chaos of the streets did not. They sought to restore, and surpass, the real or imagined harmony of long-ago crowds. On their special occasions, they summoned larger throngs than medieval kings could ever have dreamed of. Mussolini staged ostentatious pageants that deliberately echoed those of the Roman emperors whose heir he claimed to be.[29] Hitler aimed to outdo his ally in crowd size and imperial grandeur. Fortunately the spectacles he enacted on his specially created parade ground in Nuremberg were never carved in stone in the center of Berlin or Vienna. Meanwhile, the megalomania of Hitler's rival Stalin was perhaps never quite as fully expressed, but the Communist regimes of the Soviet empire did regularly turn out orderly crowds to fill their vast and otherwise lifeless streets and squares. Prominent among their spectacles were military parades, intimidating and perhaps awe-inspiring spectacles following in the tradition of nineteenth-century rulers such as the Hohenzollerns of Berlin.

In democracies, too, the twentieth-century state extended its reach into city streets. Regimes of all kinds undertook radical urban surgery to create new cities that bore little resemblance to the old ones. Their combined ambitions of state control and orderly design added up to what James Scott has labeled "high modernism." The abolition of the street is a clear example of the visible imposition of centralized power as he describes it.[30] Ambitious urban reformers steeped in the new doctrines of modern architecture looked at city streets after 1900 and saw all the encrusted failures of the past: filth, disease, poverty, unfathomable and disorderly crowds, and sluggish movement. The modernists believed their visionary sketches could enlist the power of the state to bring to life the ideals of the nineteenth-century utopians.[31] The finest nineteenth-century streets merely hid the alleys and slums of the poor (as Lenin had observed in London), but the twentieth-century state could expose and destroy them. To get rid of the traditional street was to abolish archaic privileges and hierarchies on the way to a more just society, or at least a more malleable one.

By the early twentieth century, the most ambitious of Hauss-

mann's heirs questioned the continued usefulness of streets combining such a wide variety of functions in an architectural frame
firmly rooted in the past. Their most visible targets were the often absurdly ornate façades that emphatically demarcated the space of the
street. Architects mounted an assault on the very idea of the façade.
In 1898 the young Viennese architect Adolf Loos denounced his city's
Ringstrasse as a "Potemkin City."[32] A minor but revealing rejection
of the traditional street wall appeared in Paris's 1902 building regulations, which offered incentives to property owners to set their buildings back from the street line in order to break up the visual unity
of the façades in favor of greenery and variety.[33] Among the proudest
achievements of modernist architects in the following years was the
use of steel framing and glass curtain walls to visually dissolve the
distinction between outside and inside. A more radical reimagining
of the street had already been proposed in the 1880s by Arturo Soria
y Mata, whose model of the "linear city" dissolved city and countryside alike in favor of development along spacious transportation
corridors. The rejection of the street later received its most pointed
formulation from Le Corbusier, the seductive Swiss prophet of the
bold new city, who peddled his schemes to any government willing
to take him on. For him the worst crime of the nineteenth-century
city was the "corridor street," that is, the street lined with buildings
and embedded in an urban fabric. Its obvious problems of sanitation
and circulation fed a sense of aesthetic and moral horror that rallied
many reformers to Le Corbusier's cry, "we must kill the street!"[34]

The unease with the street could be visceral, aesthetic, or political, or all at once as with Le Corbusier. For him the traditional street
was "plunged in eternal twilight" and "no more than a trench" but
also "a sea of lusts and faces." He claimed to speak for everyone:
"Although we have been accustomed to it for more than a thousand
years, our hearts are always oppressed by the constriction of its enclosing walls," whether or not we encounter crowds. On the one hand,
"the street is full of people: one must take care where one goes." But
"on Sundays, when they are empty, the streets reveal their full horror." In any guise, "the street wears us out. And when all is said and

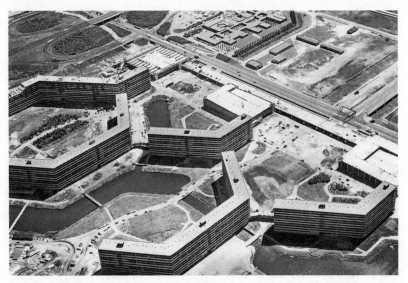

FIG. 57. Amsterdam-Bijlmermeer. Stadsarchief Amsterdam.

done we have to admit it disgusts us. . . . Heaven preserve us from those Balzacians who eagerly seek the drama of faces in the black depths of Parisian streets."[35]

Rather than reform the traditional street, Le Corbusier and his allies proposed to separate its functions. The *Charter of Athens*, an influential modernist manifesto shaped by Le Corbusier, demanded that housing be set apart from traffic routes. Another foundational text, by Sigfried Giedion, explained that Haussmann's great achievements were insufficient: "The first thing to do is abolish the rue corridor with its rigid lines of buildings and its intermingling of traffic, pedestrians, and houses. The fundamental constitution of the contemporary city requires the restoration of liberty to all three— to traffic, to pedestrians, and to residential and industrial quarters. This can be accomplished only by separating them."[36] Or as a Berlin planner put it soon after 1900, "Children, like automobiles, must be able to romp about," and obviously not in the same spaces.[37] The reorganized city would have no more street walls to keep people in the shadows, trapped in crowds between grotesque façades. Street shops and street traffic would disappear, with commerce relocated to properly specialized facilities such as shopping malls, and transportation diverted to exclusive corridors, preferably limited-access highways reserved for motor vehicles. If the traditional street was understood to have three essential functions—transportation, shopping, and recreation—then the highway, the shopping center, and the park together offered a superior replacement for Haussmann's boulevard. The sanitary and aesthetic ideal of light and air could escape the linear form entirely.

Instead of sharply defined corridor streets, planners sought to disperse urban housing across abundant open spaces that promised a pastoral ideal of sunlight and recreation. The nineteenth century had already seen influential movements to create urban parks and playgrounds in order to move recreation off the street. The English model of the "garden city" proposed to organize entire towns around green space rather than street space. Visionary plans from the 1920s, many of them coming out of Weimar Germany and the new Soviet Union, uncoupled buildings from streets. They imagined sidewalk, playground, and park flowing together in an expansive and even borderless landscape that would provide ample light, air, and recreational opportunities. The twentieth century sometimes ennobled this leftover territory by labeling it "public space" and designating it as a kind of modern agora, a truly democratic space, free of the hierarchies and encrusted traditions as well as the sensory overload of the old streets.[38] In actual projects, though, from St. Louis to Leningrad, Brasilia to Chandigarh, attention to the open space was typically an afterthought. Streets were redesigned for rapid transportation, and Le Corbusier's ideal "city made for speed" became a city made for avoiding the friction of public encounters. The spaces created by (or left over from) modernist urban designs rarely became civic gathering places, far less than the streets they were supposed to replace. Too often, public space for all turned out to be space for no one.

The destruction of the established forms of the street, intended as the abolition of old hierarchies, proved less well suited to participatory democracies than to the autocrats who sought to flatten social hierarchies into an undifferentiated mass. The new designs ensured that crowds would rarely assemble without coercion. Planners who genuinely hoped to create a civic space, a new agora, were often disappointed with the results of their work, whether in the low-density suburbs typical of the Anglo-American world (but also increasingly common on the Continent) or the high-rise satellite towns in their eastern and western European varieties.[39] Their doctrine of "functionalism," of planning and designing separate facilities for each designated purpose, codified the gradual disentangling of the street's traditional uses. It promised to replace chaotic streets with something more orderly. The result, however, usually lacked both the architectural definition and the civic traditions of the old street wall.

Conclusion

Looking Down on the Street

After 1900, European cities became the envy of the world: remarkably clean, attractive, and pleasant places to work and visit, to walk and linger, as was apparent in the appeal of the Parisian boulevards and the many attempts to imitate them. The paradox of twentieth-century cities is that they increasingly boasted streets that were clean, safe—and empty. Shopping, socializing, and politics moved elsewhere and, most conspicuously, the automobile arrived to carry people away. Streets no longer mattered as much, as the Google Ngrams of word use suggest.

There were many reasons to abandon the street. People sought greater privacy, either as solitude or as a shell around the family— that is, they tried to avoid the eyes, ears, and bodies of strangers. Stricter standards of hygiene accompanied a greater discomfort with the public display of bodily functions. Trains, planes, and automobiles created expectations of rapid mobility. The expanding scale of urban and national economies reduced the role of small-time traders while moving retail and industry into larger, enclosed establishments. The growth of mass politics and of more powerful and centralized governments sometimes drew enormous crowds into the streets but also made authorities more keen to disperse them or, better yet, to remove the opportunities for them to gather.

One result was a changed understanding of a successful street. A street thronged with people was obviously an attractive place, in a literal sense, but its very crowding came to be seen as a problem to be solved. The removal of activities from the street, and thus the removal of people, became the goal of much twentieth-century urban planning.

THE MAGISTERIAL VIEW

Streamlined and simplified streets made sense to planners and rulers who gazed at them from afar. Resistance came from others who cherished the intimacy of a crowded street or its dazzling variety of people and activities. In other words, two fundamentally different ways of thinking about streets corresponded to two ways of observing them, and two ways of designing them: the magisterial and the plebeian. The first is the view from outside or above, or perhaps from a speeding vehicle, while the second is a pedestrian's perspective from within the throng—and is, unlike the first, not merely a way of looking, since the pedestrian also hears, smells, and feels the life of the street.[1] Nineteenth-century art and literature gives us a great deal of the latter, often through the mythologized perspective of the flâneur, the knowing outsider who plunges into the crowd. But already at its nineteenth-century birth, the figure of the flâneur was under threat from those who sought to organize the crowd from outside or above it. For educated visitors more generally, the preferred image of a city became the panorama rather than the hawker or the churning crowd. The twentieth century analyzed streets as systems, not places.

Planners of streets and cities have long taken the magisterial view. Kings and other rulers surveyed streets from a hilltop castle or a palace window, or they imagined a bird's-eye perspective even before balloons and airplanes furnished them with aerial photographs. When they entered the street, they did so in a formal procession before an orderly crowd. We have records of such processions in many cities, over many centuries. Stone ruins bear witness to grand ceremonial ways dating back thousands of years in Mesopotamian and

Mesoamerican cities. European Renaissance princes who continued the processional tradition sometimes built wide, straight streets for the purpose. By the seventeenth and eighteenth centuries, Baroque avenues in many capitals directed the eye toward a palace or other monument (see fig. 2, p. 21). Beyond those central axes, rulers and administrators increasingly conceived of the city as a whole: as a grand work of art; as an organism whose life depended on circulation (of air, water, bodies, goods, and vehicles, rather than blood); or as a machine.

Their aesthetic and scientific theories set the agenda for nineteenth-century urban reforms, most visibly in their passion for wide streets. Georges-Eugène Haussmann was the most admired planner of the nineteenth century because he used the unprecedented authority granted him by Emperor Napoleon III to make the century's favorite metropolis legible to outsiders: to foreigners, rural visitors, and the Parisian upper classes. Both men approached their job as the outsiders they were. Their collaboration began with the emperor's sketch map of his proposed new streets, and the prefect then had towers built to gather survey data for a more detailed map.[2] Outsiders also gave us our standard account of pre-Haussmann Paris: the impenetrable morass of dank lanes, teeming with suspicious characters. And it was the outsiders who applauded Haussmann's wide, straight boulevards sliced through the old city, enabling their carriages to race through town while also offering dramatic vistas and spaces for middle-class leisure. Streets conceived as transportation corridors were channels, not destinations. It made sense to envision them from a distance, since what mattered was their role as arteries (in the biological metaphor) or conveyors (in the mechanical one), not the experience at any given point along them.[3]

Twentieth-century rulers and architects sought to emulate Haussmann's grand gestures on an even wider scale. His influence is most obvious in the planning of new cities and the radical reconstruction of old ones. It proved particularly well-suited to autocratic and revolutionary regimes such as Russia and China while also appealing to many other governments of widely varied political ideologies. Most democracies embarked on ambitious urban clearance and highway schemes that promised to wipe away the medically, morally, and aesthetically suspect streets and crowds. Even nations constitutionally committed to decentralized and limited government, notably the United States, embraced these sweeping powers.

Twentieth-century traffic engineers were among Haussmann's heirs. Their vantage point, like his, was the map or model that reduced a city and its streets to a network of intersecting vectors. Haussmann's early admirers included the German authors of the first manuals of urban planning, Reinhard Baumeister and Josef Stübben, who made Haussmann's boulevards the template for every new street network. With the arrival of the automobile, many of their successors rejected the traditional street entirely and produced plans to segregate motor vehicles from other street users. Their work grew out of the functionalist doctrines that condemned the street as a confused muddle of overlapping systems.

Le Corbusier, the most peremptory of the modernist ideologues, left no doubt that he took the magisterial view. The city was, "for the princes, the spirit of enlightenment: order and authority, visibility and discipline, a broad view: this was architecture." His heroes were Louis XIV and Napoleon III, who surveyed Paris from on high and decreed grand new thoroughfares. Where these were not built, the people suffered—or so Le Corbusier judged from his perch: "Like so many ants or bees, they shuffled back and forth, in and out, nested in tiny honeycomb cells, and bustled about in constricted and tortuous passageways." Like the princes, he gazed into these narrow lanes and saw trouble brewing: "Out of the jumble of hovels, from the depths of the lairs, there sometimes came a gust of rebellion, a conspiracy hatched in that chaotic darkness where any policing is a challenge."[4] With these words, Le Corbusier sought his patrons among the twentieth century's autocrats. They could give him the power he craved, and he could promise to extinguish the embers of insurrection.

Le Corbusier may have been unusually fastidious in his discomfort with crowds and bodies, and particularly vehement in expressing it, but his palpable disdain, even fear, was widely shared. Those who surveyed the street from above, actually or virtually, seldom wished to mingle with the crowd. They recoiled from the sounds and aromas and bodies of the street. They preferred the purified, deodorized space of the twentieth-century city, where commodities were neatly packaged, bodies no longer collided, and the friction of the crowd neither slowed traffic nor produced dangerous political sparks. When Europeans carried this way of thinking to the south and east of the Mediterranean, they gave it an even clearer form in colonial cities that neatly separated airy European quarters from ancient warrens of alleys and markets. The widened, segregated, simplified street was the building block of a new and rational order, at home and abroad.

THE PLEBEIAN VIEW

For all its influence on the shaping of twentieth-century cities, this magisterial way of looking can tell us little about street life: its proponents stood in bright sunshine while peering into dark alleys. In 1900, however, most citizens were still stuck on the crowded streets. Many uses of the street remained unchanged from decades or even centuries before. Labor spilled out from workshops; buyers and sellers came together in street markets; neighbors exchanged news and intrigue, argued and settled disputes, debated politics, and gathered on the way to and from the church or the pub. Some social and economic activity had moved off the streets, but much had not. There was an order to the street, or rather many kinds of order, but it was invisible to outsiders, and therefore disturbing to rulers and planners. Not everyone shared their desperate desire to burst open the intimate old streets. In full awareness of the misery of the slums and the benefits of modern innovations, some dissenters reveled in the excitement of the crowd, the personal negotiations of the market, and the unpredictable human contact on the street.

The German scholar and statesman Wilhelm von Humboldt is best known as an advocate of the bookish cultivation of classical culture and as the father of Germany's rigorous school curriculum.

We might expect him to be the kind of intellectual repelled by the "monstrous swarm" of "dirty Paris," as he described it in a 1789 letter. But he was not: "On the other hand, it gives me a pleasant feeling. In the ceaseless whirl, in the indescribable mass of humanity, the individual vanishes so completely that no one pays heed to anyone else, no one shows any consideration to anyone; indeed, one is pulled along in the current so forcefully that one feels like a mere drop in the ocean. I like it."[5]

Soon many German intellectuals embracing the new Romantic outlook developed their own attachment to cozy medieval towns, especially those they believed to be steeped in German history. The young Berlin law student Wilhelm Wackenroder's fond recollection of a 1793 journey to Nuremberg—"how happily I wander through your winding lanes!"—expressed his belief that he was absorbing the spirit of Albrecht Dürer and other medieval and Renaissance artists.[6] A more cosmopolitan Romantic was the distinguished landscape gardener Prince Hermann von Pückler-Muskau, who in the 1820s praised such towns as Utrecht and Limerick for their dark, narrow, and winding streets. "This kind of town reminds me of a natural forest, whose dark shadows, high and low, reveal a variety of sylvan streets and often a green roof like that of a Gothic church. Orderly modern cities more resemble a pruned French garden. They don't appeal to my romantic taste."[7] Later in the century, as the old lanes were being rapidly pruned, Romantic sentiment grasped at their dwindling remnants. Wilhelm Raabe's 1856 novel *The Chronicle of Sparrow Lane* opens with an affectionate look at the fast-disappearing corners of old Berlin: "In big cities I love these old neighborhoods with their narrow, crooked lanes, where sunshine is a rare visitor. . . . Here in these twisted lanes the carefree people live hard by the industrious and the serious, and the crowding presses the people together in livelier and more amusing scenes than in the more elegant but also more desolate streets."[8]

Amid the praise for the most dramatic modernization project, Haussmann's destruction of old Paris, a minority rallied to the defense of their city's vanishing charms. The most prominent critic

FIG. 58. Berlin, Fischerstrasse, 1903. Photograph by Waldemar Titzenthaler.

was Victor Hugo, whose 1831 novel *The Hunchback of Notre Dame* had popularized a sentimental vision of the lost glories of medieval Paris. It was this emerging fascination with an urban "picturesque" that Jules Janin pilloried in 1844. Janin charged that Hugo and his ilk "ridicule this city, so well paved, well guarded, well lit, and well washed every morning." They long for the "dark houses, airless lanes devoid of sun, thieves in every street. . . . Long life then to the black, gothic, filthy, feverish city, the city of darkness, disorder, violence, misery, and blood!" Their hatred of the new Paris, he continued, was laughably perverse: "As for the most beautiful streets in Paris, where the inhabitant of the city walks so serenely and so proudly, the Parisian has never been so absurdly foolish than in admiring these vast openings, filled with air, movement, space, and sun. For instance, is it possible to imagine anything more tedious than the rue de Rivoli, where you walk with dry feet, where you are sheltered from the rain in winter and the dust in summer, and where the finest shops vie with each other to offer you the treasures of the world?"[9] This was at a time when the wide, straight, arcaded rue de Rivoli, still only half built, was a rare and singular modern street. A few years later Haussmann began to replicate it (minus arcades) across central Paris, to Hugo's horror.

Photographers hurried into condemned neighborhoods to record their vanishing evils—or charms. The pioneer was Charles Marville, who received privileged access to Parisian quarters condemned by Haussmann, in order to document them for posterity. Berlin's most eminent photographers flocked to the Krögel, a rare medieval lane, after its demolition was decreed in the 1880s. For reformers like Haussmann, images of the old lanes offered evidence of the bad old days. The photographers' attitudes are less clear. Their pictures suggest more fascination than revulsion. Like his contemporaries Thomas Annan in Glasgow and Georg Koppmann in Hamburg, Marville captured an alluring sense of mystery in the old streets and avoided calling attention to their filth (see fig. 39, p. 167).[10]

Although Janin's scorn was still widely shared later in the century, Hugo's nostalgia gained adherents as the old streets disappeared. Marville's photographs revealed an intimate urban scale that was vanishing from Paris and the other burgeoning metropolises. Would-be flâneurs feared the demise of their breed. For example, Victor Fournel complained that Haussmann, the "Attila of the straight line," had robbed him of the pleasure of exploring his city's obscure corners.[11] Part of the bohemian appeal of the hilltop quarter of Montmartre at the end of the century might be explained by its steep and winding lanes that escaped redevelopment.

There is no doubt that architectural fashions in streets, as in much else, do change, but material reasons help explain these aesthetic choices. By the late nineteenth century, when the narrow lanes of old European towns were attracting many admirers, modern sewage systems and other municipal services were making them more pleasant places to linger. In 1897 the rapid electrification of Berlin's trams launched the critic Alfred Kerr into a mock eulogy for horse manure in the street, "those little piles that used to poke out from between the rails" with their "melancholy charm," evocative of a vanishing rural life.[12] Kerr's obituary was premature, since plodding horses continued to pull freight wagons through the streets for decades. But the fact that anyone could imagine being nostalgic about dung shows us how much had changed by the end of the century, and how different the atmosphere of the twentieth-century city promised to be, even if Kerr's obdurate Viennese counterpart Karl Kraus insisted that the dung would "never, ever" go away, despite the electrification of the city's trams, because Vienna's essential aroma was "paradise with horse dung."[13] A new German fastidiousness was apparent to the Berlin critic Karl Scheffler by 1908. His city had outpaced Paris in matters of cleanliness, he declared, but this was not unalloyed progress: "Order is not culture, as we see in Paris. Even the filth is picturesque there, since it is a historic ingredient of popular life."[14]

This nagging, if perverse, sense of loss contributed to a backlash against Haussmann-style redevelopment, led by influential artists, architects, and civic leaders. One notable result was a growing movement to preserve historic buildings and entire historic districts. A similar desire to retain the older scale of streets was apparent in the surprising popularity of the Viennese architect Camillo Sitte's idiosyncratic 1889 book *City Building According to Artistic Principles*. Sitte persuaded readers across Europe that the modern vogue of wide streets and windswept squares was shattering the intimate beauty of European cities. He and his acolytes heaped praise on the enclosed squares and winding lanes that had long been out of fashion among rulers and planners. Sitte traveled extensively to document the design of pre-nineteenth-century European squares and to contrast the aesthetically successful ones with those that had lost their human scale. He judged the beauty of squares by the sense of comfort they imparted to a visitor. His search for extant historical models to guide urban planning echoed many European intellectuals' growing attachment to the vanishing traces of past centuries.[15] Indeed, strikingly similar views appeared in an 1893 book by the Brussels mayor Charles Buls, even though Buls appears not to have read Sitte.[16]

Sitte charged that modern planners' obsession with circulation had left them blind to the qualities of urban places. He was appalled by the failure of Vienna's new Ringstrasse to offer any repose amid its relentless flow of traffic.[17] Buls took a similar tack, lamenting architects' tendency to "take a bird's-eye view of their plans."[18] By embracing the pedestrian perspective, Sitte offered urban planners a method to overcome their discomfort with crowds and bodies. Even if Sitte himself expressed no affinity for crowds, he did give voice to a revulsion at the desolate spaces produced by modern planning. He suggested that the "very new and modern ailment" of "agoraphobia," first named by psychiatrists in the late nineteenth century, was caused by people's uneasiness in modern squares. It was a feeling of vulnerability triggered by the removal of intimate architectural frames, "our natural craving for protection from the flank."[19] The pedestrian, finding the new boulevards inhospitable, fled into the old confined lanes.

The planners' debates seldom engaged the voices of street users. Each side claimed the support of the masses, but without any solid evidence. Certainly both could point to measurable advantages of their favored designs. Drainage, sunlight, and electric trams offered obvious benefits to the urban poor, while the destruction of their old neighborhoods, and the resulting displacement, disrupted social and economic networks and sometimes forced poor workers to move far away from their relatives and workplaces. Rarely did anyone in power stop to ponder the question of whether residents preferred to make their streets and cities anew or to preserve the places and forms that shaped their identities and sustained collective memories.

To some extent Sitte was engaging the magisterial perspective on its own terms. His book is filled with carefully drawn diagrams of old squares and the streets that issued from them, mostly sketched from church towers. But his analyses reinforced the flâneur's veneration of the crowd and suggested a model of street life at odds with that of most planners, one that reveled in the kaleidoscopic experience of the crowded street. They buttressed a modern, scholarly case for intimate urban spaces—as beautiful, as comforting, and even as effective filters for traffic. A few planners preached similar doctrines throughout the mid-twentieth century, with little success.[20]

For Sitte and others, the view from above could not replace the experience of the street. In his travels during the 1850s, the Berlin writer Theodor Fontane wearied of being led up towers to gain distance from city streets. What was the point of looking at a town from above? "Our buildings still pay proper respect to people who walk. If we ever fly, that will be the age of rooftops. All the façade decoration will find its place on the roof, the house's new front, and *then* the traveler can climb towers."[21] Three decades earlier, E. T. A. Hoffmann found that a high perch merely revived his longing for the crowd. Hoffmann, who had set several of his famously eerie tales amid the shadows and crumbling walls of Berlin's empty nighttime streets, used his story "My Cousin's Corner Window" to show how the public scene sustained the narrator's invalid cousin, a writer too infirm to leave his garret. The unfortunate man rouses himself from his lethargy as he charms his visitor with a virtual guided tour of the market day unfolding in the square below. He points down at particular women and men making their way through the crowd and turns them into his own fictional characters by inventing back stories of their haggling, flirting, squabbling, and reconciliation. Market day, the cousin concludes, is society in miniature: "Momentary needs drive the mass of people together; then, after a few brief moments, everything is deserted, the tangled din of voices falls silent, and each abandoned spot presents an all too vivid reminder of what was."

Hoffmann's own enthusiasm is apparent, tempered as it is by this melancholy note at the end. Indeed, his self-portrait is not the visiting narrator but rather the invalid cousin who keenly feels his separation from the life-sustaining crowd. Hoffmann wrote the story in 1822 while confined to his room overlooking Berlin's Gendarmenmarkt, site of a semi-weekly outdoor market. A few weeks later he succumbed to the syphilis that had already robbed him of his mobility.[22]

Haussmann's boulevards created new opportunities to watch the crowds from above. Paris's characteristic iron balconies first appeared on fashionable townhouses in the seventeenth century, but they truly flourished as standard features of the elegant apartment buildings that lined Haussmann's new boulevards.[23] They could serve various purposes, one of which might be to display oneself to the crowds below, but certainly part of their attraction was the chance to watch the passing crowd at a safe remove. They became a favored perch of Impressionist painters such as Caillebotte and Pissarro who sought to capture the color and motion of the boulevards on their canvases.

Balconies were rarer in poor neighborhoods. For generations after Hoffmann, an iconic sight in Berlin working-class districts was a head and forearms resting on a cushion planted on the sill of an upper-story apartment window. Whether the observer was noticed from the street didn't really matter, in the anonymity of the big city. On a busy street, the overhead observer could count on a degree of invisibility, since the gaze of those trapped in the throng rarely strayed upward. Too many distractions, whether eye-catching diversions or just the need to avoid collisions, ensured that their attention remained focused near at hand. Siegfried Kracauer, a keen observer of early twentieth-century Berlin, made that point in a brief feuilleton in 1933. He called his readers' attention to the heaving steam locomotives that stopped directly above central Berlin's bustling Friedrichstrasse as they waited to pull out from the elevated Friedrichstrasse station. He fancied that he alone noticed them. "Cafés, window displays, women, automats, headlines, neon signs, cops, buses, theater photos, beggars: all of these impressions at ground level occupy the

FIG. 59. Gustave Caillebotte, *Young Man at His Window*, 1875.

passerby far too much for him to notice the specter on the horizon."
On a narrow and crowded street like Friedrichstrasse, he mused,
everything above the ground floor simply evaporated, even a hulk-
ing locomotive, to say nothing of a stucco caryatid or a carved lin-
tel—or a face at a window. No matter how ornate a building's upper
façade, no matter what was happening behind it, it didn't really exist.

   "But what a show Friedrichstrasse presents to the man in the locomotive!" Kracauer proceeded to paint the scene from the perspective of the locomotive driver, just arrived from a nighttime passage
across a dark and empty countryside, and stunned by the dazzling
phantasmagoria suddenly spread out beneath him. He, at least, was
in a position to appreciate the view. The whirl of noise, lights, and
crowds on Friedrichstrasse might astonish this hypothetical visitor
from the country. Or he might be dismayed by it. But if he never dis-

FIG. 60. Berlin, Friedrichstrasse, postcard, c. 1913. © 123RF.com.

embarked and plunged into the swarm, he could not possibly understand it. His magisterial perch recalled that of rulers and planners
whose fears and obsessions increasingly shaped the modern city.

Kracauer's essay appeared in a newspaper on January 28, 1933.
While the ominous drama of German politics was undoubtedly
weighing on his mind, he probably did not intend any connection
between his rural locomotive driver and the stridently anti-urban political party whose charismatic leader took control of Berlin and Germany two days later, even though the Nazis were fond of denouncing
"asphalt democracy" and Hitler himself was obsessed with the purity
of bodies (and in later years spent hours gazing down at his model of
a new Berlin of vast boulevards and gaping squares). We can count
Kracauer, who fled into lifelong exile a few weeks later, among those
who exulted in the "swarm of vehicles and people" where "glare and
hubbub blend together in an unbridled celebration" that "encompasses rich and poor, whores and gentlemen."[24]

THE PERSISTENCE OF THE STREET

Through all reforms and regimes, this passionate love of streets has
never gone away. Nor have all the beloved streets themselves. Lon-

don, Paris, Berlin, and Vienna, along with other large and bustling cities, have maintained many lively streets. Despite the supremacy of automotive traffic on nearly all of them, sidewalk activity in familiar forms continued throughout the past century. But across Europe and beyond, that kind of street gradually became more the exception than the rule. Twentieth-century urban policy rarely attended to the quality of street space. In promoting circulation and speed, light and air, surveillance and control, distance and separation, it held to its magisterial perspective and accelerated, or completed, the nineteenth century's flight from the street, with the automobile as the primary instrument of this transformation. Cars removed the privileged few, and then many more, from the space and time of the city street. In outlying districts, in newer or smaller cities, and in suburbs, most streets were built as, or transformed into, monofunctional transportation corridors, where pedestrians, vendors, and idlers were few and far between. Even Paris, the consummate city of urban strolling, narrowed the sidewalks on its boulevards to make more room for cars.

By the end of the twentieth century, dozens of cities around the world had reached or exceeded the size of London and Paris. Many of them can boast streets as animated, thrilling, and disturbing as the now-tamed streets of Europe once were, with all the challenges to sanitation, mobility, and comfort. Complaints about cleanliness and traffic are the norm, and the prevailing response is little changed from that of Europe a century ago: sweep away vendors and other street people, make room for vehicles, move activities indoors or out of town—solutions that reflect the magisterial aversion to the chaotic crowd.

The twenty-first century also promises an insidious electronic version of the magisterial gaze. Proposals for "smart cities" envision networks of sensors that monitor activity and trigger signals from an electronic brain that can intervene far more quickly than a cop or a planner. These tools are applied most obviously to the regulation of traffic flow, but they can monitor and map any street activity. Although "big data" does not have to serve a central authority, and could be used to enhance the pedestrian experience, we can expect centralized surveillance and magisterial solutions to emerge from the systems of urban governance that developed to regulate commerce, sanitation, and circulation.[25]

The twentieth century's distaste for streets may be far from dead, but efforts to revive them have gained steam in recent decades. Discontent with amorphous and lifeless public spaces fueled interest in the shape and dynamism of the traditional European street. Yet no one really wants to return to the streets of 1900, to say nothing of 1700. Not only have standards of hygiene changed. So have thresholds of acceptable noise and odor as well as expectations of privacy and personal space. In a world of automobile drivers, earbuds, and virtual spaces, bodies in public have to devise new protocols of interaction.[26] Profound changes in retail economies and in expectations of mobility also demand different kinds of streets.

Nevertheless, Victor Gruen's mid-twentieth-century hopes for the suburban mall have returned in the recent commercial renaissance of many traffic-calmed urban streets. Ideally, everyone can now be a promenading aristocrat, or at least a bourgeois shopper, back again on the street, and engaging in time-honored social rituals. These ideals often fall short of reality in ways that do echo history. Although no one is barred from these streets, not everyone is made to feel welcome in their shops and cafés or even on the newly enhanced pavements. As in the nineteenth and twentieth centuries, the presence of too many poor people can drive away the well-to-do. Today the streets in many cities are believed to be cleaner and safer than in decades, with good reason, and they hold renewed appeal as places to linger. But that appeal depends on keeping the wrong sort of activities—and, often, the wrong sort of people—at a safe distance. As with the eighteenth-century promenade, both the right physical setting and the right mix of people are necessary for a street to thrive. Echoes of the nineteenth century can be heard in contemporary worries about ensuring the safety or comfort of women in the streets amid changing gender relations. Protests against gentrification often reflect a well-founded fear that the fashionable rediscovery of old streets is pushing the poor and the undesirable out of their remaining spaces, as in Haussmann's Paris. Some combination of custom, policing, and design always enforces the order of the street. Features designed to make middle-class visitors comfortable can also exclude the poor and the different.

For all their salutary caution, many civic leaders and urban designers sense that their communities lack something vital: the stimulation and serendipity of the crowd. Their efforts to reclaim streets for strolling, shopping, and entertainment seek to attract new crowds—if perhaps homogenous and controlled crowds. They look to the traditional street wall as an effective container for their renewed desire to bring people together. For better or worse, the thrill of the street retains its hold. Successful streets have rarely, if ever, been democratic, and they have certainly not been orderly. But they have often been diverse and vibrant places, and as such, they sustain possibilities of encounter and inclusion.

Notes

INTRODUCTION

1   Victor Dover and John Massengale, *Street Design: The Secret to Great Cities and Towns* (Hoboken, NJ: Wiley, 2014); Allan B. Jacobs, *Great Streets* (Cambridge, MA: MIT Press, 1993); Jan Gehl, *Life Between Buildings: Using Public Space* (New York: Van Nostrand Reinhold, 1987).

2   "Public space" became a metaphor for the processes of modern politics, often without any particular spatial connotation. As an abstract notion, most often derived from the theories of Jürgen Habermas, public space encompasses the civil society that emerged as a counterpart to private family life. Some confusion arises from the fact that Habermas's term "Öffentlichkeit," literally "public-ness," is sometimes translated as "public space" (otherwise as "public realm"), which suggests a geographical or spatial connotation not in the German original. Colin Jones, "Meeting, Greeting and Other 'Little Customs of the Day' on the Streets of Late Eighteenth-Century Paris," in *The Politics of Gesture: Historical Perspectives*, ed. Michael J. Braddick (Oxford: Oxford University Press, 2009), 144–71, is critical of attempts to apply Habermas's theories to physical space and streets. On more engaged and political implications of urban public space, see Lyn H. Lofland, *A World of Strangers: Order and Action in Urban Public Space* (Prospect Heights, IL: Waveland, 1973); Lofland, *The Public Realm* (New York: Aldine de Gruyter, 1998); Don Mitchell, *The Right to the City: Social Justice and the Fight for Public Space* (New York: Guilford, 2003); and the more historical approaches of Peter G. Goheen, "Public Space and the Geography of the Modern City," *Progress in Human Geography* 22 (1998): 479–96; Marshall Berman, "Take It to the Streets," *Dissent* 33 (1986): 476–85; and Mona Domosh, "Those 'Gorgeous Incongruities': Polite Politics and Public Space on the Streets of Nineteenth-Century New York City," *Annals of the Association of American Geographers* 88 (1998): 209–26.

3   Important exceptions include James Winter, *London's Teeming Streets* (London: Routledge, 1993), and the introductory sections of Thomas Lindenberger, *Strassenpolitik: Zur Sozialgeschichte der öffentlichen Ordnung in Berlin 1900 bis*

1914 (Bonn: Dietz, 1995). A book on a different era, dependent on different kinds of evidence, but in the spirit of this one, is Jeremy Hartnett, *The Roman Street: Urban Life and Society in Pompeii, Herculaneum, and Rome* (New York: Cambridge University Press, 2017). Outside Europe, see Dell Upton, *Another City: Urban Life and Urban Spaces in the New American Republic* (New Haven, CT: Yale University Press, 2008); Christine Stansell, *City of Women: Sex and Class in New York, 1789–1860* (Urbana: University of Illinois Press, 1986); Peter C. Baldwin, *Domesticating the Street: The Reform of Public Space in Hartford, 1850–1930* (Columbus: Ohio State University Press, 1999); Michael Bruce Kahan, "Pedestrian Matters: The Contested Meanings and Uses of Philadelphia's Streets, 1850s–1920s" (PhD diss., University of Pennsylvania, 2002); Andrew Brown-May, *Melbourne Street Life* (Kew: Australian Scholarly, 1997). A recent effort to place revolutions in particular streets is Mike Rapport, *The Unruly City: Paris, London and New York in the Age of Revolution* (New York: Basic Books, 2017).

4   A synthesis of architectural and political history that takes a top-down view, very unlike this book's despite an overlap of subject matter, is Donald J. Olsen, *The City as a Work of Art: London, Paris, Vienna* (New Haven, CT: Yale University Press, 1986). The discussions of design in my book do owe something to the wide-ranging, architecture-centered works of Spiro Kostof, *The City Shaped: Urban Patterns and Meanings through History* (Boston: Bulfinch, 1991), and *The City Assembled: The Elements of Urban Form through History* (Boston: Bulfinch, 1992), and Mark Girouard, *Cities and People: A Social and Architectural History* (New Haven, CT: Yale University Press, 1985), as well as his more narrowly focused *The English Town: A History of Urban Life* (New Haven, CT: Yale University Press, 1990). A recent addition is Vittorio Magnago Lampugnani, *Die Stadt von der Neuzeit bis zum 19. Jahrhundert: Urbane Entwürfe in Europa und Nordamerika* (Berlin: Wagenbach, 2017).

5   The most influential discussion of the distinctions between lived and perceived space—filtered, however, through his own terminology and his activist agenda—is that of Henri Lefebvre, *The Production of Space*, trans. Donald Nicholson-Smith (Oxford: Blackwell, 1991), 38–39. Also see David Harvey, "Space as a Key Word," in *Spaces of Global Capitalism* (London: Verso, 2006), 119–48, who argues that Lefebvre derived his categories from Ernst Cassirer, *An Essay on Man* (New Haven, CT: Yale University Press, 1944), 43. On the history of the senses, see, among others, Constance Classen, ed., *A Cultural History of the Senses*, 6 vols. (London: Bloomsbury, 2014); Mark M. Smith, *Sensing the Past* (Berkeley: University of California Press, 2007); David Garrioch, "Sounds of the City: The Soundscape of Early Modern European Towns," *Urban History* 30 (2003): 5–25; Bruce R. Smith, *The Acoustic World of Early Modern England* (Chicago: University of Chicago Press, 1999); John M. Picker, *Victorian Soundscapes* (New York: Oxford University Press, 2003); Aimée Boutin, *City of Noise: Sound and Nineteenth-Century Paris* (Urbana: University of Illinois Press, 2015); and Peter Payer, *Der Klang der Grossstadt: Eine Geschichte des Hörens, Wien 1850–1914* (Vienna: Böhlau, 2018).

6   Among the many works that use the category of "modern" to explain urban life, Marshall Berman, *All That Is Solid Melts into Air: The Experience of Modernity* (New York: Penguin, 1988), is particularly powerful.

7   All the necessary caveats about interpreting the various kinds of source material are discussed at length in Christoph Heyl, *A Passion for Privacy: Untersuchungen*

zur Genese der bürgerlichen Privatsphäre in London (1660–1800) (Munich: Oldenbourg, 2004), 28–78.

8   This, in fact, is the argument of Brian Ladd, *Autophobia: Love and Hate in the
Automotive Age* (Chicago: University of Chicago Press, 2008).

CHAPTER ONE

1   The most influential studies of social interaction, with some discussion of the
street and some cross-cultural references but not much history, have been those
of Erving Goffman, including *The Presentation of Self in Everyday Life* (Edinburgh: University of Edinburgh Social Sciences Research Centre, 1958); *Behavior
in Public Places* (New York: Free Press, 1963); and *Relations in Public* (New York:
Basic, 1971). A wide-ranging meditation on the history of bodies, motion, and
urban space is Richard Sennett, *Flesh and Stone: The Body and the City in Western
Civilization* (New York: Norton, 1994). Historical studies include Peter K. Andersson, *Silent History: Body Language and Nonverbal Identity, 1860–1914* (Montreal:
McGill-Queen's University Press, 2018); and Dell Upton, *Another City* (New Haven,
CT: Yale University Press, 2008), 86–101.

2   Virginia Woolf, "Street Haunting," *Yale Review* 17 (1927): 49. Or, in the language
of space syntax, "exterior space . . . has a higher degree of indeterminacy." Bill
Hillier and Julienne Hanson, *The Social Logic of Space* (Cambridge: Cambridge
University Press, 1984), 20.

3   For an example of this transition in ancient China, see Heng Chye Kiang, "The
Birth of the Commercial Street," in *Streets*, ed. Zeynep Çelik, Diane Favro, and
Richard Ingersoll (Berkeley: University of California Press, 1994), 45–56. On Italy:
David Friedman, "Streets and the Commune: Italy in the Late Middle Ages and
the Renaissance," in *Building Regulations and Urban Form, 1200–1900*, ed. Terry R.
Slater and Sandra M. G. Pinto (London: Routledge, 2017), 87–114. A broad over-
view is Gloria Levitas, "Anthropology and Sociology of Streets," in *On Streets*, ed.
Stanford Anderson (Cambridge, MA: MIT Press, 1978), 225–40.

4   Daniel Lord Smail, *Imaginary Cartographies: Possession and Identity in Late
Medieval Marseille* (Ithaca, NY: Cornell University Press, 1999), 13–14, 67–68,
154; Wolfgang Braunfels, *Mittelalterliche Stadtbaukunst in der Toskana* (Berlin:
Mann, 1953), 29. On the similar use of crossroads as preferred reference points in
ancient Rome, see Richard Jenkyns, *God, Space and City in the Roman Imagination*
(Oxford: Oxford University Press, 2013), 114.

5   John Brinckerhoff Jackson, "The Discovery of the Street," in *The Necessity of Ruins*
(Amherst: University of Massachusetts Press, 1980), 55–66. Also see Wolfgang
Braunfels, *Urban Design in Western Europe*, trans. Kenneth J. Northcott (Chicago:
University of Chicago Press, 1988), 32; and Erich Herzog, *Die ottonische Stadt* (Ber-
lin: Mann, 1964), 237–40, 254–56.

6   Braunfels, *Mittelalterliche Stadtbaukunst*, 88, 104–16; Jean-Pierre Leguay, *La rue
au Moyen Age* (Rennes: ouest france, 1984), 64–91; and Kathryn L. Reyerson, "Public and Private Space in Medieval Montpellier: The Bon Amic Square," *Journal of
Urban History* 24 (1997): 3–27. A Swedish example: "The medieval law, defining
the width of common land between houses by stating that a horse and a wagon
must be able to pass each other, treats the street as space between buildings. The

1619 ordinance, on the other hand, treats the street as a part of the material structure of a town, something that needs to be built and maintained." Riitta Laitinen and Dag Lindström, "Urban Order and Street Regulation in Seventeenth-Century Sweden," *Journal of Early Modern History* 12 (2008): 263.

7   Braunfels, *Mittelalterliche Stadtbaukunst*, 108-9; David Friedman, "Palaces and the Street in Late-Medieval and Renaissance Italy," in *Urban Landscapes: International Perspectives*, ed. J. W. R. Whitehand and P. J. Larkham (London: Routledge, 1992), 69-113; Richard A. Goldthwaite, *The Building of Renaissance Florence* (Baltimore: Johns Hopkins University Press, 1980), 381; F. J. D. Nevola, "'Per Ornato Della Città': Siena's Strada Romana and Fifteenth-Century Urban Renewal," *Art Bulletin* 82 (2000): 26-50; Besim S. Hakim, *Mediterranean Urbanism: Historic Urban/Building Rules and Processes* (Dordrecht: Springer, 2014), 42-43, 53.

8   Friedman, "Palaces and the Street," 93-99.

9   Ordinance reprinted in Braunfels, *Mittelalterliche Stadtbaukunst*, 250.

10   For an overview, see Braunfels, *Urban Design*.

11   John M. Najemy, "Florentine Politics and Urban Spaces," in *Renaissance Florence: A Social History*, ed. Roger J. Crum and John T. Paoletti (Cambridge: Cambridge University Press, 2006), 19-54; Nevola, "'Per Ornato,'"; Spiro Kostof, *The City Shaped* (Boston: Bulfinch, 1991), 230-32.

12   Kostof, *City Shaped*, 235-38.

13   Martha D. Pollak, *Turin, 1564-1680* (Chicago: University of Chicago Press, 1991). In general: Braunfels, *Urban Design*.

14   Nearly a century later, Diderot's famous *Encyclopédie* combined Furetière's and Richelet's definitions. These definitions are discussed in Daniel Vaillancourt, *Les urbanités parisiennes au XVIIe siècle: Le livre du trottoir* (Quebec: Presses de l'Université Laval, 2009), 138-40.

15   Le Corbusier, *Towards a New Architecture*, trans. Frederick Etchells (London: Rodker, 1930), 61. Clearly he is describing Paris. The definition is roughly applicable across much of the Continent, somewhat less so in England.

16   Quoted in Hans Blumenfeld, "Russian City Planning of the 18th and Early 19th Centuries," *Journal of the American Society of Architectural Historians* 4, no. 1 (Jan. 1944), 23. On the application of similar rules to Baltic towns, see Mart Siilivask, "Building Regulations in Livonian Towns and Their Impact on Local Urban Space, 1697-1904," in Slater, *Building Regulations*, 289-309. More generally: Spiro Kostof, *The City Assembled* (Boston: Bulfinch, 1992), 189-243.

17   Smollett, *The Expedition of Humphry Clinker*, Lydia Melford to Miss Laetitia Willis, 31 May. On the frequent use of this image, see Christoph Heyl, *A Passion for Privacy: Untersuchungen zur Genese der bürgerlichen Privatsphäre in London (1660-1800)* (Munich: Oldenbourg, 2004), 144; and the introduction to the useful compendium by Rick Allen, *The Moving Pageant: A Literary Sourcebook on London Street-Life, 1700-1914* (London: Routledge, 1998), 3-4.

18   Charles Lamb, letter to Wordsworth, 30 Jan. 1801.

19   John Trusler, *The London Adviser and Guide* (London, 1786), 115. On his and similar descriptions, see Alison O'Byrne, "The Art of Walking in London: Representing Urban Pedestrianism in the Early Nineteenth Century," *Romanticism* 14 (2008): 94-107.

20   Trusler, *London Adviser*, 132-34.

21 *Tom Jones*, bk. 8, chap. 12. The figure of the flâneur has occupied a great deal of the writing about nineteenth-century streets, partly because he (rarely she) is identified as the quintessentially rootless modern artist. O'Byrne, "Art of Walking," 97, sees a clear difference between walkers in eighteenth-century London and nineteenth-century Paris, with only the latter expressing real comfort in the crowd. In a related vein, Vic Gatrell, *The First Bohemians: Life and Art in London's Golden Age* (London: Allen Lane, 2013), 308-17, sees real pleasure in city life only late in the eighteenth century. Jonathan Conlin, however, argues that the type of the Parisian flâneur was really no different from the early eighteenth-century London literary wanderers: Conlin, *Tales of Two Cities: Paris, London, and the Birth of the Modern City* (Berkeley, CA: Counterpoint, 2013), 65-89; and Conlin, "'This Publick Sort of Obscurity': The Origins of the Flâneur in London and Paris, 1660-1780," in *The Flâneur Abroad: Historical and International Perspectives*, ed. Richard Wrigley (Newcastle: Cambridge Scholars, 2014), 14-39. Also see Penelope Corfield, "Walking the City Streets: The Urban Odyssey in Eighteenth-Century England," *Journal of Urban History* 16 (1989): 132-74. Similarly, Heyl, *Passion*, 151, argues that Richard Sennett's influential argument in *The Fall of Public Man* (New York: Knopf, 1977), 212, is wrong in dating the acceptance of anonymous street encounters to the nineteenth century rather than to eighteenth-century London. Conlin's larger claim is that the flâneur has no place in historical analysis. Or, as Rebecca Solnit puts it, "the only problem with the flâneur is that he did not exist, except as a type, an ideal, and a character in literature." Solnit, *Wanderlust: A History of Walking* (New York: Penguin, 2000), 200.

22 Susan L. Siegfried, "Boilly: de nouvelles images de la rue et de la circulation à Paris," in *La modernité avant Haussmann: Formes de l'espace urbain à Paris, 1801-1853*, ed. Karen Bowie (Paris: Editions Recherches, 2001), 280-90; Robert Alter, *Imagined Cities: Urban Experience and the Language of the Novel* (New Haven, CT: Yale University Press, 2005); Eric Hazan, *The Invention of Paris: A History in Footsteps*, trans. David Fernbach (London: Verso, 2010), 315-39; and on similar developments in Russian art and literature, Grigory Kaganov, *Images of Space: St. Petersburg in the Visual and Verbal Arts*, trans. Sidney Monas (Palo Alto: Stanford University Press, 1997), 118-33. Gatrell, *First Bohemians*, 226, agrees that eighteenth-century novels lack any sense of urban place.

23 Edmondo De Amicis, *Ricordi di Parigi* (Milan: Treves, 1879), 14, 15.

24 The vast literature on Napoleon III and Haussmann includes François Loyer, *Paris Nineteenth Century: Architecture and Urbanism* (New York: Abbeville, 1988); David P. Jordan, *Transforming Paris: The Life and Labors of Baron Haussmann* (Chicago: University of Chicago Press, 1996); and Stéphane Kirkland, *Paris Reborn: Napoléon III, Baron Haussmann, and the Quest to Build a Modern City* (New York: St. Martin's, 2013).

25 Adolf Glassbrenner, *Berliner Volksleben* (Leipzig: Engelmann, 1847), 1:34-35; also see Karl Rosenkranz, *Die Topographie des heutigen Paris und Berlin: Zwei Vorträge* (Königsberg: Bornträger, 1850), 61.

26 Henry Vizetelly, *Berlin under the New Empire* (London: Tinsley Bros., 1879), 1:63. On the evidence of early photographs, Max Osborn, *Berlin 1870-1929: Der Aufstieg zur Weltstadt* (1929; Berlin: Mann, 1994), 136, argued that artists of prephotographic prints often exaggerated the size of crowds.

27   Karl Gutzkow, *Die neuen Serapionsbrüder* (Breslau: Schottlaender, 1877), 1:1–11; Katherine Roper, *German Encounters with Modernity: Novels of Imperial Berlin* (Atlantic Highlands, NJ: Humanities Press, 1991), 67.

28   Joachim Radkau, *Das Zeitalter der Nervosität* (Munich: Hanser, 1998), esp. 310–15; Andreas Killen, *Berlin Electropolis: Shock, Nerves, and German Modernity* (Berkeley: University of California Press, 2006); Joseph Ben Prestel, *Emotional Cities: Debates on Urban Change in Berlin and Cairo, 1860–1910* (Oxford: Oxford University Press, 2017), 97–105; Peter Payer, *Der Klang der Grossstadt* (Vienna: Böhlau, 2018), 126–32.

29   Arthur Eloesser, "Grossstadt und Grossstädter" (1909), in *Die Strasse meiner Jugend: Berliner Skizzen* (Berlin: Das Arsenal, 1987), 37.

30   Ferdinand Tönnies, *Gemeinschaft und Gesellschaft* (Leipzig: Fues, 1887).

31   August Endell, *Die Schönheit der grossen Stadt* (Stuttgart: Strecker & Schröder, 1908).

32   Georg Simmel, "Die Grossstädte und das Geistesleben," in *Die Grossstadt* (*Jahrbuch der Gehe-Stiftung* 9, 1903), 185–206, widely translated as "The Metropolis and Mental Life"; "Psychologie der Koketterie," *Der Tag*, 11–12 May 1909.

CHAPTER TWO

1   J. W. von Goethe, *Italienische Reise*, journal entry of 28 May 1787.

2   Nathaniel Hawthorne, *The English Notebooks*, ed. Randall Stewart (New York: Russell & Russell, 1962), 225–26 (14 Sept. 1855). A more cynical take came from Eduard Kolloff, *Schilderungen aus Paris* (Hamburg: Hoffmann und Campe, 1839), 2:15–31, who described Paris street entrepreneurs as engaged in more or less criminal ways of taking pedestrians' money.

3   Colin Jones, "Pulling Teeth in Eighteenth-Century Paris," *Past and Present* 166 (2000): 126–29.

4   William Howitt, *The Rural and Domestic Life of Germany: Characteristic Sketches of Its Cities and Scenery* (London: Longman, 1842), 441; see also Mary Lee Townsend, *Forbidden Laughter: Popular Humor and the Limits of Repression in Nineteenth-Century Prussia* (Ann Arbor: University of Michigan Press, 1992), 25–26, 116–39; and Luc Gersal, *Spree-Athen: Berliner Skizzen von einem Böotier* (Leipzig: Reissner, 1892), 175–77.

5   *The Rambler*, nos. 170–71 (1751); Matthew Beaumont, *Nightwalking: A Nocturnal History of London, Chaucer to Dickens* (London: Verso, 2015), 127–29; Boswell's London diary, 28 July 1763.

6   Justus Conrad Müller, *Gemählde von Berlin Potsdam und Sanssouci—Politisch-moralisch-charakteristisch* (London [Nuremberg], 1792), 10. For similar examples, see Louis-Sébastien Mercier, quoted in Arlette Farge, *Vivre dans la rue à Paris au XVIIIe siècle* (Paris: Gallimard, 1979), 175–77; Jeffry Kaplow, *The Names of Kings: The Parisian Laboring Poor in the Eighteenth Century* (New York: Basic Books, 1972), 238; and Tim Hitchcock, *Down and Out in Eighteenth-Century London* (London: Hambledon and London, 2004), 88–96.

7   Dickens, "Departed Beggars," *Household Words* 144 (1852): 245. On the varying levels of poverty among street sellers, see Martin Kriele, "Strassen- und Lokal-

handel in Berlin," in *Untersuchungen über die Lage des Hausiergewerbes in Deutschland*, vol. 5 (*Schriften des Vereins für Socialpolitik* 81; Leipzig, 1899), 1–35.

8   Kriele, "Strassen- und Lokalhandel," 7.

9   Henry Mayhew, *London Labour and the London Poor* (London: Griffin, Bohn, 1861), 1:4–6; 2:1. On his slipshod use of numbers, however, see Gertrude Himmelfarb, *The Idea of Poverty: England in the Early Industrial Age* (New York: Knopf, 1984), 346–49.

10 Maximilian Rapsilber, "Bilder der Strasse," in *Spreeathener* (Berlin: Haber, 1914), 104–6.

11 Charles Hindley, *A History of the Cries of London* (London: Hindley, 1884), 239.

12 The peddler William Green described his sales patter in *The Life and Adventures of a Cheap Jack* (London: Tinsley Brothers, 1876). Also see the photographs in Willy Römer, *Ambulantes Gewerbe: Berlin 1904–1932* (Berlin: Dirk Nishen, 1983), and Imbke Behnken, "Die Strasse als Lebenswelt von Grossstadtkindern," in *Der Fotograf Willy Römer 1887–1979: Auf den Strassen von Berlin*, ed. Diethart Kerbs (Bönen: Kettler, 2004), 319–43.

13 Johann Pezzl, *Skizze von Wien* (Vienna: Krauss, 1787), 37. Similar examples in Gerhard Tanzer, "Spazierengehen—Zum ungewöhnlichen Aufschwung einer gewöhnlichen Freizeitform im Wien des ausgehenden 18. Jahrhunderts," *Beiträge zur historischen Sozialkunde* 12, no. 2 (1982): 72.

14 Pezzl, *Skizze*, 730–33.

15 Evelyn Welch, *Shopping in the Renaissance* (New Haven, CT: Yale University Press, 2005), 35–36.

16 Fred. Aug. Wendeborn, *A View of England towards the Close of the Eighteenth Century*, trans. by the author (London: Robinson, 1791), 1:333.

17 Thomas Beames, *The Rookeries of London* (London: Bosworth, 1852), 19.

18 Jean-Paul [Giovanni Paolo] Marana, *Lettre d'un Sicilien à un des ses amis* (Paris: Quantin, 1883), 13.

19 Joseph Addison, *Spectator* 251 (18 Dec. 1711).

20 Swift, *City Cries, Instrumental and Vocal: or, An Examination of Certain Abuses, Corruptions, and Enormities, in London and Dublin* (Dublin, 1732), 4–5.

21 Sean Shesgreen, *Images of the Outcast: The Urban Poor in the Cries of London* (New Brunswick, NJ: Rutgers University Press, 2002), 102–17; Jenny Uglow, *Hogarth: A Life and a World* (London: Faber and Faber, 1997), 302; Ronald Paulson, *Hogarth* (New Brunswick, NJ: Rutgers University Press, 1991), 2:115; Vic Gatrell, *The First Bohemians: Life and Art in London's Golden Age* (London: Allen Lane, 2013), 234.

22 Quoted in Roy Porter, *London: A Social History* (Cambridge, MA: Harvard University Press, 1995), 257.

23 John M. Picker, *Victorian Soundscapes* (New York: Oxford University Press, 2003), 43; on antinoise efforts also see James Winter, *London's Teeming Streets* (London: Routledge, 1993), 71–77; and Peter Payer, *Der Klang der Grossstadt* (Vienna: Böhlau, 2018).

24 Carl Georg Reginald Herloss, *Wien wie es ist*, trans. Eduard Forstmann (Leipzig: Magazin für Industrie und Literatur, 1827), 42.

25 Walter Benjamin, *Das Passagenwerk*, in *Gesammelte Schriften*, vol. 5 (Frankfurt: Suhrkamp, 1982), 536, 545; Beaumont, *Nightwalking*, 359–61.

26 Friedrich Schulz, *Über Paris und die Pariser* (Berlin: Vieweg, 1791), 114.

27   Louis-Sébastien Mercier, *Tableau de Paris* (Amsterdam, 1783), 5:66–67: "Cris de Paris." Mercier's magnum opus from the 1780s sprawls across many volumes and many editions. Failing to locate all my quotations in a single edition, I have cited the titles of his brief chapters, which are more consistent across editions than his chapter numbers.

28   Mayhew, *London Labour*, 3:158–59.

29   Karl Veit Riedel, *Der Bänkelsang: Wesen und Funktion einer volkstümlichen Kunst* (Hamburg: Museum für Hamburgische Geschichte, 1963); Leander Petzoldt, *Bänkelsang* (Stuttgart: Metzler, 1974).

30   Quoted in Tim Hitchcock and Robert Shoemaker, *London Lives: Poverty, Crime and the Making of a Modern City, 1690–1800* (Cambridge: Cambridge University Press, 2015), 312; also see Hitchcock, *Down and Out*, 65–70; and V. A. C. Gatrell, *The Hanging Tree: Execution and the English People, 1770–1868* (Oxford: Oxford University Press, 1994), 123–44.

31   Mercier, *Tableau de Paris* (Amsterdam, 1788), 9:167, "Mélange des individus." On long-distance networks, see Laurence Fontaine, *History of Pedlars in Europe*, trans. Vicki Whittaker (Durham, NC: Duke University Press, 1996).

32   Charles E. Kany, *Life and Manners in Madrid, 1750–1800* (1932; New York: AMS Press, 1970), 58–59, 97.

33   Mayhew, *London Labour*, 1:242, 3:185–94.

34   John Gay, *Trivia: or, The Art of Walking the Streets of London*, bk. 2, lines 425–39.

35   Adolphe Smith, "Halfpenny Ices," in J. Thomson and Adolphe Smith, *Street Life in London* (London: S. Low, 1877), 54.

36   Sean Shesgreen, *Hogarth and the Times-of-the-Day Tradition* (Ithaca, NY: Cornell University Press, 1983); Uglow, *Hogarth*, 302–11.

37   Jules Janin, *Un hiver à Paris* (Paris: Janet, 1846), 50; Derek Hudson, *Munby, Man of Two Worlds: The Life and Diaries of Arthur J. Munby 1828–1910* (Boston: Gambit, 1972).

38   John Sanderson, *Sketches of Paris in Familiar Letters to His Friends* (Philadelphia: E. L. Cary and A. Hart, 1838), 20–21. The opera singer Lablache was famed for his powerful voice.

39   John Trusler, *The London Adviser and Guide* (London, 1786), 138.

40   Richard Rowe, *Life in the London Streets* (London: J. C. Nimmo and Bain, 1881), 257. Stephen Jankiewicz, "A Dangerous Class: The Street Sellers of Nineteenth-Century London," *Journal of Social History* 46 (2012): 391–415, sees the hawkers more as a challenge to bourgeois identity. On the complexities of Mayhew's admiration for the "street-folk," see Richard Maxwell, "Henry Mayhew and the Life of the Streets," *Journal of British Studies* 17 (1978): 87–105.

41   Jean-Michel Baruch-Gourden, "La police et le commerce ambulant à Paris au XIXᵉ siècle," in *Maintien de l'ordre et polices en France et en Europe au XIXᵉ siècle*, ed. Philippe Vigier and Alain Faure (Paris: Créaphis, 1987), 251–67.

42   On eighteenth-century regulation, see Farge, *Vivre*, 167–72; Hitchcock and Shoemaker, *London Lives*, 387; Melissa Calaresu, "Food Selling and Urban Space in Early Modern Naples," in *Food Hawkers: Selling in the Streets from Antiquity to the Present*, ed. Melissa Calaresu and Danielle van den Heuvel (London: Routledge, 2016), 113–14; Danielle van den Heuvel, "Selling in the Shadows: Peddlers and Hawkers in Early Modern Europe," in *Working on Labor: Essays in Honor of Jan Lucassen*, ed. Marcel van der Linden and Leo Lucassen (Leiden: Brill, 2012),

125–51; Danielle van den Heuvel, "Policing Peddlers: The Prosecution of Illegal Street Trade in Eighteenth-Century Dutch Towns," *Historical Journal* 58 (2015): 367–92.

43 James Schmiechen and Kenneth Carls, *The British Market Hall: A Social and Architectural History* (New Haven, CT: Yale University Press, 1999), 27.

44 J. W. Sullivan, *Markets for the People: The Consumer's Part* (New York: Macmillan, 1913), 192–208.

45 Sullivan, *Markets*, 158–91; and see Zola's exuberant descriptions of the area in his novel *Le ventre de Paris* (*The Belly of Paris*). On German market halls, see Uwe Spiekermann, *Basis der Konsumgesellschaft: Entstehung und Entwicklung des modernen Kleinhandels in Deutschland 1850–1914* (Munich: Beck, 1999), 175–86.

46 Reprinted in Charles Hindley, *Curiosities of Street Literature* (London: Reeves and Turner, 1871), 88. On the law: Winter, *London's Teeming Streets*, 107–9. On similar Berlin regulations the same year, see Kriele, "Strassen- und Lokalhandel in Berlin," 29; *Sammlung der Polizei-Verordnungen und polizeilichen Vorschriften für Berlin* (Berlin, 1887), 301–18, 400.

47 Ordinance of 28 Dec. 1859, in *Collection officielle des ordonnances de police, Tome II (1849–1880)* (Paris: Chaix, 1881), 247–49. On a similar Berlin debate in 1880: Landesarchiv Berlin, A Rep. 000-02-01, no. 2214, vol. 2. On German regulations: Spiekermann, *Basis*, 202–17.

48 Shesgreen, *Images*, 24–25. On marketing to tourists: Melissa Calaresu, "Costumes and Customs in Print: Travel, Ethnography, and the Representation of Street-Sellers in Early Modern Italy," in *Not Dead Things: The Dissemination of Popular Print in England and Wales, Italy and the Low Countries, 1500–1820*, ed. Roeland Harms, Joad Raymond, and Jeroen Salman (Leiden: Brill, 2013), 181–209. On their appeal to upper classes: Peter Burke, "Representing Women's Work in Early Modern Italy," in *The Idea of Work in Europe from Antiquity to Modern Times*, ed. Josef Ehmer and Catharina Lis (Farnham, Surrey: Ashgate, 2009), 182–84; and Celina Fox, *Londoners* (London: Thames and Hudson, 1987), 154–67. On typical print runs, see Vincent Milliot, *Les Cris de Paris ou le peuple travesti: Les représentations des petits métiers parisiens XVIᵉ–XVIIIᵉ siècles* (Paris: Publications de la Sorbonne, 1995, 2014), 104. This is the major historical study of cries, along with the more artist-focused works of Shesgreen.

49 Catalogs and collections include Karen F. Beall, *Kaufrufe und Strassenhändler: Eine Bibliographie. Cries and Itinerant Trades: A Bibliography*, trans. Sabine Solf (Hamburg: Hauswedell, 1975); C. P. Maurenbrecher and Karen F. Beall, *Europäische Kaufrufe: Strassenhändler in graphischen Darstellungen* (Dortmund: Harenberg, 1980); Robert Massin, *Les cris de la ville: Commerces ambulants et petits métiers de la rue* (Paris: Gallimard, 1978); Wolfgang Kos, ed., *Wiener Typen: Klischees und Wirklichkeit* (Vienna: Brandstätter, 2013); *The Gentle Author's Cries of London* (London: Spitalfields Life Books, 2015).

50 This argument is made by Hitchcock, *Down and Out*, 222–23.

51 Elizabeth Grant, "John Tallis's London Street Views," *London Journal* 37 (2012): 234–51; examples at http://crowd.museumoflondon.org.uk/lsv1840/; Jeffrey A. Cohen, "A Streetscape Named Desire: Long Views through the Emerging Bourgeois City," in *Portraits of the City: Dublin and the Wider World*, ed. Gillian O'Brien and Finola O'Kane (Dublin: Four Courts Press, 2012), 22–34.

52 Massin, *Les cris*, 128.

53   All taken from Beall, *Kaufrufe*, 117–78.

54   Elisabeth Ball, "The Moving Market or Cries of London Town," in *Bibliophile in the Nursery*, ed. William Targ (Cleveland: World Publishing, 1957), 193–207; Sean Shesgreen, "The Cries of London from the Renaissance to the Nineteenth Century: A Short History," in Harms, *Not Dead Things*, 139–43; Hubert Kaut, *Kaufrufe aus Wien: Volkstypen und Strassenszenen in der Wiener Graphik von 1775 bis 1914* (Vienna: Jugend & Volk, 1970), 78.

55   Zacharias Conrad von Uffenbach, *Merkwürdige Reisen durch Niedersachen Holland und Engelland* (Ulm: Gaum, 1754), 3:218.

56   Christian Rapp, "Wiener Typen: Zu Erfindung und Karrière eines Soziotops," in *Alt-Wien: Die Stadt, die niemals war*, ed. Wolfgang Kos and Christian Rapp (Vienna: Czernin, 2004), 148.

57   On the idea of a map: Milliot, *Les* Cris, 221–22; and Sean Shesgreen, "In Search of the Marginal and the Outcast: The 'Lower Orders' in the Cries of London and Dublin," in *Others and Outcasts in Early Modern Europe*, ed. Tom Nichols (Aldershot: Ashgate, 2007), 237. On demystifying the lower classes for the upper classes: Milliot, *Les* Cris, and Shesgreen, "The Cries of London," 117–52.

58   Georges Kastner, *Les voix de Paris* (Paris: Brandus, 1857). On Mayhew's categories: Himmelfarb, *The Idea of Poverty*, 349–54.

59   Shesgreen, "In Search of the Marginal," 217–39; *The Gentle Author's Cries*, 18; Mark Bills, "The *Cries* of London by Paul Sandby and Thomas Rowlandson," *Print Quarterly* 20 (2003): 34–61. Burke, "Representing Women's Work," 184, makes a similar claim about the unusual late eighteenth-century Venetian images of Gaetano Zompini.

60   Milliot, *Les* Cris, 167–78; 192–208 on the absence of bodily deformations; 259–75 on posture and dance.

61   Vincent Milliot, "Les *Cris de Paris* ou le peuple apprivoisé, XVIe–XIXe siècles," in *Paris le peuple: XVIIIe–XXe siècle*, ed. Jean-Louis Robert and Danielle Tartakowsky (Paris: Publications de la Sorbonne, 1999), 175–81; James Cuno, "Violence, Satire, and Social Types in the Graphic Art of the July Monarchy," in *The Popularization of Images: Visual Culture under the July Monarchy*, ed. Petra ten-Doesschate Chu and Gabriel P. Weisberg (Princeton, NJ: Princeton University Press, 1994), 21. Jens Wietschorke, "Urbane Volkstypen: Zur Folklorisierung der Stadt im 19. und frühen 20. Jahrhundert," *Zeitschrift für Volkskunde* 110 (2014): 215–42, argues that later portrayals of urban "types" combined "social exclusion and cultural inclusion" (217).

62   Charles Knight, "Street Noises," in *London*, ed. Knight (London: Charles Knight, 1841), 1:136–37. The fact that Charles Hindley plagiarized this passage some forty years later (*History of the Cries*, 139) suggests that nostalgia extends beyond individual memories.

63   Victor Fournel, *Les cris de Paris: Types et physiognomies d'autrefois* (Paris: Firmin-Didot, 1887), 5.

64   Charles Booth, *Labour and Life of the People*, 3rd ed. (London: Williams and Norgate, 1891), 1:68; also quoted in Lee Jackson, *A Dictionary of Victorian London* (London: Anthem, 2006), 28.

65   Balzac, "Ce qui disparait de Paris" (1845).

66   Kolloff, *Schilderungen aus Paris*, 1:210, 227.

67 Hitchcock, *Down and Out*, 228–30; Vic Gatrell, *City of Laughter: Sex and Satire in Eighteenth-Century London* (London: Atlantic Books, 2006), 556–73. For expressions of sympathy in nineteenth-century French poetry, see Pierre Citron, *La poésie de Paris dans la littérature française de Rousseau à Baudelaire* (Paris: Les éditions de Minuit, 1961), 1:370–76.

68 Charles Lamb, "A Complaint of the Decay of Beggars in the Metropolis," 1822.

69 Dickens, "Departed Beggars," 244.

70 Lamb, "A Complaint."

71 Carl Philipp Moritz, *Reisen eines Deutschen in England im Jahre 1782*, 2nd ed. (Berlin: Friedrich Maurer, 1785), 21.

72 Ludwig Börne, *Schilderungen aus Paris* (1822; New York: Deutsche Verlags-Anstalt, 1858), 29.

73 Adalbert Stifter, *Wien und die Wiener* (1844), in *Gesammelte Werke*, ed. Konrad Steffen (Basel: Birkhäuser, 1969), 13:170.

74 Edmondo De Amicis, *Ricordi di Parigi* (Milano: Treves, 1879), 17–18.

75 Molly Loberg, *The Struggle for the Streets of Berlin: Politics, Consumption, and Urban Space, 1914–1945* (Cambridge: Cambridge University Press, 2018), 20–30. On billposting and advertising rules in Paris, see H. Hazel Hahn, *Scenes of Parisian Modernity: Culture and Consumption in the Nineteenth Century* (New York: Palgrave, 2009), 42–44, 156–58.

76 Winter, *London's Teeming Streets*, 101; Thomson and Smith, *Street Life*, 91–94; Max Schlesinger, *Saunterings in and about London* (London: Nathaniel Cooke, 1853), 15–16; Hahn, *Scenes of Parisian Modernity*, 31. On women: Hahn, 136; and Arthur J. Munby, diary, 25 Mar. 1887, in Hudson, *Munby*, 411.

77 Quoted in Jackson, *Dictionary of Victorian London*, 3–4.

78 Schlesinger, *Saunterings*, 23. On Paris: Hahn, *Scenes of Parisian Modernity*, 133, 152–53.

79 See esp. Peter Fritzsche, *Reading Berlin 1900* (Cambridge, MA: Harvard University Press, 1996).

80 Charles Vincent, "Les dernières échoppes," in *Paris Guide* (Paris: Libraire Internationale, 1867), 972.

81 Goethe, *Italienische Reise*, journal entry of 16 Sept. 1786.

82 Wolfgang Braunfels, *Mittelalterliche Stadtbaukunst in der Toskana* (Berlin: Mann, 1953), 39; David Friedman, "Palaces and the Street in Late-Medieval and Renaissance Italy," in *Urban Landscapes: International Perspectives*, ed. J. W. R. Whitehand and P. J. Larkham (London: Routledge, 1992), 73. The fact that spinning was women's work probably influenced official sentiment.

83 Frances Trollope, *Paris and the Parisians in 1835* (London: Bentley, 1836), 1:113–15.

84 Alain Corbin, *Time, Desire and Horror*, trans. Jean Birrell (Cambridge: Polity, 1995), 175.

85 Jon Stobart, "The Shopping Streets of Provincial England, 1650–1840," in *The Landscape of Consumption: Shopping Streets and Cultures in Western Europe, 1600–1900*, ed. Jan Hein Furnée and Clé Lesger (London: Palgrave, 2014), 18; Derek Keene, "Sites of Desire: Shops, Selds and Wardrobes in London and other English Cities, 1100–1550," in *Buyers and Sellers: Retail Circuits and Practices in Medieval and Early Modern Europe*, ed. Bruno Blondé et al. (Turnhout, Belgium:

Brepols, 2006), 138–39. On the use of girls as a lure, also see Martha Carlin, "The Senses in the Marketplace," in *A Cultural History of the Senses in the Middle Ages*, ed. Richard Newhauser (London: Bloomsbury, 2014), 85.

86 Welch, *Shopping in the Renaissance*, 32, on Italy.

87 Kathryn A. Morrison, *English Shops and Shopping: An Architectural History* (New Haven, CT: Yale University Press, 2003), 7; Welch, *Shopping in the Renaissance*, 97, 143.

88 Quoted in Laura Gowing, " 'The Freedom of the Streets': Women and Social Space, 1560–1640," in *Londinopolis*, ed. Paul Griffiths and Mark S. R. Jenner (Manchester: Manchester University Press, 2000), 143.

89 Gowing, " 'Freedom of the Streets,' " 143.

90 On the New Exchange, see Linda Levy Peck, *Consuming Splendor: Society and Culture in Seventeenth-Century England* (Cambridge: Cambridge University Press, 2005), 46–61; J. F. Merritt, *The Social World of Early Modern Westminster* (Manchester: Manchester University Press, 2005), 156–59; and Holly Dugan, *The Ephemeral History of Perfume* (Baltimore, MD: Johns Hopkins University Press, 2011), 147–48.

91 Quoted in Emily Cockayne, *Hubbub: Filth, Noise, and Stench in England, 1600–1770* (New Haven, CT: Yale University Press, 2007), 177.

92 J.-H. Ronesse, *Vues sur la propreté des rues de Paris* (Paris, 1782), 32.

93 Kai Kauffmann, *Es ist nur ein Wien! Stadtbeschreibungen von Wien 1700 bis 1873* (Vienna: Böhlau, 1994), 273–74. On a similar trend in London, see Claire Walsh, "Shop Design and the Display of Goods in Eighteenth-Century London," *Journal of Design History* 8 (1995): 169–70.

94 Georg Christoph Lichtenberg, letter to Ernst Gottfried Bailinger, 10 Jan. 1775.

95 Balzac, *Histoire de la grandeur et de la décadence de César Birotteau*, in *Œuvres complètes de H. de Balzac* (Paris: Houssiaux, 1855), 10:211.

96 Charles Dickens, *Sketches by Boz*, "Gin-Shops" (1836), quoted in Porter, *London*, 200. On the movement of shops off the street and on the competition for façades, see Claire Walsh, "Stalls, Bulks, Shops and Long-Term Change in Seventeenth- and Eighteenth-Century England," in Furnée and Lesger, *Landscape of Consumption*, 37–56.

97 Moritz, *Reisen*, 258.

98 Sophie von La Roche, *Tagebuch einer Reise durch Holland und England* (Offenbach: Weiss und Brede, 1788), 480: diary, 28 Sept. 1787. For more on astonished German visitors, see Heidrun Homburg, "German Landscapes of Consumption, 1750–1850: Perspectives of German and Foreign Travellers," in Furnée and Lesger, *Landscape of Consumption*, 126–33. On Paris: Hahn, *Scenes of Parisian Modernity*, 20, 26.

99 Börne, *Schilderungen*, 28.

100 Robert Southey, *Letters from England: By Don Manuel Alvarez Espriella. Translated from the Spanish*, 3rd ed. (1808; London: Longman, Hurst, Rees, Orme, and Brown, 1814), 3:71.

101 Nikolaus Theodor Mühlibach, *Wien von seiner übelsten Seite betrachtet* (Vienna: Camesina, 1815), 133.

102 Anneleen Arnout, "Something Old, Something Borrowed, Something New: The Brussels Shopping Townscape, 1830–1914," in Furnée and Lesger, *Landscape of Consumption*, 165.

103 Paris ordinances of 24 Apr. 1817, 8 Apr. 1819, and 20 Jan. 1832, in *Collection offi-cielle des ordonnances de police: Depuis 1800 jusqu'à 1844* (Paris: Paul Dupont, 1845), 2:77–78, 2:130–31; 3:1–2; Kriele, "Strassen- und Lokalhandel in Berlin"; and see Winter, *London's Teeming Streets*, 107–9, on the 1867 London law.

104 Herloss, *Wien wie es ist*, 12.

105 Johanna Schopenhauer, *Ausflug an den Niederrhein und nach Belgien im Jahr 1828* (Leipzig: Brockhaus, 1831), 1:147.

106 Thomas Hughes, *The Stranger's Handbook to Chester and Its Environs* (Chester: Catherall, 1856), 46, quoted in David Alexander, *Retailing in England during the Industrial Revolution* (London: Athlone, 1970), 9.

107 Johann Friedrich Geist, *Arcades: The History of a Building Type* (Cambridge, MA: MIT Press, 1985), 48–51; Marie Gillet, "Innovation and Tradition in the Shopping Landscape of Paris and a Provincial City, 1800–1900," in Furnée and Lesger, *Landscape of Consumption*, 185–90; on women: Morrison, *English Shops*, 93.

108 Contemporary guidebooks and visitors' accounts typically describe its attractions at length. Particularly thorough descriptions are in Schulz, *Über Paris*, 397–544, and François-Marie Mayeur de St. Paul, *Tableau du Nouveau Palais-Royal*, 2 vols. (London: Maradan, 1788). Also: Olivier Daumestre, "La promenade: Un loisir urbain universel? L'exemple du Palais-Royal à Paris à la fin du XVIIIe siècle," *Histoire urbaine* 3 (2001): 83–102.

109 Benjamin, *Das Passagenwerk*, 93.

110 See the thorough catalog in Geist, *Arcades*.

111 Benjamin, *Das Passagenwerk*, 140.

112 Victoria Kelley, "The Streets for the People: London's Street Markets, 1850–1939," *Urban History* 43 (2016): 391–411; Judith R. Walkowitz, *Nights Out: Life in Cosmopolitan London* (New Haven, CT: Yale University Press, 2012), 144–82.

113 Quoted in Spiekermann, *Basis*, 210.

114 Petition from 1900, quoted in Loberg, *Struggle for the Streets*, 82; see also 81–90; and Peter T. A. Jones, "Redressing Reform Narratives: Victorian London's Street Markets and the Informal Supply Lines of Urban Modernity," *London Journal* 41 (2016): 60–81.

115 Georg Simmel, *Soziologie* (Leipzig: Duncker und Humblot, 1908), 685.

CHAPTER THREE

1 Mario Damen, "The Town as a Stage? Urban Space and Tournaments in Late Medieval Brussels," *Urban History* 43 (2016): 47–71.

2 Richard Alewyn and Karl Sälzle, *Das grosse Welttheater: Die Epoche der höfischen Feste in Dokument und Deutung* (Hamburg: Rowohlt, 1959), 22, 30.

3 Laurent Turcot, *Le promeneur à Paris au XVIIIe siècle* (Paris: Gallimard, 2007); Turcot, "The Rise of the *Promeneur*: Walking the City in Eighteenth-Century Paris," *Historical Research* 88 (2015): 67–99; Gudrun M. König, *Eine Kulturgeschichte des Spaziergangs: Spuren einer bürgerlichen Praktik 1780–1850* (Vienna: Böhlau, 1996); Gerhard Tanzer, "Spazierengehen—Zum ungewöhnlichen Aufschwung einer gewöhnlichen Freizeitform im Wien des ausgehenden 18. Jahrhunderts," *Beiträge zur historischen Sozialkunde* 12, no. 2 (1982): 67–72; James Amelang, "The Myth of the Mediterranean City: Perceptions of Sociability," in *Mediterranean Urban Cul-*

ture, 1400–1700, ed. Alexander Cowan (Exeter: University of Exeter Press, 2000), 28.

4   Charles de Forster, *Quinze ans à Paris, 1832–1848: Paris et les Parisiens* (Paris: Didot, 1848), 1:108.

5   *London and Paris; or, Comparative Sketches by the Marquis de Vermont and Sir Charles Darnley, Bart* [both pseudonyms] (London: Longman, 1823), 37.

6   *Journal des dames et des modes*, 25 Thermidor, year XII (13 Aug. 1805), quoted in Denise Z. Davidson, "Making Society 'Legible': People-Watching in Paris after the Revolution," *French Historical Studies* 28 (2005): 285–86.

7   Anaïs Bazin [Anaïs de Raucou], *L'epoque sans nom: Esquisses de Paris, 1830–1833* (Paris: Alexandre Mesnier, 1833), 2:152. For the appearance of the boulevards in 1853, see the panoramic print reproduced in John Russell, *Paris* (New York: Abrams, 1983), 338–48.

8   Henry W. Lawrence, "Origins of the Tree-Lined Boulevard," *Geographical Review* 78 (1988): 355–74; Laurent Turcot, "L'émergence d'un espace plurifonctionnel: Les boulevards parisiens au XVIIIᵉ siècle," *Histoire urbaine* 12 (2005): 89–115; A. Parmentier, "Les boulevards de Paris au XVIIIᵉ siècle," *Revue du XVIIIᵉ siècle* 1 (1913): 121–37; Anne-Marie Châtelet, Michaël Darin, and Claire Monod, "Formation et transformation," in *Les grands boulevards: Un parcours d'innovation et de modernité*, ed. Bernard Landau, Claire Monod, and Evelyne Lohr (Paris: Action artistique de la Ville de Paris, 2000), 42–51; Yoann Brault, "Une regeneration de la promenade au milieu du XVIIIᵉ siècle? Evolution et influence du boulevard du Temple à Paris," in *La promenade au tournant des XVIIIᵉ et XIXᵉ siècle (Belgique—France—Angleterre)*, ed. Christophe Loir and Laurent Turcot (Brussels: Editions de L'université de Bruxelles, 2011), 23–39.

9   Ernest Despres, "Le dimanche à Paris," in *Nouveau tableau de Paris au XIXᵉ siècle* (Paris: Charles-Bechet, 1844), 2:44. For a similar description from the 1770s, see *Memoirs of Carlo Goldoni* (New York: Knopf, 1926), 426–27.

10   Luc Sante, *The Other Paris* (New York: Farrar, Straus and Giroux, 2015), 102.

11   Jean-Baptiste Rigaudy, "L'appropriation haussmannienne," in Landau, *Les grands boulevards*, 59–62; Anne-Marie Châtelet, "Formation et transformation des Grands Boulevards," in *La modernité avant Haussmann: Formes de l'espace urbain à Paris, 1801–1853*, ed. Karen Bowie (Paris: Editions Recherches, 2001), 244–50. On what became known as street furniture, see Marie de Thézy, "Histoire du mobilier urbain parisienne de second Empire à nos jours," in *Paris, la rue: Le mobilier urbain parisien du second Empire à nos jours à travers les collections photographiques de la Bibliothèque historique de la ville de Paris* (Paris: Société des Amis de la Bibliothéque historique, 1976), 11–79.

12   David Scobey, "Anatomy of the Promenade: The Politics of Bourgeois Sociability in Nineteenth-Century New York," *Social History* 17 (1992): 203–27.

13   London streets (as opposed to its parks) proved less congenial to promenading, but the same was not true of other English cities. See Simon Gunn, *The Public Culture of the Victorian Middle Class* (Manchester: Manchester University Press, 2000), 60–78; Andrew Davies, *Leisure, Gender, and Poverty: Working-Class Culture in Salford and Manchester, 1900–1939* (Buckingham: Open University Press, 1992); and Jenny Birchall, "'The Carnival Revels of Manchester's Vagabonds': Young Working-Class Women and Monkey Parades in the 1870s," *Women's History Review* 15 (2006): 229–52.

14   Marianne Baillie, *First Impressions on a Tour upon the Continent in the Summer of 1818 through Parts of France, Italy, Switzerland, the Borders of Germany, and a Part of French Flanders* (London: John Murray, 1819), 146-47.

15   Pepys's diary, 10 Jan. 1660. François-Marie Mayeur de St. Paul describes a similar difficulty with his own sword in the crowds of the Palais-Royal in *Tableau du Nouveau Palais-Royal* (London: Maradan, 1788), 1:131-32.

16   *Journal du voyage de Michel de Montaigne en Italie*, March 1581.

17   Giovanna P. Del Negro, *The Passeggiata and Popular Culture in an Italian Town: Folklore and the Performance of Modernity* (Montreal: McGill-Queen's University Press, 2004). On informal class and gender segregation of promenades, see John K. Walton, "Policing the Alameda: Shared and Contested Leisure Space in San Sebastián, c. 1863-1920," in *Identities in Space*, ed. Simon Gunn and Robert J. Morris (Aldershot: Ashgate, 2001), 228-41; and Miren Llona, "Las mujeres de las clases medias bilbaínas en los años veinte," in *El rumor de lo cotidiano*, ed. Luis Castells (Bilbao: Universidad del Pais Vasco, 1999), 207-23.

18   Winfried Löschburg, *Unter den Linden: Gesichter und Geschichten einer berühmten Strasse* (Berlin: Der Morgen, 1973), 23.

19   Adapted from John Louis Miller's translation: http://www.eaglesweb.com/John _Louis_Miller/R_Gluck.PDF.

20   Max Osborn, *Berlin 1870-1929* (Berlin: Mann, 1994), 16-18; also see the panoramic engravings of the street from 1820 and 1849, reprinted in Winfried Löschburg, ed., *Panorama der Strasse Unter den Linden* (Berlin: Koehler und Amelang, 1986).

21   Karl Rosenkranz, *Die Topographie des heutigen Paris und Berlin* (Königsberg: Bornträger, 1850), 16, 72.

22   M. Lapeyre, *Les Moeurs de Paris* (Amsterdam: Castel, 1747), 149.

23   Quoted in Colin Jones, *Paris: Biography of a City* (New York: Viking Penguin, 2004), 194. On the decay of old hierarchies, see Robert B. Shoemaker, *The London Mob: Violence and Disorder in Eighteenth-Century England* (London: Hambledon and London, 2004), 1-26.

24   König, *Kulturgeschichte*, 259.

25   Joachim Christoph Nemeitz, *Séjour de Paris* (Leiden: Jean van Aecoude, 1727), 118. On London and England, see Christoph Heyl, *A Passion for Privacy: Untersuchungen zur Genese der bürgerlichen Privatsphäre in London (1660-1800)* (Munich: Oldenbourg, 2004), 143, 148; and Penelope J. Corfield, "Dress for Deference and Dissent: Hats and the Decline of Hat Honour," *Costume* 23 (1989): 64-79.

26   König, *Kulturgeschichte*, 259-79.

27   König, *Kulturgeschichte*, 280-87; Bernd Jürgen Warneken, "Bürgerliche Gehkultur in der Epoche der Französischen Revolution," *Zeitschrift für Volkskunde* 85 (1989): 177-87.

28   George Sand, *Story of My Life*, group trans. ed. Thelma Jurgrau (Albany: SUNY Press, 1990), 892-93.

29   Stendhal, *Souvenirs d'Egotisme* (1832), chap. 6. On class mixing, also see Davidson, "Making Society 'Legible.'" On the combination of promenade and shopping, see Natacha Coquery, "Promenade et *shopping*: La visibilité de l'échange économique dans le Paris du XVIIIe siècle," in Loir, *La promenade*, 61-75.

30   Balzac, "Another Study of Womankind," trans. Jordan Stump, in *The Human*

Comedy: Selected Stories, ed. Peter Brooks (New York: New York Review Books, 2014), 38–39. A few years earlier, Balzac turned his observations of walking style into an essay on the theory of walking ("Theorie de la démarche").

31   John Sanderson, *Sketches of Paris* (Philadelphia: E. L. Cary and A. Hart, 1838), 40.

32   Adolf Glassbrenner, *Berliner Volksleben* (Leipzig: Engelmann, 1847), 1:22.

33   Georg Christoph Lichtenberg, letter of 17 Apr. 1770.

34   Johann Friedrich Reichardt, *Vertraute Briefe: Geschrieben auf einer Reise nach Wien und den österreichischen Staaten zu Ende des Jahres 1808 und zu Anfang 1809* (Amsterdam: Kunst- und Industrie-Comtoir, 1810), 1:460.

35   *The Autobiography of Francis Place*, ed. Mary Thale (Cambridge: Cambridge University Press, 1972), 64–65; William Hone, *The Every-Day Book* (1825; London: William Tegg, 1866), 1:29.

36   Pierce Egan, *Real Life in London* (1821; London: Methuen, 1905), 68–69. On the melding of shopping and the promenade in The Hague, see Jan Hein Furnée, "'Our Living Museum of Nouveautés': Visual and Social Pleasures in The Hague's Shopping Streets, 1650–1900," in *The Landscape of Consumption*, ed. Jan Hein Furnée and Clé Lesger (London: Palgrave, 2014), 208–31.

37   James D. McCabe, Jr., *Paris by Sunlight and Gaslight* (Philadelphia: National Publishing Company, 1869), 75.

38   Heinrich Heine, letter 37, 11 Dec. 1841, in *Lutezia* (1854).

39   I am indebted to Marshall Berman's powerful reading of the poem in *All That Is Solid Melts into Air* (New York: Penguin, 1988), 148–55. See also David Harvey, *Paris, Capital of Modernity* (New York: Routledge, 2003), 220–21; and Edward Ahearn, "A Café in the High Time of Haussmannization: Baudelaire's Confrontation with the Eyes of the Poor," in *The Thinking Space: The Café as Cultural Institution in Paris, Italy and Vienna*, ed. Leona Rittner, W. Scott Haine, and Jeffrey H. Jackson (Farnham, Surrey: Ashgate, 2013), 93–100. Note that Robert Smith's lyrics to the English rock band The Cure's 1987 song "How Beautiful You Are" are a slightly altered translation of the poem.

40   Jennifer Jones, "*Coquettes* and *Grisettes*: Women Buying and Selling in Ancien Régime Paris," in *The Sex of Things*, ed. Victoria de Grazia (Berkeley: University of California Press, 1996), 25–53; Erika Rappaport, *Shopping for Pleasure: Women in the Making of London's West End* (Princeton, NJ: Princeton University Press, 2000).

41   Tobias Smollett, *Travels through France and Italy* (1766; Fontwell, Sussex: Centaur Press, 1969), 322. Decades later, Willibald Alexis, *Wiener Bilder* (Leipzig: Brockhaus, 1833), 129, observed that all Viennese on the street were identically dressed and that foreigners were immediately recognizable. By 1888, though, Victor Tissot, *Un hiver à Vienne: Vienne et la vie viennoise* (Paris: Dentu, 1888), 156–57, lamented that the uniformity of dress was now international and exotic foreigners were no longer identifiable.

42   Nemeitz, *Séjour de Paris*, 81.

43   On veils, see Marni Kessler, "Dusting the Surface, or the *Bourgeoise*, the Veil, and Haussmann's Paris," in *The Invisible Flaneuse? Gender, Public Space, and Visual Culture in Nineteenth-Century Paris*, ed. Aruna D'Souza and Tom McDonough (Manchester: Manchester University Press, 2006), 49–64. On masks: Heyl, *Passion*, 305–49.

44   Matthew Beaumont, *Nightwalking: A Nocturnal History of London, Chaucer to Dickens* (London: Verso, 2015), 141–68. Previously the English word "nightwalk-

ing" had denoted crime and disorder. See Paul Griffiths, "Meanings of Nightwalking in Early Modern England," *Seventeenth Century* 13 (1998): 212–38. Later in the century came Nicolas Edme Rétif de la Bretonne's nocturnal accounts of Paris, followed by Joseph Aloys Mercy, *Berlinische Nächte* (Leipzig: Darnmann, 1803–4). Histories of the night: Joachim Schlör, *Nights in the Big City: Paris, Berlin, London, 1840–1930* (London: Reaktion, 1998); Craig Koslovsky, *Evening's Empire: A History of the Night in Early Modern Europe* (Cambridge: Cambridge University Press, 2011); Alain Cabantous, *Histoire de la nuit, XVIIe–XVIIIe siècle* (Paris: Fayard, 2009); Simone Delattre, *Les douze heures noires: La nuit à Paris au XIXe siècle* (Paris: Albin Michel, 2000); Wolfgang Schivelbusch, *Disenchanted Night: The Industrialization of Light in the Nineteenth Century*, trans. Angela Davies (Berkeley: University of California Press, 1988).

45 Julien Lemer, *Paris au gaz* (Paris: Jung-Treuttel, 1861), 1.

46 Edmondo De Amicis, *Ricordi di Parigi* (Milan: Treves, 1879), 26–27.

47 Seth Koven, *Slumming: Sexual and Social Politics in Victorian London* (Princeton, NJ: Princeton University Press, 2004), 14.

48 Abraham Flexner, *Prostitution in Europe* (New York: Century, 1914), 158. See also Schlör, *Nights*, 178–88. Useful studies of prostitution include Alain Corbin, *Women for Hire: Prostitution and Sexuality in France after 1850*, trans. Alan Sheridan (Cambridge, MA: Harvard University Press, 1990); Tony Henderson, *Disorderly Women in Eighteenth-Century London: Prostitution and Control in the Metropolis, 1730–1830* (London: Longman, 1999); Robert D. Storch, "Police Control of Street Prostitution in Victorian London: A Study in the Contexts of Political Action," in *Police and Society*, ed. David H. Bayley (Beverly Hills: Sage, 1977), 49–72; Vic Gatrell, *The First Bohemians: Life and Art in London's Golden Age* (London: Allen Lane, 2013), 70–113; and Nancy M. Wingfield, *The World of Prostitution in Late Imperial Austria* (New York: Oxford University Press, 2017).

49 Corbin, *Women for Hire*, 85.

50 Corbin, *Women for Hire*, 205.

51 Schlör, *Nights*, 217–34.

52 Jules Michelet, *La Femme* (Paris: Hachette, 1860), xxxiv; Harvey, *Paris*, 286–93.

53 "The Girl of the Period," *Saturday Review* 25 (1868): 340. See Lynda Nead, *Myths of Sexuality: Representations of Women in Victorian Britain* (Oxford: Blackwell, 1988), 179–81.

54 On gendered regulations and the fear of prostitution, see esp. Victoria E. Thompson, *The Virtuous Marketplace: Women and Men, Money and Politics in Paris, 1830–1870* (Baltimore: Johns Hopkins University Press, 2000), 86–118. An overview of scholarship on earlier centuries is Danielle van den Heuvel, "Gender in the Streets of the Premodern City," *Journal of Urban History* 45, no. 4 (July 2019).

55 Lynda Nead, *Victorian Babylon: People, Streets and Images in Nineteenth-Century London* (New Haven, CT: Yale University Press, 2000), 62–67.

56 Thomas Lindenberger, *Strassenpolitik: Zur Sozialgeschichte der öffentlichen Ordnung in Berlin 1900 bis 1914* (Bonn: Dietz, 1995), 69. On cases of mistaken identity and arrest in Berlin, see Joseph Ben Prestel, *Emotional Cities: Debates on Urban Change in Berlin and Cairo, 1860–1910* (Oxford: Oxford University Press, 2017), 88–97. On 1880s London, see Judith R. Walkowitz, *City of Dreadful Delight* (Chicago: University of Chicago Press, 1992), 127–29.

57 Schlör, *Nights*, 174–77; Lindenberger, *Strassenpolitik*, 70–71.

58 *Vossische Zeitung*, 21 Sept. 1911, quoted in Lindenberger, *Strassenpolitik*, 71.

59 *Vossische Zeitung*, 19 Jan. 1927, quoted in Schlör, *Nights*, 176.

60 Judith R. Walkowitz, "Going Public: Shopping, Street Harassment, and Street-walking in Late Victorian London," *Representations* 62 (Spring 1998): 1-30; James Winter, *London's Teeming Streets, 1830-1914* (London: Routledge, 1993), 173-89; Lynda Nead, "'Many little harmless and interesting adventures . . .': Gender and the Victorian City," in *The Victorian World*, ed. Martin Hewitt (London: Routledge, 2012), 291-95; Birchall, "'The Carnival Revels.'" On Berlin: Schlör, *Nights*, 177; Ben Prestel, *Emotional Cities*, 86-88.

61 Quoted in Karl Gutzkow, "Das Kastanienwäldchen in Berlin" (1869).

62 *Berliner Tageblatt*, 20 Feb. 1878, 8.

63 Quoted in Henry Vizetelly, *Berlin under the New Empire* (London: Tinsley Bros., 1879), 1:142. Similar New York examples are collected in James McCabe, *Lights and Shadows of New York Life* (Philadelphia: National Publishing, 1872), 611-14. On stories of fortuitous encounters and missed connections, see Tyler Carrington, *Love at Last Sight: Dating, Intimacy, and Risk in Turn-of-the-Century Berlin* (New York: Oxford University Press, 2019), 23-34; on personal ads, 126-43.

64 Diane Shaw, "The Construction of the Private in Medieval London," *Journal of Medieval and Early Modern Studies* 26 (1996): 447-66. On its significance for policing: Peter K. Andersson, *Streetlife in Late Victorian London: The Constable and the Crowd* (Basingstoke: Palgrave Macmillan, 2013), 49.

65 Daniel Jütte, *The Strait Gate: Thresholds and Power in Western History* (New Haven, CT: Yale University Press, 2015), 82-89, argues that doors were not typically left open. Looking at a later period, in England, Melanie Tebbutt, "Women's Talk? Gossip and 'Women's Words' in Working-class Communities, 1880-1939," in *Workers' Worlds*, ed. Andrew Davies and Steven Fielding (Manchester: Manchester University Press, 1992), 61, asserts that they were.

66 Friedrich Justinian von Günderrode, *Beschreibung einer Reise aus Teutschland durch einen Theil von Frankreich, England und Holland* (Breslau: Johann Ernst Meyer, 1783), 2:235. Louis-Sébastian Mercier made a similiar observation about London house doors by contrast to Paris: Mercier, *Parallèle de Paris et de Londres* (Paris: Didier Erudition, 1982), 140.

67 Jonathan Conlin, *Tales of Two Cities* (Berkeley: Counterpoint, 2013), 41; Charles Booth, *Life and Labour of the People in London* (London: Macmillan, 1892), 2:40, 46-82; Ellen Chase, *Tenant Friends in Old Deptford* (London: Williams and Norgate, 1929), 87.

68 M. J. Daunton, *House and Home in the Victorian City: Working Class Housing, 1850-1914* (London: Arnold, 1983), 12-13.

69 Yvonne Elet, "Seats of Power: The Outdoor Benches of Early Modern Florence," *Journal of the Society of Architectural Historians* 61 (2002): 444-69.

70 Jütte, *The Strait Gate*, 104; Alexander Cowan, "Seeing Is Believing: Urban Gossip and the Balcony in Early Modern Venice," in *Gender and the City before Modernity*, ed. Lin Foxhall and Gabriele Neher (Chicester: Wiley-Blackwell, 2013), 231-48. Tebbutt, "Women's Talk?" makes a similar point about doorways and working-class women.

71 René Brunschweiler, "Aneignung von Raum mit und ohne physische Präsenz: Prostituierte und Freier im Zürcher Niederdorf, 1870-1920," in *Stadt—Raum—Geschlecht: Beiträge zur Erforschung urbaner Lebensräume im 19. und 20. Jahrhun-*

dert, ed. Monika Imboden, Franziska Meister, and Daniel Kurz (Zurich: Chronos, 2000), 225–26. On warnings to all women: Natalie Tomas, "Did Women Have a Space?" in *Renaissance Florence: A Social History*, ed. Roger J. Crum and John T. Paoletti (Cambridge: Cambridge University Press, 2006), 311–28.

72   Heyl, *Passion*, 158–59; Steen Eiler Rasmussen, *London: The Unique City* (Harmondsworth: Penguin, 1960), 219–20.

73   Heyl, *Passion*, 166–67; Max Schlesinger, *Saunterings in and about London* (London: Nathaniel Cooke, 1853), 3–4.

74   Chase, *Tenant Friends*, 23–24, 57, 58.

75   Relevant here is the well-known study of the relationship between automobile traffic and sociability in San Francisco streets by Donald Appleyard, *Livable Streets* (Berkeley: University of California Press, 1981), 15–29.

76   Otto von Leixner, *1888–1891: Soziale Briefe aus Berlin* (Berlin: Pfeilstücker, 1891), 76–87. Anna Davin, *Growing Up Poor: Home, School and Street in London 1870–1914* (London: Rivers Oram, 1996), 63–68, 180–84, collects similar examples of children's activities. On Manchester and Salford, see Davies, *Leisure*, and Robert Roberts, *The Classic Slum: Salford Life in the First Quarter of the Century* (Manchester: University of Manchester Press, 1971). Also see the photographs in Willy Römer, *Kinder auf der Strasse, Berlin 1904–1932* (Berlin: Dirk Nishen, 1983). A systematic analysis is Imbke Behnken, *Urbane Spiel- und Strassenwelten: Zeitzeugen und Dokumente über Kindheit am Anfang des 20. Jahrhunderts* (Weinheim: Juventa, 2006). On eating in the street, see Keith R. Allen, *Hungrige Metropole: Essen, Wohlfahrt und Kommerz in Berlin* (Hamburg: Ergebnisse, 2002), 19.

77   Jane Jacobs, *The Death and Life of Great American Cities* (New York: Vintage, 1961), 50–54.

CHAPTER FOUR

1   Mark Twain, *A Tramp Abroad* (1880), ch. 119.

2   Walter King, "How High is Too High? Disposing of Dung in Seventeenth-Century Prescot," *Sixteenth Century Journal* 23 (1992): 443–57; Thomas Bauer, *Im Bauch der Stadt: Kanalisation und Hygiene in Frankfurt am Main 16.–19. Jahrhundert* (Frankfurt: Waldemar Kramer, 1998), 35; Carlo M. Cipolla, *Miasmas and Disease: Public Health and the Environment in the Pre-industrial Age*, trans. Elizabeth Potter (New Haven, CT: Yale University Press, 1992), 12–22; Emily Cockayne, *Hubbub: Filth, Noise, and Stench in England, 1600–1770* (New Haven, CT: Yale University Press, 2007), 188.

3   *Mistrichter*, elsewhere called *Mistmeister*. Felix Czeike, *Historisches Lexikon Wien*, vol. 5 (Vienna: Kremayr & Scheriau, 1997), 367–68. In modern Austrian German, *Mist* can mean "trash," but the earlier and more general meaning is "dung."

4   On Berlin: Johann Friedrich Karl Grimm, *Bemerkungen eines Reisenden durch die königlichen preussischen Staaten in Briefen* (Altenburg: Richter, 1779), 1:363–64; Julius Friedrich Knüppeln, *Charakteristik von Berlin: Stimme eines Kosmopoliten in der Wüsten* (Philadelphia [Leipzig and Gera], 1784), 1:12; *Schattenriss von Berlin* (Amsterdam, 1788), 81. On Vienna: Bertrand Michael Buchmann, "Dynamik des Städtebaus," in *Wien: Geschichte einer Stadt*, vol. 3, ed. Peter Csendes and Ferdinand Opll (Vienna: Böhlau, 2006), 72.

5   Repr. in *Bulletin de la Société de l'histoire de Paris et de l'Ile-de-France* 30 (1905): 175.

6   "Bittschrift eines D . . . haufens an die Polizei, eingereicht am Sonnabend," *Spener'sche Zeitung*, 1755, repr. in *Schriften des Vereins für die Geschichte Berlins* 11 (1874): 145.

7   *Encyclopédie méthodique*, vol. 1: *Médicine*, ed. Félix Vicq d'Azyr (Paris: Panckoucke, 1787), 587; Alain Corbin, *The Foul and the Fragrant: Odor and the French Social Imagination* (Cambridge, MA: Harvard University Press, 1986), 211.

8   Paul Jacob Marperger, *Von Reinigung der Gassen und Strassen in grossen und volckreichen Städten* (Dresden, 1724), 7.

9   Samuel Johnson, *Debates in Parliament*, in *The Yale Digital Edition of the Works of Samuel Johnson*, 11:216.

10 Daniel Vaillancourt, *Les urbanités parisiennes au XVIIe siècle* (Quebec: Presses de l'Université Laval, 2009), 241-45.

11 *Chronique scandaleuse, ou Paris ridicule* (Amsterdam, 1668), reprinted in *Le petit journal illustré*, 31 Jan. 1909. On the importance of clean clothes, see Georges Vigarello, *Concepts of Cleanliness: Changing Attitudes in France since the Middle Ages*, trans. Jean Birrell (Cambridge: Cambridge University Press, 1988), 61-77; and Karen Newman, *Cultural Capitals: Early Modern London and Paris* (Princeton, NJ: Princeton University Press, 2007), 80-81.

12 Arthur Young, *Travels in France and Italy During the Years 1787, 1788 and 1789* (London: J. M. Dent, 1915), 85: journal, 25 Oct. 1787.

13 Pierre-Jean Grosley, *A Tour to London; or, New Observations on England, and Its Inhabitants*, trans. Thomas Nugent (London: Lockyer Davis, 1772), 1:34.

14 Despite its subtitle, the compilation of evidence in Cockagne, *Hubbub*, supports this conclusion.

15 Quoted in Vigarello, *Concepts of Cleanliness*, 88. On perfuming in general, see Corbin, *The Foul and the Fragrant*, 61-77.

16 Quotations in Cipolla, *Miasmas*, 16-17.

17 Vigarello, *Concepts of Cleanliness*, 145; Corbin, *The Foul and the Fragrant*, 58-61.

18 N. M. Karamzin, *Letters of a Russian Traveler, 1789-1790*, trans. Florence Jonas (New York: Columbia University Press, 1957), 184-85.

19 Friedrich von Cölln, *Wien und Berlin in Parallele* (Amsterdam and Cologne [Leipzig]: Hammer, 1808), 93, 160.

20 Karamzin, *Letters*, 53.

21 William Howitt, *The Rural and Domestic Life of Germany* (London: Longman, 1842), 429.

22 Frances Trollope, *Paris and the Parisians in 1835* (London: Bentley, 1836), 1:233.

23 Quoted in Donald Reid, *Paris Sewers and Sewermen: Realities and Representations* (Cambridge, MA: Harvard University Press, 1991), 23.

24 Smollett, *The Expedition of Humphry Clinker* (Matthew Bramble to Dr. Lewis, June 8).

25 J.-H. Ronesse, *Vues sur la propreté des rues de Paris* (Paris, 1782), 15.

26 Louis-Sébastien Mercier, *Tableau de Paris* (Hamburg, 1781), 117 ("Reverbères").

27 Pierre Chauvet, *Essai sur la propreté de Paris, par un citoyen français* (Paris, 1797), 3-6.

28 Jean-Louis Harouel, "Les fonctions de l'alignement dans l'organisme urbain," *Dix-huitième siècle* 9 (1977): 135-49. See also chap. 6 in this book.

29   Richard Etlin, "L'air dans l'urbanisme des Lumières," *Dix-huitième siècle* 9 (1977): 123-34; David S. Barnes, *The Great Stink of Paris and the Nineteenth-Century Struggle against Filth and Germs* (Baltimore: Johns Hopkins University Press, 2006), 100-104; Marianne Rodenstein, *"Mehr Licht, Mehr Luft": Gesundheits-konzepte im Städtebau seit 1750* (Frankfurt: Campus, 1988); Brian Ladd, *Urban Planning and Civic Order in Germany, 1860-1914* (Cambridge, MA: Harvard University Press, 1990), 45-48.

30   James Fenimore Cooper, *Gleanings in Europe: The Rhine*, ed. Thomas Philbrick and Maurice Geracht (Albany: SUNY Press, 1986), letter 12 (1832), 117.

31   Carolyn Purnell, *The Sensational Past: How the Enlightenment Changed the Way We Use Our Senses* (New York: Norton, 2017), 110-14; Corbin, *The Foul and the Fragrant*, 142-60, on "the stench of the poor."

32   Manfred Gailus, "Rauchen in den Strassen und anderer Unfug: Kleine Strassen-konflikte (Polizeivergehen) in Berlin 1830 bis 1850," in *Berlin-Forschungen*, vol. 3, ed. Wolfgang Ribbe (Berlin: Colloquium, 1988), 11-42. On the smell of tobacco, see Corbin, *The Foul and the Fragrant*, 149-50.

33   James Winter, *London's Teeming Streets, 1830-1914* (London: Routledge, 1993), 101.

34   André Guillerme, *Les temps de l'eau: La cité, l'eau et les techniques: Nord de la France, fin IIIe-début XIXe siècle* (Seyssel: Champ Vallon, 1983), 174; Cipolla, *Miasmas*, 17.

35   Tiffany Stern, *Documents of Performance in Early Modern England* (Cambridge: Cambridge University Press, 2009), 50.

36   Swift, *City Cries, Instrumental and Vocal: or, An Examination of Certain Abuses, Corruptions, and Enormities, in London and Dublin* (Dublin, 1732), 8-9.

37   Quoted in Dan Cruickshank and Neil Burton, *Life in the Georgian City* (London: Viking, 1990), 15-17. Similarly, Lee Jackson, *Dirty Old London* (New Haven, CT: Yale University Press, 2014), 156, on London in 1832.

38   Trollope, *Paris*, 1:113.

39   *Mémoires*, quoted in Roger-Henri Guerrand, *Les lieux: Histoire des commodités* (Paris: La Découverte, 1985), 79.

40   *Johann Friedrich Reichardt's Vertraute Briefe aus Paris geschrieben in den Jahren 1802 und 1803* (Hamburg: B. G. Hoffmann, 1804), 253-54.

41   Early nineteenth-century examples cited in Manuel Frey, *Der reinliche Bürger: Entstehung und Verbreitung bürgerlicher Tugenden in Deutschland, 1760-1860* (Göttingen: Vandenhoeck und Ruprecht, 1997), 297-98.

42   Quoted in Jackson, *Dirty Old London*, 157.

43   Chauvet, *Essai sur la propreté*, 6.

44   Alphonse L, *De la salubrité de la ville de Paris* (Paris: Huzart, 1826), 6.

45   William Hazlitt, *Notes of a Journey through France and Italy* (London: Hunt and Clarke, 1826), 130-31.

46   Letter quoted in Christophe Studeny, *L'invention de la vitesse: France, XVIIIe-XXe siècle* (Paris: Gallimard, 1995), 105.

47   Bassana-Richard Forot, *Propreté et gestion des déchets à Paris hier et aujourd'hui* (Nice: Editions Bénévent, 2007), 45; Jean-Pierre Leguay, *La rue au Moyen Age* (Rennes: ouest france, 1984), 78-90. Marc Raeff, *The Well-Ordered Police State: Social and Institutional Change through Law in the Germanies and Russia, 1600-1800* (New Haven, CT: Yale University Press, 1983), 123, argues that because these

"rules applied to everyone," with no exceptions for privileged nobles, they marked "the beginning of treating all urban inhabitants in a uniform and equal manner for the sake of general benefit and breaking down traditionally privileged groups."

48   Henry Mayhew, *London Labour and the London Poor* (London: Griffin, Bohn, 1861), 2:294.

49   *The Autobiography of Francis Place*, ed. Mary Thale (Cambridge: Cambridge University Press, 1972), 68–70; *Scenes from My Life, by a Working Man* (London: Seeley, 1858), 30–31; Winter, *London's Teeming Streets*, 58.

50   Max Schlesinger, *Saunterings in and about London* (London: Nathaniel Cooke, 1853), 64.

51   *Journal of the Society of Arts*, 13 Feb. 1857, 196. Also see Mayhew, *London Labour*, 2:185.

52   James Grant, *Travels in Town* (London: Saunders and Otley, 1839), 1:9.

53   Mayhew, *London Labour*, 2:195. Paris statistics in Sabine Barles, *La ville délétère: Médecins et ingénieurs dans l'espace urbain, XVIIIe–XIXe siècle* (Seyssel: Champ Vallon, 1999), 239.

54   Nathaniel Hawthorne, *The English Notebooks*, ed. Randall Stewart (New York: Russell & Russell, 1962), 105, journal entry of 26 Dec. 1856.

55   Goethe, *Italienische Reise*, journal entry of 28 May 1787.

56   E. J. Tilt, *Elements of Health, and Principles of Female Hygiene* (Philadelphia: Lindsay and Blakiston, 1853), 193; also cited in Lee Jackson, http://www.victorian london.org. Photographic and film evidence of skirt-lifting is examined in Peter K. Andersson, *Silent History* (Montreal: McGill-Queen's University Press, 2018); examples from painting and graphic art in Temma Balducci, "*Aller à pied*: Bourgeois Women on the Streets of Paris," in *Women, Femininity and Public Space in European Visual Culture, 1789–1914*, ed. Temma Balducci and Heather Belnap Jensen (Farnham, Surrey: Ashgate, 2014), 154–56.

57   Lady F. W. Harberton, "Symposium on Dress," *Arena* 6 (1892): 334, quoted in Jackson, *Dirty Old London*, 4.

58   *Punch* 21 (1851): 29. In earlier centuries, men had assumed this duty as well, dragging their fashionably droopy sleeves through the mud.

59   *Berliner Tageblatt*, 5 May 1878.

60   Pierce Egan, *Real Life in London* (1821; London: Methuen, 1905), 325–26.

61   Mark Bills, "William Powell Frith's 'The Crossing Sweeper': An Archetypal Image of Mid-Nineteenth-Century London," *Burlington Magazine* 146, no. 1214 (May 2004): 300–307.

62   Arthur J. Munby, diary, 30 Dec. 1862, in Derek Hudson, *Munby, Man of Two Worlds* (Boston: Gambit, 1972), 143.

63   Tim Hitchcock, *Down and Out in Eighteenth-Century London* (London: Hambledon and London, 2004), 58.

64   Mayhew, *London Labour*, 2:465. Similarly, Charles Manby Smith, *Curiosities of London Life* (London: Cash, 1857), 46–47. Hitchcock, *Down and Out*, 58, describes a 1736 case in which a sweeper helped solve a theft.

65   Mayhew, *London Labour*, 2:475.

66   Ludwig Kalisch, "Pariser Bilder und Geschichten: Allerlei sonderbare Erwerbsquellen und Geschäfte," *Die Gartenlaube* (1874): 259.

67   Elizabeth L. Banks, "How the Other Half Lives: The Crossing-Sweeper," *English Illustrated Magazine* 11 (1894): 845–50. Long before that, John Gay's 1716 poem *Trivia* made the same claim.

68   *Punch* 2 (1842): 41. See also Hitchcock, *Down and Out*, 56–58; Jackson, *Dirty Old London*, 33–35; and, on Savoyard sweepers in Paris, John Sanderson, *Sketches of Paris* (Philadelphia: E. L. Cary and A. Hart, 1838), 39.

69   Abbé Pierre Jaubert, *Dictionnaire raisonné universel des arts et métiers* (1773), excerpted in Marguerite Pitsch, *La vie populaire à Paris au XVIIIᵉ siècle* (Paris: Picard, 1949), 95; Vincent Milliot, *Un policier des Lumières* (Seyssel: Champ Vallon, 2011), 587–90.

70   Pierre-Denis Boudriot, "Essai sur l'ordure en milieu urbain à l'époque pré-industrielle: Boues, immondices et gadoue à Paris au XVIIIᵉ siècle," *Histoire, économie et société* 5 (1986): 518.

71   Ludwig Geiger, *Berlin 1688–1840: Geschichte des geistigen Lebens der preussischen Hauptstadt*, vol. 1 (Berlin: Paetel, 1893), 640–41.

72   Czeike, *Historisches Lexikon Wien*, 5:368.

73   *The Life and Remarkable Adventures of Israel R. Potter* (Providence, RI: Henry Trumbull, 1824), 78.

74   See the images and especially the engraved drinking glass reproduced in Wolfgang Kos, ed., *Wiener Typen* (Vienna: Brandstätter, 2013), 280.

75   Notably in Paris: Simone Delattre, *Les douze heures noires: La nuit à Paris au XIXᵉ siècle* (Paris: Albin Michel, 2000), 218–37; Pierre Citron, *La Poésie de Paris dans la littérature française de Rousseau à Baudelaire* (Paris: Les éditions de Minuit, 1961), 2:315–18; Patrice Higgonet, *Paris: Capital of the World* (Cambridge, MA: Harvard University Press, 2002), 221–24.

76   Joseph Durieu, *Les Parisiens d'aujourd'hui: Les types sociaux de simple récolte et d'extraction* (Paris: Giard et Brière, 1910), 92–93; Alain Faure, "Sordid Class, Dangerous Class? Observations on Parisian Ragpickers and Their *Cités* during the Nineteenth Century," *International Review of Social History* 41 (1996): 157–76.

77   Faure, "Sordid Class." On London: Andrea Tanner, "Dust-O! Rubbish in Victorian London, 1860–1900," *London Journal* 31 (2006): 157–78.

78   Thomas J. Campanella, "Broom with a View," www.slate.com, 16 Apr. 2018.

79   Grimm, *Bemerkungen eines Reisenden*, 1:365.

80   Friedrich Schulz, "Kleine Wanderungen durch Teutschland," *Teutscher Merkur*, 1785, 2nd quarter, 71.

81   Lee Jackson, *A Dictionary of Victorian London* (London: Anthem, 2006), 179.

82   Guerrand, *Les lieux*, 67; Pierre Saddy, "Le cycle des immondices," *Dix-huitième siècle* 9 (1977): 208–9; Reid, *Paris Sewers*, 11, 72–8; Barnes, *Great Stink*, 68–69, 81–83.

83   Czeike, *Historisches Lexikon Wien*, 5:368.

84   Guerrand, *Les lieux*, 41 (quotation), 56, 78. Other examples in Bauer, *Im Bauch der Stadt*, 35–36; Peter Payer, *Unentbehrliche Requisiten der Grossstadt: Eine Kulturgeschichte der öffentlichen Bedürfnisanstalten von Wien* (Vienna: Löcker, 2000), 18.

85   Clé Lesger, "Urban Planning, Urban Improvement and the Retail Landscape in Amsterdam, 1600–1850," in *The Landscape of Consumption*, ed. Jan Hein Furnée and Clé Lesger (London: Palgrave, 2014), 105–6.

86   Ernest Hemingway, *A Moveable Feast* (New York: Bantam, 1964), 3–4; Reid, *Paris*

Sewers, 79–82; Gérard Jacquemet, "Urbanisme parisien: La bataille du tout-a-l'égout à la fin du XIXe siècle," *Revue d'histoire moderne et contemporaine* 26 (1979): 505–48.

87   Payer, *Unentbehrliche Requisiten*, 23, 44–45. The trade was sometimes depicted in printed collections of "cries" during that period.

88   Willibald Alexis, *Wiener Bilder* (Leipzig: Brockhaus, 1833), 150–51; Payer, *Unentbehrliche Requisiten*, 45–46; Frey, *Der reinliche Bürger*, 298. On the disappearance of the earlier accommodations in London, see James Stevenson, *Report on the Necessity of Latrine Accommodation for Women in the Metropolis* (London: Parish of Paddington, Vestry, 1879).

89   Guerrand, *Les lieux*, 62–63, 89.

90   Adolf Schmidl, *Wien und seine nächsten Umgebungen* (Vienna: Schmidt, 1847), 130–31.

91   Payer, *Unentbehrliche Requisiten*, 46–49.

92   Landesarchiv Berlin, A Rep. 000-02-01, no. 2019; Payer, *Unentbehrliche Requisiten*, 48–124; Jackson, *Dirty Old London*, 155–80. On other cities: Nicolas Kenny, *The Feel of the City* (Toronto: University of Toronto Press, 2014), 184–91, on Montreal and Brussels; Maureen Flanagan, "Private Needs, Public Space: Public Toilets Provision in the Anglo-Atlantic Patriarchal City: London, Dublin, Toronto and Chicago," *Urban History* 41 (2014): 265–90; Peter C. Baldwin, "Public Privacy: Restrooms in American Cities, 1869–1932," *Journal of Social History* 48 (2014): 264–88.

93   Ordinance of 1 Apr. 1843, in *Collection officielle des ordonnances de police: Depuis 1800 jusqu'à 1844* (Paris: Paul Dupont, 1845), 3:585; ordinance of 23 Feb. 1850, in *Collection officielle des ordonnances de police, Tome II (1849–1880)* (Paris: Chaix, 1881), 19.

94   Frey, *Der reinliche Bürger*, 298; Payer, *Unentbehrliche Requisiten*, 35.

95   David Higgs, ed., *Queer Sites: Gay Urban Histories since 1600* (London: Routledge, 1999); Payer, *Unentbehrliche Requisiten*, 172–76.

96   Denis Caillaud et al., *Les grands boulevards* (Paris: Musées de la ville de Paris, 1985), 206–7.

97   Stevenson, *Report on the Necessity*.

98   Quoted in Guerrand, *Les lieux*, 116.

99   Landesarchiv Berlin, A Rep. 000-02-01, no. 2019. Payer, *Unentbehrliche Requisiten*, 58, quotes a nearly identical objection from Vienna. On similar objections in London and Dublin, see Maureen A. Flanagan, *Constructing the Patriarchal City: Gender and the Built Environments of London, Dublin, Toronto, and Chicago, 1870s into the 1940s* (Philadelphia: Temple University Press, 2018), 125, 153–54.

100   Quoted in Marie Thézy, "Histoire du mobilier urbain parisienne du second Empire à nos jours," in *Paris, la rue* (Paris: Societé des Amis la Bibliothèque historique, 1976), 66.

101   Landesarchiv Berlin, A Rep. 000-02-01, nos. 2020–21; Jackson, *Dirty Old London*, 172–80; Barbara Penner, "A World of Unmentionable Suffering: Women's Public Conveniences in Victorian London," *Journal of Design History* 14 (2001): 35–51; Payer, *Unentbehrliche Requisiten*, 65–84, and 112–24 on underground facilities; Thézy, "Histoire du mobilier," 63–67. On another city: Andrew Brown-May and Peg Fraser, "Gender, Respectability, and Public Conveniences in Melbourne,

Australia, 1859–1902," in *Ladies and Gents: Public Toilets and Gender*, ed. Olga Gershenson and Barbara Penner (Philadelphia: Temple University Press, 2009), 75–89.

CHAPTER FIVE

1   Martin Lister, *A Journey to Paris in the Year 1698* (London: Jacob Tonson, 1699), 13; Annik Pardailhé-Galabrun, "Les déplacements des Parisiens dans la ville aux XVIIème et XVIIIème siècles," *Histoire, économie et société* 2 (1983): 228.

2   Quoted in Christophe Studeny, *L'invention de la vitesse* (Paris: Gallimard, 1995), 66.

3   John Taylor, *The World Runs on Wheels* (1623), xix; Tatsuya Mitsuda, *The Horse in European History, 1550–1900* (DPhil diss., Cambridge University, 2007), 14–25.

4   Pater Hilarion [Joseph Richter], *Bildergalerie weltlicher Missbräuche* (Frankfurt and Leipzig, 1785), 141–43.

5   Louis-Sébastien Mercier, *Tableau de Paris* (Amsterdam, 1783), 8:231–36, "Aller à pied." Other examples cited in Studeny, *L'invention*, 66.

6   John Moore, *A View of Society and Manners in France, Switzerland, Germany, and Italy*, 2nd ed. (London: Strahan, 1779), 1:34. On Mercier, see Colin Jones, "Meeting, Greeting and Other 'Little Customs of the Day' on the Streets of Late Eighteenth-Century Paris," in *The Politics of Gesture: Historical Perspectives*, ed. Michael J. Braddick (Oxford: Oxford University Press, 2009), 152–53.

7   Quoted in John Lough, *France on the Eve of Revolution: British Travellers' Observations, 1763–1788* (London: Croon Helm, 1987), 75. Similarly in Arthur Young, *Travels in France and Italy* (London: J. M. Dent, 1915), 85: journal, 25 Oct. 1787. More examples in Studeny, *L'invention*, 67–71; and Mitsuda, *Horse*, 236–45.

8   Quoted in Studeny, *L'invention*, 119.

9   Quoted in Studeny, *L'invention*, 119.

10   Goncourt journal, 22 Feb. 1857, quoted in Studeny, *L'invention*, 120.

11   See Marshall Berman, *All That Is Solid Melts into Air* (New York: Penguin, 1988), 210–11.

12   Paul Schmidt, *Die ersten 50 Jahre der Königlichen Schutzmannschaft zu Berlin* (Berlin: Mittler, 1898), 5–6.

13   Mrs. Humphry Ward, *A Writer's Recollections* (London: W. Collins, 1918), 197; quoted in Jerry White, *London in the Nineteenth Century* (London: Jonathan Cape, 2007), 123.

14   Arthur J. Munby, diary, 12 Jan. 1863, in Derek Hudson, *Munby* (Boston: Gambit, 1972), 147.

15   Henry James, "London," in *Essays in London and Elsewhere* (New York: Harper, 1893), 19.

16   On the railroad, see Wolfgang Schivelbusch, *The Railway Journey* (Berkeley: University of California Press, 1986), 53. On cars, see Brian Ladd, *Autophobia* (Chicago: University of Chicago Press, 2008), 17–21.

17   Nicholas Papayanis, *Horse-Drawn Cabs and Omnibuses in Paris* (Baton Rouge: LSU Press, 1996), 16–21; Daniel Vaillancourt, *Les urbanités parisiennes au XVIIᵉ siècle* (Quebec: Presses de l'Université Laval, 2009), 273–74; Joan DeJean, *How Paris*

Became Paris: The Invention of the Modern City (New York: Bloomsbury, 2014), 114-22.

18   Jo Guldi, *Roads to Power: Britain Invents the Infrastructure State* (Cambridge, MA: Harvard University Press, 2012); on the French *Turgotines*: Studeny, *L'invention*, 78-81.

19   Hermann von Pückler-Muskau, *Briefe eines Verstorbenen*, ed. Heinz Ohff (Berlin: Kupfergraben, 1986), 389 (letter 48, 14 Jan. 1829).

20   Ernest Fouinet, "Un voyage en omnibus," in *Paris, ou le livre des cent-et-un* (Paris: L'advocat, 1831), 2:61-62. A similar account is in Eduard Kolloff, *Schilderungen aus Paris* (Hamburg: Hoffmann und Campe, 1839), 1:398-413.

21   Edmondo De Amicis, *Ricordi di Londra*, 2nd ed. (Milan: Treves, 1874), 32.

22   Max Schlesinger, *Saunterings in and about London* (London: Nathaniel Cooke, 1853), 166. Georg Simmel's later discussion of the social changes wrought by buses has been much cited: Simmel, *Soziologie* (Leipzig: Duncker und Humblot, 1908), 650.

23   Schivelbusch, *Railway Journey*, 70-71.

24   Paul Lindenberg, *Berlin in Wort und Bild* (Berlin: Dümmler, 1895), 135.

25   Kolloff, *Schilderungen*, 1:413-14.

26   Charles Dickens, "Omnibuses," *Sketches by Boz* (1836).

27   Joseph Roth, *Frankfurter Zeitung*, 15 Nov. 1924, in *What I Saw: Reports from Berlin, 1920-1933*, trans. Michael Hofmann (New York: Norton, 2003), 101-2.

28   Quoted in Studeny, *L'invention*, 117.

29   Papayanis, *Horse-Drawn Cabs*, 66.

30   Studeny, *L'invention*, 208.

31   Guy de Maupassant, "Le père Mongilet" (1883).

32   Ordinance of 12 July 1879, in *Collection officielle des ordonnances de police, Tome II (1849-1880)* (Paris: Chaix, 1881), 693.

33   Alfred Kerr, letter of 12 July 1896, in *Mein Berlin: Schauplätze einer Metropole* (Berlin: Aufbau, 1999), 114; Isidor Kastan, *Berlin wie es war*, 2nd ed. (Berlin: Rudolf Mosse, 1919), 69. Vienna did not have double-decker buses before the motor age.

34   Virginia Woolf, diary, 3 Feb. 1905; Nadezhda Krupskaya, *Memories of Lenin*, trans. E. Verney (New York: International Publishers, 1930), 71. Also see Brian Stokoe, "Viewing the Metropolis: The Experience of London by Bus," *London Journal* 41 (2016): 150-69.

35   Kitty J. Buckman, quoted in Katrina Jungnickel, "'One needs to be very brave to stand all that': Cycling, Rational Dress and the Struggle for Citizenship in Late Nineteenth-Century Britain," *Geoforum* 64 (2015): 362.

36   Fouinet, "Un voyage en omnibus," 78-79.

37   Richard Jenkyns, *God, Space and City in the Roman Imagination* (Oxford: Oxford University Press, 2013), 143-62; Monica Hellström, "Fast Movement through the City: Ideals, Stereotypes and City Planning," in *The Moving City: Processions, Passages and Promenades in Ancient Rome*, ed. Ida Östenberg, Simon Malmberg, and Jonas Bjørnebye (London: Bloomsbury, 2015), 47-58.

38   Victor Auburtin, "Wie sie spazieren gehen," *Berliner Tageblatt*, 1 May 1911. Also see Joanna Guldi, "The History of Walking and the Digital Turn: Stride and Lounge in London, 1808-1851," *Journal of Modern History* 84 (2012): 116-44.

39   Matthew Beaumont, *Nightwalking* (London: Verso, 2015), 377-78.

40   Pepys's diary, 10 Dec. 1661. Also see John Gay, *Trivia: or, The Art of Walking the Streets of London*, bk. 3, lines 17–34. Contemporaneous Paris examples are in Vaillancourt, *Les urbanités*, 267–68.

41   On Boileau: Vaillancourt, *Les urbanités*, 171–77. On the tradition: Vincent Milliot, *Paris en bleu: Images de la ville dans la littérature de colportage (XVIᵉ–XVIIIᵉ siecles)* (Paris: Parigramme, 1996), 81; and Pierre Citron, *La poésie de Paris dans la littérature française de Rousseau à Baudelaire* (Paris: Les éditions de Minuit, 1961), 1:90, 353.

42   Gay, *Trivia*, bk. 3, lines 35–50.

43   Pepys's diary, 27 Nov. 1660.

44   Studeny, *L'invention*, 67.

45   *London Post*, 16–18 Feb. 1702, from "Early Eighteenth-Century Newspaper Reports: A Sourcebook Compiled by Rictor Norton," http://grubstreet.rictor norton.co.uk/insolent.htm.

46   Guy Patin, letter, 26 Jan. 1655, in *Lettres de Guy Patin*, ed. Loïc Capron, at http://www.biusante.parisdescartes.fr/patin/; Vaillancourt, *Les urbanités*, 211–12. These examples cast doubt on Richard Sennett's assertion that "our pre-modern ancestors were more relaxed" about traffic delays, in *Building and Dwelling: Ethics for the City* (New York: Farrar, Straus and Giroux, 2018), 36.

47   Nathaniel S. Wheaton, *A Journal of a Residence during Several Months in London* (Hartford, CT: Huntington, 1830), 191.

48   Horace Walpole, letter of 18 April 1791.

49   Parking rules: Paris decree of 22 June 1820, in *Collection officielle des ordonnances de police: Depuis 1800 jusqu'à 1844* (Paris: Paul Dupont, 1845), 2:175; Felix Czeike, *Historisches Lexikon Wien* (Vienna: Kremayr & Scheriau, 1994), 3:532–33; Wiener Stadt- und Landesarchiv, 2.8.16.A1.1 (carriage licenses from the 1830s and 1840s).

50   F. Hervé, *How to Enjoy Paris in 1842: Intended to Serve as a Companion and Monitor, Containing Historical, Political, Commercial, Artistical, Theatrical and Statistical Information* (Paris: Amyot, 1842), 116–17.

51   John Sanderson, *Sketches of Paris* (Philadelphia: E. L. Cary and A. Hart, 1838), 52.

52   Delphine de Girardin, letter of 21 June 1837, in *Œuvres complètes de Madame Émile de Girardin* (Paris: Plon, 1861), 4:141–42. It should be noted that she published her "letters" under a male pseudonym, Vicomte de Launay.

53   Hervé, *How to Enjoy Paris*, 117.

54   1767 quotation in David Garrioch, *Neighbourhood and Community in Paris, 1740–1790* (Cambridge: Cambridge University Press, 1986), 213; also see Arlette Farge, *Vivre dans la rue à Paris au XVIIIᵉ siècle* (Paris: Gallimard, 1979), 168–71.

55   Nicholas Papayanis, *Planning Paris before Haussmann* (Baltimore: Johns Hopkins University Press, 2004), 103, on the 1840s. Studeny, *L'invention*, 102–4, makes a similar claim about the 1830s. There is no definitive way to pin down such a general assessment. Vaillancourt, *Les urbanités*, identifies an embrace of circulation in the seventeenth century, although he describes it as "more virtual than actual" (17).

56   Girardin, *Œuvres*, 4:143.

57   The quoted line comes from the ordinance of 20 Jan. 1832: *Collection officielle des ordonnances de police: Depuis 1800 jusqu'à 1844*, 3:1–2. Also see the related ordinance of 8 Feb. 1819, in *Collection officielle*, 2:130–31; and Sabine Barles, "La voie

publique est spécialement affectée à la circulation," in *La modernité avant Hauss-mann: Formes de l'espace urbain à Paris, 1801–1853*, ed. Karen Bowie (Paris: Editions Recherches, 2001), 200.

58   Felix Czeike, "Regelung und Sicherung des grossstädtischen Strassenverkehrs seit dem 18. Jahrhundert dargestellt am Beispiel der Stadt Wien," *Zeitschrift für Verkehrssicherheit* 8 (1962): 205.

59   Carl Philipp Moritz, *Reisen eines Deutschen in England im Jahre 1782*, 2nd ed. (Berlin: Friedrich Maurer, 1785), 20.

60   Daly cited by Studeny, *L'invention*, 113. On attitudes and policies in nineteenth-century London, see James Winter, *London's Teeming Streets, 1830–1914* (London: Routledge, 1993), 42–48; Peter K. Andersson, *Streetlife in Late Victorian London* (Basingstoke: Palgrave Macmillan, 2013), 89–96, 128–29; and Carlos Lopez Gal-viz, "Mobilities at a Standstill: Regulating Circulation in London *c.* 1863–1870," *Journal of Historical Geography* 42 (2013): 62–76. Mark Jenner, " 'Nauceious and Abominable'? Pollution, Plague, and Poetics in John Gay's *Trivia*," in *Walking the Streets of Eighteenth-Century London: John Gay's* Trivia *(1716)*, ed. Clare Brant and Susan E. Whyman (Oxford: Oxford University Press, 2007), 97, argues that attitudes had changed by 1700.

61   Czeike, "Regelung," 212.

62   Landesarchiv Berlin, A Rep. 000-02-01, Nr. 2397. Frances Trollope, *Vienna and the Austrians* (London: Bentley, 1838), 2:33, makes this observation of Viennese coachmen; William Howitt, *The Rural and Domestic Life of Germany* (London: Longman, 1842), 366, describes it as "a horrid groan."

63   Quoted in Adolf Wolff, *Berliner Revolutions-Chronik: Darstellung der Berliner Bewegungen im Jahre 1848*, vol. 1 (Berlin: Hempel, 1851), 87.

64   William Morris, "Free Speech in the Streets," *Commonweal* 2 (31 July 1886): 137. Also see Krista Cowman, "The Battle of the Boulevards: Class, Gender and the Purpose of Public Space in Later Victorian Liverpool," in *Identities in Space*, ed. Simon Gunn and Robert J. Morris (Aldershot: Ashgate 2001), 152–64. On class and mobility in Paris, see Victoria E. Thompson, "Telling 'Spatial Stories': Urban Space and Bourgeois Identity in Early Nineteenth-Century Paris," *Journal of Modern History* 75 (2003): 523–56. More broadly, Richard Sennett, *Flesh and Stone* (New York: Norton, 1994), 256–57, argues that motion desensitizes the body and circulation promotes indifference.

65   Thomas Lindenberger, *Strassenpolitik: Zur Sozialgeschichte der öffentlichen Ord-nung in Berlin 1900 bis 1914* (Bonn: Dietz, 1995), 347.

66   *Berliner Illustrirte Zeitung*, 6 Mar. 1910, repr. in *Als die Deutschen demonstrieren lernten: Das Kulturmuster "friedliche Strassendemonstration" im preussischen Wahlrechtskampf 1908–1910*, ed. Bernd Jürgen Warneken (Tübingen: Ludwig-Uhland-Institut für empirische Kulturwissenschaft der Universität Tübingen, 1986), 67.

67   Josef Stübben, *Der Städtebau* (Darmstadt: Bergsträsser, 1890), 32.

68   *First Report from the Select Committee on Metropolis Improvements*, House of Commons, 23 May 1838, iv, repr. in *Irish University Press Series of British Parliamentary Papers, Urban Areas, Planning*, vol. 1 (Shannon: Irish University Press, 1968).

69   Quoted in Gareth Stedman Jones, *Outcast London* (New York: Pantheon, 1971), 180.

70   *Mémoires du Baron Haussmann*, 3rd ed. (Paris: Victor-Havard, 1890), 2:257.

71   Peter D. Norton, *Fighting Traffic: The Dawn of the Motor Age in the American City* (Cambridge, MA: MIT Press, 2008). For a different and more Eurocentric analysis of the ascendancy of the automobile, one more compatible with the argument here, see Gijs Mom, *Atlantic Automobilism: Emergence and Persistence of the Car, 1895-1940* (New York: Berghahn, 2015); also Ladd, *Autophobia*. On 1920s Berlin, see Molly Loberg, *The Struggle for the Streets of Berlin* (Cambridge: Cambridge University Press, 2018), 119-50.

72   Quoted in Harald Bodenschatz, "Berlin West: Abschied von der steinernen Stadt," in *Neue Städte aus Ruinen*, ed. Klaus von Beyme et al. (Munich: Prestel, 1992), 74.

CHAPTER SIX

1   "Government created itself in the act of claiming the city streets and squares." Peter Arnade, Martha Howell, and Walter Simons, introduction to the special issue "Fertile Spaces: The Productivity of Urban Space in Northern Europe," *Journal of Interdisciplinary History* 32:4 (Spring 2002), 547. Among the many studies of royal and ducal entries in the Middle Ages and Renaissance, see Fabrizio Nevola, *Siena: Constructing the Renaissance City* (New Haven, CT: Yale University Press, 2007), 29-45; Gordon Kipling, *Enter the King: Theatre, Liturgy and Ritual in the Medieval Civic Triumph* (New York: Oxford University Press, 1998); Bernard Guenée and Françoise Lehoux, *Les entrées royales françaises de 1328 à 1515* (Paris: CNRS, 1968); Lawrence M. Bryant, *The King and the City in the Parisian Royal Entry Ceremony: Politics, Ritual, and Art in the Renaissance* (Geneva: Droz, 1986); and R. M. Smuts, "Public Ceremony and Royal Charisma: The English Royal Entry into London, 1485-1642," in *The First Modern Society*, ed. A. L. Beier, David Cannadine, and James M. Rosenheim (Cambridge: Cambridge University Press, 1989), 65-93. Studies that also reach into related aspects of ceremony and streets include Miri Rubin, *Corpus Christi: The Eucharist in Late Medieval Culture* (Cambridge: Cambridge University Press, 1991), 243-71; Barbara A. Hanawalt and Kathryn Reyerson, eds., *City and Spectacle in Medieval Europe* (Minneapolis: University of Minnesota Press, 1994); and Peter Arnade, *Realms of Ritual: Burgundian Ceremony and Civic Life in Late Medieval Ghent* (Ithaca, NY: Cornell University Press, 1996. On eighteenth-century Paris, see Arlette Farge, *Fragile Lives: Violence, Power and Solidarity in Eighteenth-Century Paris*, trans. Carol Shelton (Cambridge, MA: Harvard University Press, 1993), 172-73.

2   Maximilian Rapsilber, "Bilder der Strasse," in *Spreeathener* (Berlin: Haber, 1914), 102.

3   Quoted in Arlette Farge, *Vivre dans la rue à Paris au XVIIIᵉ siècle* (Paris: Gallimard, 1979), 197. In general: Marc Raeff, *The Well-Ordered Police State: Social and Institutional Change through Law in the Germanies and Russia, 1600-1800* (New Haven, CT: Yale University Press, 1983).

4   Helmut Angelmahr, "Transport: Die Überwindung wachsender Distanzen," in *Wien: Wirtschaftsgeschichte, 1740-1938*, ed. Günther Chaloupek, Peter Eigner, and Michael Wagner (Vienna: Jugend und Volk, 1991), 2:860.

5   Simon Devereaux, "Recasting the Theatre of Execution: The Abolition of the

Tyburn Ritual," *Past and Present* 202 (2009): 127-74; Thomas W. Laqueur, "Crowds, Carnival and the State in English Executions, 1604-1868," in Beier, *The First Modern Society*, 305-55.

6   V. A. C. Gatrell, *The Hanging Tree: Execution and the English People, 1770-1868* (Oxford: Oxford University Press, 1994), 297, makes this point; also see 589-611; and Richard J. Evans, *Rituals of Retribution: Capital Punishment in Germany, 1600-1987* (Oxford: Oxford University Press, 1996), 305-17; David D. Cooper, *The Lesson of the Scaffold: The Public Execution Controversy in Victorian England* (Athens: Ohio University Press, 1974); Randall McGowen, "Civilizing Punishment: The End of the Public Execution in England," *Journal of British Studies* 33 (1994): 257-82; Laurence Guignard, "Les supplices publics au XIXe siècle: L'abstraction du corps," in *Le corps violenté: Du geste à la parole*, ed. Michel Porret (Geneva: Droz, 1998), 157-84; and Pieter Spierenburg, *The Spectacle of Suffering: Executions and the Evolution of Repression: From a Preindustrial Metropolis to the European Experience* (Cambridge: Cambridge University Press, 1984), 183-99. France continued public executions until 1939, but, after moving them off the Place de Grève in 1830, usually not in prominent sites or in front of large crowds.

7   John Stuart Mill, "Civilization," quoted, in part, in Gatrell, *Hanging Tree*, 595.

8   Quoted in Eric Hazan, *The Invention of Paris: A History in Footsteps*, trans. David Fernbach (London: Verso, 2010), 161. On Oxford Street: Gatrell, *Hanging Tree*, 602-3.

9   Geoffrey Pearson, *Hooligan: A History of Respectable Fears* (London: Macmillan, 1983); Joan Neuberger, *Hooliganism: Crime, Culture, and Power in St. Petersburg, 1900-1914* (Berkeley: University of California Press, 1993).

10 Examples: "Early Eighteenth-Century Newspaper Reports: A Sourcebook Compiled by Rictor Norton," http://grubstreet.rictornorton.co.uk/insolent.htm; Farge, *Vivre dans la rue*, 151-59, 188-89, 217-22; Arlette Farge and Jacques Revel, *The Vanishing Children of Paris: Rumor and Politics before the French Revolution* (Cambridge, MA: Harvard University Press, 1991); Jeffry Kaplow, *The Names of Kings: The Parisian Laboring Poor in the Eighteenth Century* (New York: Basic, 1972), 137-38; Michael John, "'Strassenkrawalle und Exzesse': Formen des sozialen Protestes der Unterschichten in Wien 1880 bis 1918," in *Wien-Prag-Budapest*, ed. Gerhard Melinz and Susan Zimmermann (Vienna: Promedia, 1996): 230-44; Thomas Lindenberger, *Strassenpolitik: Zur Sozialgeschichte der öffentlichen Ordnung in Berlin 1900 bis 1914* (Bonn: Dietz, 1995), 107-72.

11 Rene S. Marion, *The Dames de la Halle: Community and Authority in Early Modern Paris* (PhD diss., Johns Hopkins University, 1994), 319.

12 Elaine A. Reynolds, *Before the Bobbies: The Night Watch and Police Reform in Metropolitan London, 1720-1830* (Palo Alto, CA: Stanford University Press, 1998); Alan Williams, *The Police of Paris, 1718-1789* (Baton Rouge: LSU Press, 1979), 71-111; Catherine Denys, "The Development of Police Forces in Urban Europe in the Eighteenth Century," *Journal of Urban History* 36 (2010): 332-44.

13 Robert D. Storch, "The Policeman as Domestic Missionary: Urban Discipline and Popular Culture in Northern England, 1850-1880," *Journal of Social History* 9 (1976): 481-509; Lindenberger, *Strassenpolitik*, 82-106.

14 Quentin Deluermoz, *Policiers dans la ville: La construction d'un ordre public à Paris, 1854-1914* (Paris: Publications de la Sorbonne, 2012), 45-46, 103-35;

Peter K. Andersson, *Streetlife in Late Victorian London* (Basingstoke: Palgrave Macmillan, 2013); Lindenberger, *Strassenpolitik*, 72–82.

15   Anthony Sutcliffe, *Towards the Planned City: Germany, Britain, the United States and France, 1780–1914* (Oxford: Blackwell, 1981); Brian Ladd, *Urban Planning and Civic Order in Germany, 1860–1914* (Cambridge, MA: Harvard University Press, 1990).

16   Paul Léon, *Paris, Histoire de la rue* (Paris: La Taille Douce, 1947), 108–9, 222–28.

17   Léon, *Paris*, 105.

18   Louis-Sébastien Mercier, *Tableau de Paris* (Amsterdam, 1782), 2:204, "Les écriteaux des rues." Also see Jeanne Pronteau, *Les numérotages des maisons de Paris du XVᵉ siècle à nos jours* (Paris: Commission des travaux historiques, 1966), 81–86; and special section on house numbering in *Urban History* 39 (2012): 607–79.

19   Voltaire, "Des embellissements de Paris," 1749.

20   Johann Georg Krünitz, *Oekonomische Encyklopädie*, entry "Strasse," available at http://www.kruenitz1.uni-trier.de.

21   Krünitz, *Oekonomische Encyklopädie*. Diderot's *Encyclopédie* also insisted on the need for wide streets in cold and temperate climates.

22   Jean-Jacques Rousseau, *The Confessions*, trans. J. M. Cohen (Harmondsworth: Penguin, 1953), 155.

23   George Sand, "La Rêverie à Paris," in *Paris Guide* (Paris: Libraire Internationale, 1867), 1196–97.

24   Most often quoted is an 1860 line from the Goncourts' diary, "life threatens to become public." Sharon Marcus, however, in "Haussmannization as Anti-Modernity: The Apartment House in Parisian Urban Discourse, 1850–1880," *Journal of Urban History* 27 (2001): 727–28, and *Apartment Stories* (Berkeley: University of California Press, 1999), 139–49, argues that Haussmannization sharpened the division between interior and exterior, pushing the bourgeoisie's lives more into their homes.

25   Heinrich Heine, *Französische Zustände*, chap. 3, art. 1, 28 Dec. 1831.

26   Otto Wagner, *Die Groszstadt: eine Studie über diese* (Vienna: Schroll, 1911), 5. See also Carl Schorske, *Fin-de-siècle Vienna* (New York: Random House, 1979), 24–115. On the international connections between simplified, horizontal façades, and rapid mobility, see Barbara Miller Lane, "Changing Attitudes to Monumentality: An Interpretation of European Architecture and Urban Form," in *Growth and Transformation of the Modern City*, ed. Thomas Hall and Ingrid Hammarstrøm (Stockholm: Almquist & Wiksell, 1979), 104–14.

27   On Gruen, see M. Jeffrey Hardwick, *Mall Maker: Victor Gruen, Architect of an American Dream* (Philadelphia: University of Pennsylvania Press, 2003).

28   Anthony Vidler, *The Scenes of the Street and Other Essays* (New York: Monacelli, 2011), 43–59. Richard Sennett, *The Conscience of the Eye: The Design and Social Life of Cities* (New York: Knopf, 1990), links the "fear of exposure" (xii) to Ferdinand Tönnies's influential distinction later in the nineteenth century between cold, mechanical Gesellschaft and warm, organic Gemeinschaft (23–24).

29   Diane Ghirardo, "Architecture and Theater: The Street in Fascist Italy," in *"Event" Arts and Art Events*, ed. Stephen C. Foster (Ann Arbor: UMI Research Press, 1988), 175–99.

30   James C. Scott, *Seeing like a State: How Certain Schemes to Improve the Human*

Condition Have Failed (New Haven, CT: Yale University Press, 1998); James Holston, *The Modernist City: An Anthropological Critique of Brasilia* (Chicago: University of Chicago Press, 1989).

31 Half a century ago, Leonardo Benevolo identified utopian socialism as a key root of modern urban planning in *The Origins of Modern Town Planning* (London: Routledge, 1967).

32 Adolf Loos, "Die Potemkin'sche Stadt," *Ver Sacrum* 1, no. 7 (July 1898): 15–17.

33 Anthony Sutcliffe, *Paris: An Architectural History* (New Haven, CT: Yale University Press, 1993), 123; François Loyer, *Paris Nineteenth Century: Architecture and Urbanism* (New York: Abbeville, 1988), 413–14.

34 See his 1925 drawing reprinted in Eric Mumford, *Designing the Modern City: Urbanism since 1850* (New Haven, CT: Yale University Press, 2018), 165.

35 Le Corbusier, "La rue," *L'intransigeant*, May 1929, repr. in *Oeuvre complète 1910–1929* (Zurich: Éditions d'architecture, 1964), 112. From another canonical modernist work, see E. A. Gutkind, *International History of City Development*, vol. 1: *Urban Development in Central Europe* (Glencoe: Free Press, 1964), 200, on the pernicious "cult of the street."

36 Sigfried Giedion, *Space, Time, and Architecture*, 3rd ed. (Cambridge, MA: Harvard University Press, 1954), 725.

37 Hermann Jansen, quoted in Friedrich Lenger, *European Cities in the Modern Era, 1850–1914*, trans. Joel Golb (Leiden: Brill 2012), 171.

38 In a related vein but a different context, Kirk Savage, *Monument Wars: Washington, D.C., the National Mall, and the Transformation of the Memorial Landscape* (Berkeley: University of California Press, 2011), discusses a shift from a notion of "public grounds" to a more abstract "public space" in the early twentieth century.

39 An example of this dissatisfaction is the desire to restore "animation" to streets in 1960s France. See Kenny Cupers, *The Social Project: Housing Postwar France* (Minneapolis: University of Minnesota Press, 2014), 123–28.

CONCLUSION

1 Without reference to a bird's-eye view, Georg Simmel made a related claim about the exclusive reliance on sight in the modern metropolis, adding that "those who see without hearing are much more confused, perplexed, and uneasy than those who hear without seeing." Simmel, *Soziologie* (Leipzig: Duncker und Humblot, 1908), 650.

2 David P. Jordan, *Transforming Paris: The Life and Labors of Baron Haussmann* (Chicago: University of Chicago Press, 1996), 170–74. The original map has not survived.

3 Nick Yablon, "'A Curious Epitome of the Life of the City': New York, Broadway, and the Evolution of the Longitudinal View," *Journal of Urban History* 44 (2018): 953–84, distinguishes between the view from above and a "longitudinal" view down the street, characteristic of the nineteenth century. Similarly, see Jeffrey A. Cohen, "A Streetscape Named Desire: Long Views through the Emerging Bourgeois City," in *Portraits of the City*, ed. Gillian O'Brien and Finola O'Kane (Dublin: Four Courts Press, 2012), 22–34, on nineteenth-century commercial prints in Europe and the United States.

4   Le Corbusier, *La ville radieuse* (Paris: Editions Vincent, 1933), 120. On his fear of touching, see Anthony Vidler, "Le Corbusier, Ayn Rand, and the Idea of 'Ineffable Space,'" in *Warped Space* (Cambridge, MA: MIT Press, 2000), 51–64.

5   Wilhelm von Humboldt, letter to Caroline von Beulwitz and Caroline von Dachröden, Aug. 1789, in Wilhelm von Humboldt, *Briefe 1781 bis Juni 1791*, ed. Philip Mattson (Berlin: Akademie, 2014), 1:210.

6   W. H. Wackenroder and Ludwig Tieck, *Herzensergiessungen eines kunstliebenden Klosterbruders* (1796; Leipzig: Diederichs, 1904), 68; Michael Brix, *Nürnberg und Lübeck im 19. Jahrhundert* (Munich: Prestel, 1981), 22.

7   Hermann von Pückler-Muskau, *Briefe eines Verstorbenen*, ed. Heinz Ohff (Berlin: Kupfergraben, 1986), 158, letter 33, 22 Sept. 1828, on Limerick. Also see 425, letter 2, 25 Sept. 1826, on Utrecht. On the overlooked urban focus of German Romanticism, see Marianne Thalmann, *Romantiker entdecken die Stadt* (Munich: Nymphenburger, 1965).

8   Wilhelm Raabe, *Die Chronik der Sperlingsgasse* (Berlin: Franz Stage, 1857), 9.

9   Jules Janin, *Un été à Paris* (Paris: L. Curmer, 1844), 13, 17, 19–20. Looking at England, Malcolm Andrews argues that the old rural picturesque, with its aestheticization of poverty, became intolerable when applied to the urban poor: "The Metropolitan Picturesque," in *The Politics of the Picturesque*, ed. Stephen Copley and Peter Garside (Cambridge: Cambridge University Press, 1994), 282–98.

10   Sarah Kennel, *Charles Marville: Photographer of Paris* (Washington, DC: National Gallery of Art, 2013); Robert Evans, "History in Albumen, Carbon, and Photogravure: Thomas Annan's Old Glasgow," in *Nineteenth-Century Photographs and Architecture*, ed. Micheline Nilsen (Farnham, Surrey: Ashgate, 2013), 59–74; Amanda Maddox and Sara Stevenson, *Thomas Annan: Photographer of Glasgow* (Los Angeles: Getty Publications, 2017); Katja Zelljadt, "Capturing a City's Past," *Journal of Visual Culture* 9 (2010): 425–38, on Berlin; Steven Jacobs and Bruno Notteboom, "Photography and the Spatial Transformations of Ghent, 1840–1914," *Journal of Urban History* 44 (2018): 203–18; Ellen Handy, "Dust Piles and Damp Pavements: Excrement, Repression, and the Victorian City in Photography and Literature," in *Victorian Literature and the Victorian Visual Imagination*, ed. Carol T. Christ and John O. Jordan (Berkeley: University of California Press, 1995), 111–33; Micheline Nilsen, *Architecture in Nineteenth-Century Photographs: Essays on Reading a Collection* (Farnham, Surrey: Ashgate, 2011), 43–55.

11   Victor Fournel, *Paris nouveau et Paris futur* (Paris: Lecoffre, 1865), 220.

12   Alfred Kerr, letter of 25 July 1897, in *Mein Berlin: Schauplätze einer Metropole* (Berlin: Aufbau, 1999), 46.

13   Karl Kraus, "Der Traum ein Wiener Leben," *Die Fackel* 307–8 (1910), quoted in *Wien—Die Stadt und die Sinne: Reportagen und Feuilletons um 1900*, ed. Peter Payer (Vienna: Löcker, 2016), 288.

14   Karl Scheffler, *Paris: Notizen* (Leipzig: Insel, 1908), 220.

15   On Sitte and his influence, see George R. Collins and Christiane Crasemann Collins, *Camillo Sitte: The Birth of Modern City Planning* (New York: Rizzoli, 1986); also Brian Ladd, "The Closed versus the Open Cityscape: Rival Traditions from Nineteenth-Century Europe," *Change over Time* 4 (2014): 58–74. Le Corbusier and Sitte are the respective exemplars of the "progressist" and "culturalist" models of urban planning for Françoise Choay in *The Modern City: Planning in the 19th*

Century, trans. Marguerite Hugo and George R. Collins (New York: Braziller, 1969).

16   Charles Buls, *Esthétique des villes*, 2nd ed. (Brussels: Bruylant-Christophe, 1894). A similar case that also played out without reference to Sitte is described by Patrick Luiz Sullivan De Oliveira, "Imagining an Old City in Nineteenth-Century France: Urban Renovation, Civil Society, and the Making of Vieux Lyon," *Journal of Urban History* 45 (2019): 67-98.

17   Carl Schorske, *Fin-de-siècle Vienna* (New York: Random House, 1979), 32-36, 62-72.

18   Buls, *Esthétique*, 17.

19   Camillo Sitte, *City Planning According to Artistic Principles*, trans. George R. and Christiane Crasemann Collins, in Collins and Collins, *Camillo Sitte*, 183, 233; Anthony Vidler, "Agoraphobia: Psychopathologies of Urban Space," in *Warped Space*, 25-50. Abram de Swaan, however, in "The Politics of Agoraphobia," *Theory and Society* 10 (1981): 359-85, attributes the outbreak of agoraphobia to the loosening of restrictions on women going out in public, a variation on similar speculations by Freud (see Vidler, 37-38).

20   Thomas Sharp in England was one; see his *Town and Townscape* (London: John Murray, 1968); Sharp, *The Anatomy of the Village* (1946; Abingdon: Routledge, 2014); also John Pendlebury, "Making the Modern Townscape: The Reconstruction Plans of Thomas Sharp," in *Alternative Visions of Post-War Reconstruction*, ed. John Pendlebury, Erdem Erten, and Peter J. Larkham (London: Routledge, 2015), 125-41. Efforts to maintain a tradition of street-oriented design are surveyed by Wolfgang Sonne, *Dwelling in the Metropolis: Reformed Urban Blocks 1890-1940* (Glasgow: University of Strathclyde and Royal Institute of British Architects, 2005).

21   Theodor Fontane, *Ein Sommer in London* (Dessau: Katz, 1854), 21.

22   Hoffmann, "Des Vetters Eckfenster." This is, of course, the same allegory that Eduard Kolloff found in a bus ride a few years later (see chap. 5). On Raabe and other writers who used their perch at a window or tower to enrich the experience of the street, see Susanne Hauser, *Der Blick auf die Stadt: Semiotische Untersuchungen zur literarischen Wahrnehmung bis 1910* (Berlin: Reimer, 1990), 107-11. Hoffmann's involuntary distance from the scene was not without its incidental benefits: a visitor to the same market, years later, described the "long row of green, slimy, moss-covered fishtanks, with fish floating belly-up in stagnant, reeking water," where "the cadavers were pushed around by women with long paddles in an effort to make them look alive. . . . At the butcher stands along Markgrafenstrasse bottle-flies hummed around moldering carcasses, pools of blood coagulated in the street, and starving dogs fought over bits of gristle and guts. Worse still were the cheese stalls." Sebastian Hensel, quoted in David Clay Large, *Berlin* (New York: Basic, 2000), 18.

23   François Loyer, *Paris Nineteenth Century* (New York: Abbeville, 1988), 138-39, 200-208.

24   Siegfried Kracauer, "Lokomotive über der Friedrichstrasse," *Frankfurter Zeitung*, 28 Jan. 1933, repr. in *Der Berliner zweifelt immer*, ed. Heinz Knobloch (Berlin: Der Morgen, 1977), 488-90. The account of Hitler comes from his architect: Albert

Speer, *Inside the Third Reich*, trans. Richard and Clara Winston (New York: Avon, 1971), 187–88.

25   This is similar to the point that Richard Sennett makes in *Building and Dwelling: Ethics for the City* (New York: Farrar, Straus and Giroux, 2018), 158–63.

26   On standards of bodily privacy in a contemporary US legal and political context, see Don Mitchell, "The S.U.V. Model of Citizenship: Floating Bubbles, Buffer Zones, and the Rise of the 'Purely Atomic' Individual," *Political Geography* 24 (2005): 77–100.

Index